Advance Praise for *The Imita...*

"As I began cheering wildly after reading th... the woodpeckers started pecking, the swa... and the Mississippi River started rippling: cosmic applause for this magnificent modern rendering of *The Imitation of Christ*. Bill Griffin has given an invaluable gift to the Body of Christ."

—Brennan Manning, author of *Ruthless Trust*

"Reading the manuscript of Bill Griffin's revival of *The Imitation of Christ* was sheer enjoyment. I could never imagine how anyone could put that masterpiece into a modern idiom. But Bill accomplished the impossible and with humor and tongue-in-cheek all throughout. I could tell he was enjoying the task immensely because it shows in the lightness of the read and the clarity of the thought. I am sure it will be widely read and for a long time."

—Fr. Joseph Girzone, author of *Joshua*

"Like Griffin, I had read the *Imitatio* fifty years ago as a Jesuit novice, and when I got some distance from novice fervor, I wondered why everyone thought it a spiritual classic. Now I know why. This translation is a gem. It brings out the fresh, down-to-earth, straight-from-the-shoulder wisdom of the author. Thomas à Kempis once again can engage his readers to pull them into serious reflection on the fundamental issues of the spiritual life, indeed of life itself. A classic has been given a translation it deserves."

—Fr. William Barry, author of
The Practice of Spiritual Direction

THE IMITATION OF CHRIST

✠ ✠ ✠

THE IMITATION OF CHRIST

How Jesus Wants Us to Live

Thomas à Kempis

✠ ✠ ✠

A Contemporary Version
William Griffin

HarperSanFrancisco
A Division of HarperCollins*Publishers*

HarperCollins books may be purchased for educational, business, or sales
promotional use. For information please write: Special Markets Department,
HarperCollins Publishers, Inc., 10 East 53rd Street, New York, NY 10022.

HarperCollins Web site: http://www.harpercollins.com
HarperCollins®, 🏭®, and HarperSanFrancisco™ are trademarks of
HarperCollins Publishers, Inc.

FIRST EDITION

Library of Congress Cataloging-in-Publication Data
Griffin, William
    The imitation of Christ : a contemporary version / by William Griffin.
        p. cm.
    Includes bibliographical references.
    ISBN 0–06–063400–6 (cloth)
    1. Meditations.   I. Imitatio Christi. English.   II. Title.

BV4821.G75   2001
242—dc21   00-044860

00 01 02 03 04 RRD(H) 10 9 8 7 6 5 4 3 2 1

For

WILLIAM CLARK RUSSELL, S.J.

Contents

✠ ✠ ✠

BOOK ONE

The Spiritual Life

What It Is & How It Works

✠ ✠ ✠

BOOK TWO

The Interior Life

Where It Is & How to Find It

✠ ✠ ✠

BOOK THREE

Internal Consolation

How Jesus Describes It & How the Soul Experiences It

✠ ✠ ✠

BOOK FOUR

The Sacrament of the Altar

How to Prepare for It & What It Tastes Like

✠ ✠ ✠

Preface

✠ ✠ ✠

For over half a millennium the *Imitation of Christ* has been the unchallenged devotional masterpiece for Christians everywhere. Its surpassing popularity is witnessed to by the fact that it has been translated into more than fifty different languages. Although there have been many English translations, this fresh effort by William Griffin is a genuine cause for celebration. Mr. Griffin takes with utmost seriousness the need for a translation that will elicit in us an emotional experience similar to that of the original readers. This is no simple task and one fraught with many dangers, but it is one in which William Griffin has succeeded. This fresh rendering causes the *Imitation* to once again become a *devotio moderna*, a modern devotion, constantly challenging us to new spiritual depths.

Many fine translations of the *Imitation* have had the unintended consequence of replacing the common, serviceable, spiritual-instruction Latin of the fifteenth-century European monastery with an English that is cadenced, beautiful, and harmonious. And although this is comforting to the ear and lends an aura of serenity to the work, it also distances it from the bumpy, messy, scattered reality of our everyday lives. The result is that though we may admire, even honor, the *Imitation*, it is the admiration and honor we might give to a museum piece.

But this original translation changes all that, giving us instead what the Welsh poet Dylan Thomas describes as "the gusts and grunts and hiccups and heehaws of the common fun of the earth."

Bill Griffin is an old friend, and although he is quite serious and sensible, he is at the same time an extremely funny guy. I mean, who else would have the imagination (and the daring) to translate *"Trahunt desideria sensualitatis ad spatiandum: sed cum hora transierit, quid nisi gravitatem conscientiae, et cordis dispersionem, reportas?"* as "Our sensual desires promise us a promenade, but deliver us only a dragonnade." And then, I all but fell out of my chair when I came upon this line: "All-nighters of roister-doistery lead only to mornings of hugger-muggery, that's to say, of sickness and sadness." Funny, but at the same time right to the point, because such behavior does indeed produce sickness and sadness.

What I am trying to say is that this fresh translation of the *Imitation* puts back into Kempis's writings all of those glorious emotions of love and terror and pity and pain and wonder and sorrow that make our lives dangerous and great and bearable. Consider, for example, this discussion on humility: "Yes, there are rascals who spend their days standing on the corner . . . waiting for just such an oaf as yourself to trip up on your own defects. One moment you're humble, and the next? Well, you've given the ruffians a good laugh. Anyone humbled in this way God shields from further harm, dusts him off, patches him up. . . . What's the result of this sudden humility? Whenever the person trips, he falls, but the bloodied nose no longer shakes his peace of mind. That's because his standing is not with the rowdies on the next corner, but with the Angels in the next world."

When I agreed to write this brief preface, Bill Griffin thanked me more than he needed to, but I am the one who should be thanking him—profusely. It is a genuine honor to have even a small part in introducing such a surpassing translation of *De Imitatione Christi*.

—RICHARD J. FOSTER,
author of *A Celebration of Discipline*

Foreword

✠ ✠ ✠

THE ORIGINAL

It may have been the best of times or the worst of times, but who knew? Not the Netherlanders. For them it was just another century—the fourteenth, as it happens—and few if any knew what was going on in the next town or village, let alone on the rest of the continent of Europe. But historians have come to know . . .

Flamboyant traceries were lightening the interiors of those Gothic blockhouses called cathedrals. Castles were abuilding, but not without battlements. Crusaders were afoot and a danger to themselves as well as to others, especially to the infidels, who by this time were on the run. Knighthood was in flower, albeit out to deflower much of the maidenhood of Christendom. Rumor had it that the heavily armored Europeans had already defoliated much of the Holy Land. England exported wool; the Netherlands imported wool and made all sorts of textured textiles, exporting them to the rest of the clothéd world, leaving the merchant class back at home to wive it wealthily. And, oh yes! Death came aknocking.

The Black Death, appearing as both bubonic and pneumonic plague from 1348 to 1350, killed one-third of the population between Iceland and India, according to French chronicler Jean Froissart; it returned four times before the end of the century. Then there was the Hundred Years' War in France, from roughly 1328 to 1429, "an epic of brutality and bravery checkered by disgrace," as one historian called it.

Literarily, chaste knights wooed distant ladies they knew they'd never win—that's to say, happily married ladies—at least in that new genre of continental literature, the romance. Chaucer's *Canterbury Tales* and Boccaccio's *Decameron* flooded the market with brief entertainments in a variety of literary styles. Petrarch pursued Laura, a woman he saw in a church, with a seemingly endless sorites of sonnets.

By 1429 there was a little book with limited circulation called *De Imitatione Christi* written by a fairly anonymous Augustinian monk named Thomas Hämerken or Hämerlein (his father was a man of the forge, and the family name was his chiefest implement, albeit in the diminutive) from a modest town in Germany named Kempen. He was also a member of a small faith community in the Netherlands known as the Brethren of the Common Life.

De Imitatione Christi

The *Imitation* has four parts, but they appear to be four separate works, all short treatises, all written at different times, perhaps between 1420 and 1427. Book One has to do with the spiritual life, what it is and how it works. Book Two, with the interior life, where it is and how to find it. Book Three, with the consolation within, how Jesus describes it and how a monk or would-be monk experiences it. Book Four, with the Sacrament of the Altar, how to prepare for it and what it tastes like. Someone put the four parts together under the general title; someone else put in subtitles; still another person inserted Kempis's name as author; and the rest has been spiritual and indeed publishing history.

Thematic threads run through this Flemish tapestry. Vanity mummers as virtually everything under the sun. One should cloak oneself in the love of God. One gets out of the spiritual life only what one puts into it, but sometimes one gets rather more, like inner consolation. Jesus is in dialog with the willing soul; even with the unwilling soul He's always trying to start a conversation. All the good soul needs to survive imprisonment in the body is food and light; that's to say, Sacrament and Scripture.

Devotio Antiqua

In the fourteenth century most of the diocesan clergy were upwardly mobile chaps for whom ordination, if not theological sophistication, was a way out of poverty. On the other hand, the educated clergy were swanning about the universities, divvying up, and in the process multiplying, the abstract perfections of the Godhead. But if the clergy failed to inspire, to whom was the pious Netherlander to turn, the Church?

Church was still a place of worship, but in many instances it was also the only place for social gathering. Is it any wonder, then, that the holy precincts disintegrated into a dance hall, gambling parlor, house of ill repute. The Church itself was even described as something like "a prostitute found at the scene of a debauch"; that's to say, pulled now one way, now another, by the pope and the antipope, Rome and Avignon. If neither to the clergy nor to the Church, then, to whom could the desperate Netherlander turn?

Devotio Moderna

Dissenters from the *devotio antiqua*—they were assenters, really, to the core doctrines and practices of the Church—began to gather around the sort of pious men with piercing eyes who ofttimes over the centuries have been found roaming the streets of our finer cities. Small communities of laypersons began to form, pooling their resources into a common purse, and a *devotio moderna* emerged. It stressed things like the humanity of Christ, method in meditation, knowledge of self, fulfillment of obligations, the practice of virtue, the avoidance of vice, retirement from the world, devotional reading of the Scriptures, and a prickly restlessness with intellectuality for its own sake. Because of their enthusiasm for the movement, the Brethren quickly became known as the "Devouts."

By the end of the fourteenth century there were in northern Europe a hundred houses for the Brethren and three hundred for the Sistern. Yes, women too were attracted to the Common Life; they were the thoroughly modern Millies of their own age. And since that time, may it be said, centuries of nuns have slept more holily, if not more comfortably, with a copy of the *Imitation* under their pillows.

Auctoritas

Clearly the *Imitation* was the work of at least three men: Gerard Groote, founder of the Brethren; Florent Radewijns, sometimes listed as founder of the group and certainly the formulator of the *devotio moderna;* and Thomas à Kempis, a member of the Brethren from about 1400 until his death in 1471. Thomas was also a priest, Augustinian monk, author of a dozen works, and copyist extraordinaire.

Anonymous copies of the *Imitatio* were made in the fifteenth century, but the first name to appear on a title page was Kempis's. No doubt his imperial position in the *scriptorium,* as the copy room was called, allowed him access to and supervision of all the writings of the Brethren to that date. In addition, he'd have had access to the *rapiaria* or *florilegia* of the deceased members of the group; that's to say, their personal logs or diaries dutifully containing quotable quotes from the very best wisdom literature of the West, sacred as well as profane. So in a sense there lay in his very own *scriptorium,* if not on his very own *scrinium,* the golden treasury of *devotio moderna* as it appeared in written form.

That trove Kempis consumed at a rapid rate in order to fulfill his own obligations as *quondam* master of novices, preacher in the church attached to the Augustinian monastery of St. Agnes near Zwolle, a municipality in north-central Netherlands, and spiritual director of the lay members of the Brethren. Needless to say, the best

of that written material eventually found its way into his own confer-
ence notes. From there it was only a *saltatio, exaltatio, exsultatio*
(Latin for "hop, skip, and jump") to his own personal condensation or
summation of *devotio moderna*.

All that needs to be said about the author of the *Imitatio*, then, is
that "Kempis" may and indeed should be construed as a collective
noun for himself and the Brethren who preceded him.

Devotio Perennis

Recent translators and publishers have adopted the habit of trotting
out some celebrity readers of the *Imitatio* over the centuries. One
listed holy people like Thomas More, Ignatius of Loyola, Robert
Bellarmine, John Wesley, Thomas Merton, and even John Paul I, who
died in bed while reading the book on the thirty-third night of his
papacy.

Another has paraded readers of some notoriety but with no profes-
sional connection to Christianity: German philosopher Gottfried
Wilhelm von Leibniz, French playwright Pierre Corneille, Irish
politician Daniel O'Connell, and English writers Thomas De Quincey,
Charles Kingsley, Samuel Johnson, Thomas Carlyle, and Matthew
Arnold.

Still another, going further afield, has added General Charles
George ("Chinese") Gordon, who, despite his affection for the
Imitation, was beheaded with a scimitar in the battle of Khartoum;
Victorian novelist and freethinker George Eliot, who referred to it as
"a small, old-fashioned book," but applied its healing influence in her
novel *The Mill on the Floss;* mystery writer Agatha Christie, who
mentioned in passing that Miss Marple's bedtime reading was often a
chapter from the *Imitation;* and twentieth-century novelist Graham
Greene, who in *A Burnt-Out Case* described the Ryckers, a Catholic
couple of the strict observance—the wife dutifully read her husband
to sleep with the *Imitation*, then picked up a fashionable women's
magazine to feast on the dreamy fiction.

Of this motley crew the most interesting to me is the fictional Jane Marple. She lived in a small town, but grew to know that all the evil in the world, as well as all the good, dwelt in the hearts and souls of the town of St. Mary Meade. Her experience was confirmed by what she read in the *Imitation*. Presumably, that's what made her so helpful to the English constabulary. To this day, sad to say, the *Imitation*, the spiritual classic first composed in the fifteenth century, has yet to make the required reading list at Scotland Yard.

And so it is, on into our own time. The *devotio* whose modernity was immediately apparent in the fourteenth century, is also apparent in the twenty-first. Perhaps it should be renamed *devotio perennis;* that's to say, the devotion that's never gone out of fashion because it describes the disorder within, the chaos that knows no century, and what can be done about it.

Translatio Antiqua

The *Imitatio* first found its way into English in the translation by William Atkinson and Lady Margaret Beaufort; printed in 1503, it went through four editions by 1528. A second round of translation began with Richard Whitford in 1530; by 1585 it had run through at least ten editions. But from then on, Whitford's work all but disappeared from studies devoted to the development of English prose style, only to reappear in 1941 in an edition prepared by the Reverend Edward J. Klein.

In admiration, Harold C. Gardiner, S.J., at the time literary editor of *America,* the national Jesuit weekly magazine, decided to make the Whitford translation more accessible to the American audience. He de-archaized the work, leaving most of the original prose intact. His version of Whitford's translation was published in 1955 and has been in print ever since.

Other translations have come along with fair regularity. The translators have described themselves as faithful to the Latin original, by which they meant they were fairly faithful not only to the Latin vocabulary, but also to the Latin word order. But this well-intentioned fidelity seems to have grown gray hairs; once current vocabulary has lost much of its color; once fluid word order has hardened many of its arteries.

Translatio Moderna

Most translators have praised the Latinity of Kempis's original text; that's to say, "the grand style of the original," as one of them put it. Historian Will Durant has even hailed Kempis's style as "simple" and "mellifluous."

A recent translator, however, has expressed just the opposite point of view; in other words, he had the courage to say the obvious. "The original Latin of the *Imitation* is not very polished"; moreover, he thinks a good translation of the classic should have an English that's unpolished too. But one tinkers with the patina of five centuries, however dulled, at the peril of spoiling the literary antique. If, however, that patina is making the original less understandable to truly modern readers, what's the truly modern translator to do?

A word about Kempis's Latin, which, we must remember, was his second language, his first being the vernacular of the Netherlands. Mellifluous it certainly wasn't. But it was clear enough to communicate with his peers, containing as it does the technical vocabulary of the spiritual life, and pure enough to allow him to read and copy classical and ecclesiastical Latin in the *scriptorium;* yet it was becoming brackish, beginning to blend with the grammar and vocabulary of the emerging vernacular. But in the end, if it can sell millions of copies in that language and the subsequent languages of translation over a number of centuries, then it can certainly be construed today as Latin good enough to get the job done.

Translator Proprius

I first encountered the *Imitation of Christ* as a novice in the Society of Jesus, also known as the Jesuits, nearly fifty years ago. Fifteen minutes a day were devoted to the silent reading of this so-called masterpiece of ascetical literature. At lunch and dinner, which were generally silent meals, a novice read some verses from the Scriptures in Latin and some paragraphs from the *Imitation* in English. I took my turn in the pulpit and soon became vain about my ability to read Latin at sight and out loud before the most critical audience in the world.

But the *Imitation* quickly became my unfavorite spiritual book. Its message of "advance to the rear" or "hold the line" seemed in direct contradiction to the spirituality of Ignatius of Loyola, founder of the Jesuits and a former military man, as it was being purveyed to me by the novice master. "Be a monk whole and entire," Ignatius seemed to be saying, "but bring your monkishness into the marketplace and make a joyful shout!" An incarnational thrust rather than an eschatological feint. Other novices didn't seem to have the same difficulty. They persevered. I didn't.

What, then, leads me back to this book of unhappy memory? Latinity and its several fruits.

In the novitiate I continued the study of Latin literature I'd begun four years before in high school, and I began to speak Latin, the official language in most Catholic seminaries around the world at that time. I learned the words for turnip and cabbage *(rapa, brassica),* knife and fork *(culter, furca),* long meal and short meal *(prandium, cena),* coffee and tea *(coffeum, thea)*—all in use in the dining room *(triclinium).* To this day I've retained it all. Indeed, I could make a reservation at the finest Latin restaurant in the world, joke casually with the *major domus,* order the costliest meal, and leave the largest tip—if only there were such a place!

In all I've had eleven years of Latin study in one form or another and read widely—then and since—in the classical and ecclesiastical authors. Motivated by *Winnie Ille Pooh,* I even translated *Peter Rabbit* into *De Petro Cuniculo.* "A pretty fair job," said a sister of the Love of God, Benedicta Ward, a patristic scholar in Oxford, whose own tea things bore the Beatrix Potter figures. "Too bad it's already been done."

In the 1960s, while a senior editor at Harcourt Brace doing high-school literature anthologies, I was asked to take on an additional task, editing *Our Latin Heritage,* a high-school Latin series with a variety of ancillary materials. The chief author was an impossible nun, whom Mao Tse Tung knew when they both were pups; that's to say, when she was a young missionary in China and he just a boy learning to pillage and burn. If he'd put the torch to her, she'd have refused to ignite!

Well, in that four-book series, there were, among others, Caesar, Cicero, Virgil; there were macrons, stress marks, grammars, vocabularies, a dozen formats and type sizes; and there were agreeable coauthors with whom the *Soror Impossibilis* couldn't get along. Nonetheless, I learned to count in Latin, write letters in Latin, even date my interoffice memoranda in Latin. I survived to the bitter end, but just, with my Latinity intact.

In 1971, when Cardinal József Mindszenty left the U.S. embassy in Budapest after fifteen years of asylum from Hungary's Communist government, he was immediately besieged by publishers for the exclusive right to bring out his memoirs. At the time I was an acquiring editor at Macmillan in New York. The Jewish editor-in-chief assumed that since I was a Catholic, I could get the project. "Spare no expense," he encouraged. "Use whatever guile, but get the project!"

My problem was that I *was* a Catholic and hence knew how hard it was to get to the cardinal, any cardinal. Best thing I could come up with was to write him a letter in Latin explaining why he should consider Macmillan. Well, as things turned out, the good cardinal got a $300,000 advance, paid equally by the German, British, and American publishers, and I was the editor of both the British and American editions. *Latinitas vincit omnia!*

In recent years my wife, Emilie, invited me to join her and Charles Till Davis, a Dante scholar and a former professor of hers who'd gone blind, in reading Latin for pleasure. They'd already covered a good deal of the *Aeneid* and some essays of Cicero's—I pass over in silence (if I may be permitted a *praeteritio*) their reading much of the *Commedia* in Italian—when I was asked to join. So refreshing and indeed so rollicking were the sessions that Emilie and I decided to translate two essays on friendship, with Charles's help, and dedicate them to Charles himself: Cicero's *De Amicitia* and Aelred of Rievaulx's *De Spiritali Amicitia*. To cap the proposed work I even volunteered to translate into Latin C. S. Lewis's essay on friendship, as found in *The Four Loves!* Alas, the project has stalled, Charles having died suddenly, swept away by an exotic infection. Soon Emilie and I will resume and dedicate the project to his holy memory.

All of which are roundabout ways of answering the question of what led me back to this book of unhappy memory.

Vanity. My vanity. I'm vain about my Latinity, and even vainer about my English. But if my vanity has any value at all, why should I continue trafficking with a treatise whose main thrust is the eradication of all vanity? Alas, I've not been able to come up with a satisfactory answer.

Restauratio

When J. B. Phillips sent C. S. Lewis a version of his modern paraphrase of Colossians, Lewis was astonished. He thought he knew the King James Version pretty well, and he had a passing knowledge of the Latin Vulgate text, but, he wrote back to the Anglican vicar, it was like seeing a classical painting cleaned and restored.

That was in 1943. In 2000 I've attempted much the same thing. That's to say, I've attempted to restore *De Imitatione Christi*, a spiritual classic of the fifteenth century, so that it can be read and heard with relish in the twenty-first century. My cleansing agents have been, among other things, a dramatic rather than a literary style, a recognizable voice for Kempis himself, colloquialisms, contractions, vintage words and references, and a larger vocabulary than Kempis's.

A fair amount of humor has been uncovered, as has a multitude of university referents. Then there are the masculinity of monasticism, the virtual omnipresence of scriptural quotation and allusion, the ornamentation of allegory, and some brushes with can only be called Lowlands earthiness.

I've been at some pains to recreate the monastery and university settings in the *Imitation*. I've come to see that the work deserves a prominent position in the genre of friendship literature—a welcome antidote to what has seemed to be Self-Abnegation's centuries-old Black Death grip on the text. As for the university's being thought the root of all intellectual evil, just the opposite seems to be true; what Kempis developed wasn't a species of anti-intellectualism, but rather a respectable spirituality for intellectuals.

More details in the Afterword.

Kempis himself makes reference to a restoration process in his work (Book Four, Chapter 1), that's to say, the Eucharist at work. "When you receive this Sacrament, Spiritual Grace is conferred, and Virtue dimmed is restored to its original beauty. Once covered with soot and sin, the pallid soul will soon blush into a full palette of colors."

One thing about restorations. The first reaction is invariably one of shock. Readers remember their favorite English translations of the *Imitation*, which, though the translators tried heroically to be faithful, are eventually hobbled by their Latinate vocabulary and word order. That's to say, they're really dimmed down—and in some cases, dumbed down—versions of the Latin original. Exposure to something new, like my version, seems to have a blinding effect. Like the recent restoration in the Sistine Chapel, the colors may seem too bright, verging even on the garish. Too quickly do our eyes become accustomed to the dirt and grime of the ages.

All of which is another way of saying that, for all the brightness of my version, the *Imitation* is still the same old *Imitation*. And Kempis is still the same old Kempis. He's not the Good Shepherd, and he's not one of the sheep. Rather, he's still the scrappy border collie routing and rousting the sheep, nipping at their heels, nipping at their souls, heading the flock toward its final fold.

Correctio

As I've said, my first encounter with Kempis was disastrous. No introduction was given to the *Imitation*. Reading it, I thought it was the preamble to an exclusively contemplative life, and yet I had joined a religious order that was supposed to combine the contemplative life with the active life.

Some decades later, stumbling onto the *Imitation* again, I discovered that Kempis has said more, and hinted much more, about the active life than previous translators had let appear. Not only was he a bustling copyist and archivist, he also served the community as sub-prior and procurator. As the latter, all monies entering and leaving the monastery passed though his hands; the temporal and spiritual care of the lay brothers and externs fell to him; he bought and sold cattle; he developed some monastery properties. In other words, the prosperity of the community was put into his holy hands. All of which is to say that Kempis, presumably a pure contemplative, was also vigorously involved in the active life.

Some critics have said that he was a disaster both as sub-prior and procurator, and well he may have been, but that's not my point here. With good monastic form he accepted the jobs when offered to him, even going so far as to tell his superiors what they already knew, that he seemed to have little talent for the active life. Perhaps that was because they knew there was one task for which he was admirably suited. As procurator, he was also chief alms procurer of the monastery.

Already Kempis had learned to see Jesus in his fellow religious, but now he had the chance to find Jesus in that leprous and pauperous crew that tended to congregate in the neighborhood of all religious houses. According to all reports he developed a high style of dealing with God's poor; giving them food and drink, clothes and coins, as needed; and spiritual nourishment too, reminding them that they were truly God's chosen in this world and the next. No wonder there was always a queue at the monastery gate!

Ever a slave to the stylus and the inkpot, Kempis eventually put down his thoughts on almsgiving in *De Fideli Dispensatore (On the Faithful Steward)*. The *locus classicus* was the New Testament story of Martha, Lazarus's sister, and the focus was on her industry during Jesus's visit to the family home. In the course of this work Kempis made several striking observations about the active life. First, during non-business hours the material interests of the community were more than enough reason to draw him from the contemplative activities in his cell. Second, he had to be reckless when giving to the poor. He had to save for the future, yes, but that shouldn't prevent him from giving today. "As long as you have one loaf," he wrote, "you should halve it with Christ."

With these additional instances from Kempis's life outside of his cell, the reader can now approach the more rarefied air of *The Imitation of Christ,* knowing that the end result will be neither solely contemplative, nor solely active, but perhaps somewhere in the middle; perhaps, a contemplative in action. Something I wish I'd known some fifty years ago.

Caveat Lector!

The Imitation of Christ has been acknowledged by virtually all Christian denominations as a spiritual classic for some centuries now, but that doesn't mean that readers have to accept everything in it as gospel. Kempis makes mention of things that not all Christians hold dear. Purgatory, for example, as well as the Eucharist and Marian devotion.

And there are some passages that may not ring true. In Book One, Chapter 21, Kempis argues that when divine consolation abandons us, the reason is sin. Not necessarily so. "This statement must be accepted with reservation," says a noted previous translator, Monsignor Ronald

A. Knox. "Most spiritual writers teach that the lack of consolation is a test of our faith, not the punishment of infidelity."

Careful readers may find other such passages, but they'll note that Kempis tends to approach each topic from more than one perspective and use more than one argument or illustration. Which means that careful and pious readers will be able to find interest and profit in virtually every chapter of the *Imitation*.

As always, let the Spirit be your guide!

—WILLIAM GRIFFIN
Alexandria, Louisiana
Kalendis Aprilibus, MM°

"Many are wowed by His miracles.
Few are wooed by His Cross."

BOOK ONE

✠ ✠ ✠

The Spiritual Life

✠ ✠ ✠

What It Is
&
How It Works

1

IMITATING CHRIST
&
CONDEMNING THE WORLD

"Whoever shadows my every move won't lose me in the dark." At least that's what Christ says, or what the Evangelist John heard Him say (8:12). He tells us to walk on, through the darkness, with Christ as our only torch. That way, when morning comes, we mayn't have gained a step, but we won't have lost one either. And on into the day we must pursue with doggéd tread the life of Jesus Christ.

We Devouts know more about Christ than we do about the Saints. For example, whoever finds the spirit of Christ discovers in the process many "unexpected delights," if I may use an expression of the Apostle John's from the Last Book of the New Testament (2:17).

But that isn't often the case. Many who've heard the Gospel over and over again think they know it all. They've little desire to discover if there's more to the story. That's because, as the Apostle Paul diagnosed it in his Letter to the Romans (8:9), "they don't have the spirit of Christ."

On the other hand, whoever wants to understand the words of Christ and fully and slowly savor their sweetness has to work hard at making himself another Christ.

If you're not humble, you make the Trinity nervous, and in that wretched state what possible good do you get out of standing up in public and disputing to high heaven about the Trinity as an intellectual entity? The real truth, if only you'd learn it, is that highfalutin words don't make us Saints. Only a virtuous life can do that, and only that can make God care for us.

"Compunction" is a good example. The Schoolmen at the University—that's to say, the Philosophers and the Theologians—could produce lengthy, perhaps even lacy, definitions of this holy word, but that wouldn't move them one inch closer to the Gate of Heaven. The humble Devout, on the other hand, who can neither read nor write, might very well have experienced compunction every day of his life; he's the one, whether he knows it or not, who'll find himself already waiting at that very gate when the Final Day comes.

By the way, I do know what *compunction* means, and so should you: a prickling or stinging of the conscience.

Are you any the richer, if I may put it the way Paul did in his First Letter to the Corinthians (13:3), for knowing all the proverbs of the Bible and all the axioms of the Philosophers, when you're really all the poorer for not knowing the charity and the grace of God?

"Vanity of vanities, and everything is vanity," says the Ancient Hebrew Preacher in Ecclesiastes (1:2). The only thing that isn't vanity is loving God and, as Moses preached to the Israelites in Deuteronomy, serving him alone (6:13). That's the highest wisdom, to navigate one's course, using the contempt of the World as a chart, toward that Heavenly Port.

Just what is vanity? Well, it's many things. A portfolio of assets that are bound to crash. A bird breast of medals and decorations. A brassy solo before an unhearing crowd. Alley-catting one's "carnal desires," as Paul so lustily put it to the Galatians (5:16), only to discover that punishment awaits further up and farther in. Pining for a long life and at the same time paying no attention to the good life. Focusing both eyes on the present without casting an eye toward the future. Marching smartly in the passing parade instead of falling all over oneself trying to get back to that reviewing stand where Eternal Joy is queen.

Don't forget the hoary wisdom of the Ancient Hebrew Preacher: "The eye is never satisfied by what it sees; nor the ears, by what they hear" (1:8). With that in mind, try to transfer your holdings from the visible market into the invisible one. The reason? Those who trade in their own sensualities only muck up their own account and in the process muddy up God's Final Account.

2
KNOWLEDGE ABOUT KNOWLEDGE

Everyone has a natural desire to know things. That's what Aristotle said a long time ago in his *Metaphysics* (1.1). I say to you now, what good is all that knowledge unless it's accompanied by fear of God? Certainly better is the humble farmer who serves God than the proud Philosopher who entertains thoughts about the heavens. At least that's what Augustine noted in his *Confessions* (5.4).

The Devout who knows himself well has proper self-esteem, one that isn't swept away by the blustering winds of human praise. If his head contained all the knowledge in the world and yet his soul was "empty of all charity"—the words of Paul in his First to the Corinthians (13:2)—what leg would he have left to stand on in front of his judge, the Lord God; all He wants to know are the facts.

Hunt for knowledge, yes, but don't let the hunter become the hunted. That way lies the wrong end of a blunderbuss. Often the studious want not so much to know everything as to be seen swanning about as authority figures.

But many areas of knowledge have little or nothing to offer to the soul. Yet these are the very ones the harebrained often turn to instead of the topics that truly serve their own spiritual well-being.

A shower of glitter doesn't slake the thirst of a soul. A life well lived, on the other hand, refreshes the mind, and a conscience well formed develops the confidence one needs when it comes to dealing with God.

Antsy? Don't get antsy. Stay in line. Don't push others aside just to get ahead. If you do, you'll get slapped with a fine by the Final Judge. That's to say, unless you've lived a holy life. Therefore, don't, every time you learn something new about art or science, break into a *trompette volontaire!* Rather, have some respect for the knowledge you already have.

You may know a lot, yes, but there's also a lot you don't know. "Don't be a wiseacre," wrote Paul to the Romans (11:20). Admit you're not omniscient. And when it comes to standing in line, what about the people ahead of you? Apparently, they know more than you do. Get used to knowing less than God. Get used to the middle of the line. That's where you belong.

What's the most profound, and yet the most practical, lesson you can learn? That you *look like* an ant! What's the deepest wisdom and yet the highest perfection? That you *are* an ant! Have no illusions about yourself—that's what Paul laid upon the Romans (11:20). Hold high opinions only about others.

If you come upon a couple *in flagrante delicto*, don't think for a moment you're better than they. Why? No one's perfect, said the Great Bernard somewhere in his *Third Sermon on Christmas Day*. We're all crockery. We all break when we hit the floor. And what's more, no one is more of a crock than you!

3

TRUTH ABOUT TRUTH

Unhappy are you who've heard about Truth only through riddles, that's to say, the figures of speech and the literary genres of the day, as the Author of Numbers suggested so felicitously (12:8). But happy are you to whom Truth has revealed herself in all her glory.

Alone, Sound Reason and Common Sense often fail us, preventing us from seeing any farther than our nose. What good is a lot of piffling and trifling about the great unknowns? We'll never be convicted at the Final Bar because we didn't solve all the mysteries of the world.

Isn't it great folly, then, for you to spend so little time on the practical and necessary things of the soul, and yet so much time on the intellectual curiosities and travesties of our time? We do have eyes, the dolorous Jeremiah once observed, but sometimes we just don't see (5:21).

Why do the Schoolmen go on so, haggling about what's a species, what's a genus? That may be Philosophy, but it's in one ear and out the other. And yet, when the Eternal Word whispers—and this may be Theology—you should stop and listen. That's what John says in the beginning of his Gospel (1:3).

From the One Word all words flow, as the same John reminds us (8:25), and all words bespeak the One Word. Without this concept of the Eternal Word, the pupil can neither understand one entity nor distinguish among many.

All are one. All to one. All in one. When you realize all this, you can forget about Philosophy and Theology as they're taught in the University; you're already at home with God. O God, as John embraced Jesus as Truth (14:6), so I embrace You as the Truth the University's seeking! May You in turn, as You embraced the prophetic Jeremiah (31:3), embrace me as a seeker of the Truth!

Endless lectures, pointless tomes, majuscule, minuscule, my poor head splits, and yet all I want and desire is You. Learned doctors may giggle, dumb creatures may gaggle, and yet in all the babel Yours is the only voice I hear.

A man harnesses the unruly affections of his heart and trains them to trot as one. The surer he does that, the quicker he comes to understand the great and the deep. That's because they receive strong direction from the Powerful Hand above.

The impure, complex, unstable spirit is pulled in a variety of directions at once and never gets any work done; but the docile, willing, and powerful spirit puts all its efforts into pulling for the honor of God, even to the degradation of blinders. How's this possible? It's the great gray drays of your unmortified heart that cause all the delays.

The devout monk takes time to plan ahead for market day. But his sinful desires will suggest that any other day of the week would be just as good for carting and hauling. Nonetheless, the holy person bends them to his own purpose; that's to say, subjects the willful horses to the tight reins in his strong hands.

What's the moral?

No one has a greater struggle than the one who tries to conquer himself? And this ought to be our business each and every day, to harness ourselves and pull our ever increasing weight.

Every perfection in this life comes with its own imperfection. For example, every window glass, every polished piece of metal, returns to the viewer's eye a distorted image. No great matter!

Every humble person, when he looks at his own likeness, may see just a lump. But in that lumpkin, that unpromising mass of Humankind, is more of a portrait of God than the most profound scientific experiment can produce.

Now there's no need to blame the complexities of logical inquiry or the simplicities of natural observation. Both ways of looking at things have their own perfections and are themselves mirrors of God.

But preferred to them have to be Good Conscience and Virtuous Life! Why? Because a lot of us spend more time studying hard than living well. That's such a mistake! All that does is produce a tree that bears no fruit, except perhaps the odd pear or single peach.

Plowing vices under and planting virtues in their place—that's hard work. Harder even than the grunt and the grind of the great philosophical issues. But if the priestly scholar had already done that hard and serious work in his own life, he'd find it easier now dealing with those Devouts traipsing about in sandals and monks processing around in ermines.

With the certain advent of that Final Event, the question to be posed isn't whether we read the right books, but whether we did the good deeds; not whether we said the right things, but whether we made the right choices.

Tell me now, where are those celebrity professors who taught you when they were at the height of their careers and you were starting out? They're dead and gone. You occupy their chairs of learning now, and now you're spending their stipends. Doctors they once were; now they're only dodoes, and you can hardly remember their names.

How soon the glory of the World sets, wrote John in his first letter to an early group of Christians (2:17)! Would that the professors' lives had matched their doctrinal teachings! Yet they fell far short. If they had it to do over again, I suppose they'd have studied longer and read till their eyes turned red. But that would've done them little good. That's what Paul had in mind when he wrote to the Romans (1:21).

How many of the professors have perished because they followed the unreliable wisdom of the World! Because they gave scant attention to the service of God. They had their choices, though. They picked greatness rather than humility, and as a result logicked themselves right out of their own holy syllogisms.

But when the sun finally sets, there'll be other, happier people.

The truly great? Those who didn't make a lot of themselves; they gathered honors as their due, but they didn't display their trophies in the window.

The truly prudent? Those who gave the world its due; they wouldn't mind sweeping up after elephants if that's what would keep them on the path to God, as Paul put it so earthily to the Philippians (3:8).

The truly educated? Those who engaged God's will and disengaged their own in one and the same transaction.

4

WISDOM ABOUT WISDOM

Words and feelings come in a rush. We can't help it. That's just the way it is. Should we believe them? That's the sort of question Jesus son of Sirach would ask in his book of Wisdom (19:14). The answer is both yes and no. Each and every one should be carefully weighed in the scale of God, that's to say, magnanimously and longanimously.

But, oh, what a pain it is! If we don't do the pondering, the complaint about someone will be swallowed whole while the compliment is left untouched on the plate. What excuse can we come up with, except that old canard that we're poor, weak human beings?

But once gullible people don't fall for the same lame story a second time. They know the kind of infirmity Humankind is heir to. They know that it's a slippery slope from the good to the bad, as Jesus son of Sirach put it (14:1), and that words, merry messengers that they are, are the first ones down the hill.

Wisdom, how great thou art! Not to be hasty in what has to be done. Not to be stubborn in what doesn't have to be done. Not to believe every word uttered by Humankind. And of the utterings judged believable, not to ladle them too eagerly into the empty ears of others.

But how does one distinguish the Believables from the Unbelievables? The only way is to take counsel with a wise and conscientious person, as the Author of Tobit advised (4:18). Seek to be instructed on how to become a better Christian; and that certainly doesn't include how to become a better prankster.

A good life makes you wise in God's eyes. But is that all? In many ways it also makes you an expert in the World's eyes, as Jesus son of Sirach had it (34:9). Is that all? You grow in humility and openness to God. Is that all? Simultaneously, surreptitiously, you become wiser and more peaceful in the rest of life. That's all there is and needs to be.

5

READING HOLY SCRIPTURE

When it comes to reading the Holy Scriptures, look for Truth, not style. That's to say, every verse of Sacred Scripture ought to be read in the spirit in which it was written. But what should we look for? For the spirituality of the Scripture verse rather than the subtlety of a sermon about the Scripture verse.

So in addition to reading learned tomes and leathered volumes, we should feel free to dip into sacred and simple books. Don't be distracted by trying to figure out who the author is. Don't get nervous if you find the author trying too hard. Don't waste time trying to determine if the style is too highbrow, too lowbrow.

If read you must, then read on, letting the love of Truth be your guide. Don't ask who wrote it. Just pay attention to what's said. At least with regard to the Scriptures.

Humankind comes and goes, but "the Truth of the Lord remains forever." That's what the Psalmist says (116:2). But through it all God speaks to us. At least, that's as the Letters to the Hebrews (1:1) and the Romans (2:11) express it. How? Through Devouts, of course, but also in a variety of other ways. Scripture among them, and the reading is easy.

Except perhaps for Scripture scholars. Intellectual curiosity often gets in their way. They isolate a verse, do a tarantella on it, and then seem surprised to learn they've stomped it to death.

For the rest of us, when we have trouble reading a verse, we should read the next one, then the one after that, and so on until the muddy pool clears.

If you want to satisfy your thirst for the Scriptures, forget about scholarship. Read humbly, simply, faithfully; that's the way they were written.

This isn't to say that we can't ask questions of and about Scripture anytime we want. But we should pay quiet attention to the Scripture writers themselves, accepting their words as though the ink were still damp.

A cautionary word. There's going to be stuff in the Scriptures you don't like. What to do? Don't fuss. The writers had their reasons, and in them God had His.

6

OUTRAGEOUS AFFECTIONS

The person who lusts for something breaks out into hives. The person who's proud produces pouches under his eyes. The person who's greedy develops hollows in his cheeks. The person who hasn't died to himself is easy game for the Enemy's guile.

Whoever finds himself flooded with weakness and clinging to the flesh is mired in desire. He can still extract himself from this sort of life, but only with the greatest difficulty. When a person like this holds himself back, he grows sad. When someone else holds him back, he flies off into a rage.

By way of contrast, the person who's poor and the one who's humble in spirit may seem to live a humdrum life; nonetheless they experience a measure of control and even a modicum of concord.

You may go for the gusto, that's to say, aggressively pursue something you lust for; but when you grab it, it will grab you and twist you to the floor.

By allowing a thousand such small passions to enslave you, you will never find True Peace of Heart. You must resist, fight back, if you ever hope to escape, to find what you're looking for.

In the same way anyone who revels and drivels his life away can't find True Peace; only the fervent and spiritual know where to look for that.

7

RELIANCE ON GOD

Without a prayer is anyone who puts his hope in anthropoids and hominoids, said Jeremiah (17:5). He should put it in Jesus Christ, for the love of whom he should serve the poor and even be mistaken for the poor. What shame can there be in that? asked Paul in his Second Letter to the Corinthians (2 Cor. 4:5).

Don't rise above your station. Just place your hope in God who's above all stations. Do what you think you should do, and God will be the witness of your goodwill.

Don't rely on your own counsel or seek the counsel of another. Rely instead on the grace of God, who helps the humble and humbles those who think they have no need of help. That's the encouragement of the Letter of James (4:6).

Don't glory in wealth, said the pauperous Jeremiah (9:23), especially if you have a stash. Don't brag about your friends, especially if they have positions of importance. If you have to glory at all, then take great pride in God, who surpasses all created things and desires above all else to give Himself as a gift. That's what Paul urged the First Corinthians to do (1:31).   beauty

Don't boast about your magnitude or your pulchritude! It takes only a sniffle to snuff your life out, corrupt your corpse, bury your bones.

Don't whistle at the snappiness of your talent or the snazziness of your attire. God won't like that, and He's the whole of whom you're only a part.

Don't think better of yourself than others. Why? Because at that very moment God might just think you worse than others. He, if anybody, should know what stuffings are found in Humankind, as the Gospel of John has hinted (2:15).

Don't be proud of your good works. Why? Because your judgments aren't necessarily God's. What tickles your fancy might make God sneeze, and then who would say *Gesundheit?*

If you do something good, believe better in others; that'll keep your humility fresh.

Prefer others to yourself, and there's no skin off your nose. But prefer yourself to another, and there's no telling which of your legs God'll break first.

The humble soul's vista is shimmering with peace. The heart of the proud soul, however, is frequently clouded with jealousy or rage.

8

FAMILIARITY FLOUTED

"Don't unfold your heart to anyone," said the cautious Jeremiah (17:5).

When you get a problem, present it to a counselor who knows what he's doing and doesn't hesitate to tell you. The Book of Proverbs suggests much the same (25:9).

Don't hang on the youngsters and don't dawdle with the outsiders.

Don't dally with the rich and famous; or so says the Book of Proverbs (25:6).

The humble and the simple, the devout and the obedient, these are the ones to associate with. And with them busy yourself only in the Edifiables.

Don't commend yourself to any one woman in particular, but commend all women as a group to God. That's what Jesus son of Sirach would have us do (9:1–9).

Don't draw attention to yourself in a crowd.

But if you must have some familiars, then choose God and his Holy Angels.

Charity knows no bounds, but familiarity, apparently, has its limits. For example, we hear of a person who has a glowing reputation and immediately we think we could be such good friends. But when we meet him face to face, of course we're polite, but once he opens his mouth, our eyes begin to glaze.

And we're just vain enough to think that the opposite isn't true. But how true it is! Others should be quite pleased to meet us, we think, but, astonishingly, as soon as we begin to speak, and of course we speak so very well, their eyes grow steely, staring right through us; that's to say, they sense the latent load that's in us.

9

OBEDIENCE & SUBJECTION

It's a great thing you're living under obedience; that's to say, doing things the way a superior wants them, not the way you think they ought to be. And it's safer too. Nobody blames an inferior when something goes wrong.

But many Devouts under obedience today feel they're prisoners, and their complaints rise like murmurings from the cell block. But these Devouts will never achieve freedom of mind until they whole-heartedly subject themselves to the will of God.

But don't let me stop you. Hit the road if you want, hithering and thithering wherever you like! Mark you, you won't find rest until you humbly subject yourself to the superior's regime.

But if you're so dreamy, then dream this: Yourself in front of the last monastery at the end of the world, ringing the bell at the gate—things will definitely be better here! Sweet dream, I grant you, but it's still a dream. And how many of today's Devouts have fallen for it!

Yes, it's true, each one of us does what he feels in his bones is right. And yes, each one of us associates with those who feel the same way. But God is among us now. We have to leave behind what we feel if ever we hope to achieve peace of soul. Is that too much to ask?

Who's so wise that he can know everything there is to know? No one, of course. Therefore, don't rely too much on how you feel on any given day. But don't hesitate to listen to the way others feel.

At any given moment we all feel we know what's the right and good thing to do. But next time it happens to you, take God's advice and drive it out of your mind. Why? Follow yourself, and you'll end up in ever decreasing circles. Follow another, and you'll find yourself farther down the path toward perfection than you could've ever dreamed.

Good Counsel, or so the Proverb goes (12:15): to accept it keeps one's spirituality fresh, but to give it to the young of soul on a daily basis ages the counselor prematurely.

Advice is one thing, but it's not the only thing. There are also Sound Reason and Good Cause. They too can encourage one to acquiesce to others.

No matter whence the wisdom, not to defer to another is a clear indication that, no matter what your age, you're either a pompous twit or a willful snot.

10

CLASHING CONVERSATIONS

Shun the madding crowd. Turn a deaf ear to the histories of the World. Whether original works or just condensations, they crowd out our knowledge of the world of the spirit. And the vanity in these volumes—a light dusting at first, but before you know it, it's snowing soot!

Many's the time I wish I hadn't gone outside the walls. All I did was talk. I yammered and listened to the yammerings of others, but when it was time to return to the realm of silence, my ears were battered the color of plum.

Tittlers and tattlers I suppose we all are when it comes to our bruiséd hearts; talk helps, and someone needs to listen. But why is it that jokes and japes are so good at relieving the stress, the depression? Well, it must be the magpies in us, and though I hesitate to say it, it's not so bad every now and then to give them voice to jabber and to chatter and to tell you what the matter is with you.

These klatches outside the walls, they're such a pain! At best, in vain. At worst, inane. They're for exterior consolation only, for they clash with the very consolation that's interior and divine.

Inside the walls we Devouts must watch and pray, as the Gospel of Matthew urges us (26:41), that none of our time is spent idly. But if we have to speak and have the permission, we should do so but only about *bona fide* Edifiables; Paul'd have the Ephesians do just that

(4:29). Otherwise, abuse of this rule in particular and negligence of our own spiritual progress in general will lead us to lose control of our tongue.

Nevertheless, because you're in a religious community devoted to the Lord, conversational topics related to spiritual progress should come up from time to time.

11

LOSING SPIRITUAL PEACE

We want peace, of course, but sometimes we don't want to spend a lot of time trying to acquire it. Instead, we lose ourselves in the crowd, intrude ourselves into foreign affairs—that's to say, in affairs outside the monastery walls. Continue to do that, and we'll surely lose what little peace we have.

What's the attraction outside? Why do we pounce on every invitation, attend every function? Why do we ignore every chance to gather ourselves within? Blessed are those who live uncomplicated lives, for they shall have heads without headaches.

Why have some of the Saints been such perfect models of the contemplative life? Because they strove to deaden their earthly desires. In doing so they weren't without some spiritual guile. They emptied out the innermost parts of their hidden hearts so they could cling to God.

Inside the walls we play too much with our pet distractions; outside, we mingle too often with the passing parade.

Rarely do we stamp out a vice completely. Daily do we forget to light a candle under ourselves.

Rarely do we achieve the perfection that's possible within one day. And so we remain neither hot nor cold, just a bit of each, a puddle of no particular pretension.

If we were maximally dead to ourselves and only minimally involved with others, then we could divine the divine, that's to say, experience some of the delights in the Heavenly Garden. But we aren't, so we can't. Our passions and concupiscences are plants, wildly successful plants choking everything in sight.

About to swing on down the road to perfection in the merry hope of following the Saints, we take a header on the first cobble and howl to high heaven! Bruised knees, bruised feelings, we decide to stay home and nurse our hurts, not all that unhappy, it has to be admitted, about postponing the trip for the thousandth time.

Hold your ground like the brave embroiled in battle; that's what we should do. Have no fear. God'll give us a sign from above. For He's prepared to help those who slug it out for the greater glory. After all, He promotes the fights, He says, so we can enjoy the victories.

Spiritual progress, that's what we're concerned about here. Observing only the externals of our religion is not enough. Devotion will dry up if that's all we're going to do.

Our garden's overrun. Let's put ax to the root. Let's purge ourselves of the spurge, the gorse and the vetch, the cattail and the creeper. That's to say, as the Gospel of Matthew exhorts (3:10), let's root out our passions, the deadly nightshades that haunt our patch. Only then will the roses emerge.

Stamp out just one vice a year, and you'll soon be a perfect individual. That's a piece of common wisdom but, apparently, experience tells us otherwise. In the beginning of our monastic life, we were more obedient and more observant than we are today, many years after our first vows. Or so it seems in retrospect.

Fervor and progress ought to inch along each day—that's the way it was in the Great Bernard's day, or so he said in one of his sermons (27:5), when many of his monks managed to retain their first fervor for a lifetime. But nowadays it's an eyebrow raiser if some bloke can retain just a smidge of his first fervor for a few weeks!

What's the moral?

No pain, no gain. If we'd undergone more pain at the beginning, we'd have made more gain by now. And wouldn't that be nice?

Not to do what you're used to is hard. Harder still, to do what you're not accustomed to. But if you don't make it a practice of dealing with the small annoyances, you'll be helpless in the face of a big challenge. Make no mistake about it. Self-denial is what we're talking about here.

Now's the time to make a new start. Resist your inclination. Unlearn your bad behavior, lest it lead you little by little to worse behavior.

Oh, if you'd only make a turnaround! You'd start pleasing yourself and stop annoying others. Living your life well, that's the way to pay more attention to your spiritual progress.

12

WHEN BAD IS GOOD

It's good to be dumped on. How often? Occasionally. Why? It's a reminder. Of what? That this isn't our world; that we're exiles somewhere between this world and the next. It's all right to hope, but not to put hope in this world.

It's not so bad to be lied about. How often? Every now and then. Why? It's an experience. It draws us toward humility and shields us against vainglory.

By and large we Devouts are virtuous gents. But to be vilified in the marketplace, crucified in the monastery! That's what often happens, but who knows the real story? God knows. He's our witness. He'll vouch for us when the Final Time comes.

What happens when a person plants himself firmly in God? He learns he doesn't have to stray far for nourishment.

What happens when that same person is tried and tested or besieged with bad thoughts? He comes to understand there's nothing without God, as John has written (15:5), and that he needs God more.

What happens when that person cries, groans, and puts to prayer all the miseries he suffers? It wears him down to the point that he desires death to come, that "he can be dissolved and be with Christ," as Paul wrote to the Philippians (1:23).

One or all these calamities will help the person of goodwill to take note. Perfect Security and Plentiful Peace—these commodities can't be had, at least in this world.

13

TEMPTATION HAPPENS

As long as we live in this world, trials and tribulations will dog our steps. Job had it right. "Human life on this earth is just one unending trudge" (7:1). Each one of us, therefore, ought to take care. Don't underestimate the power of a temptation. Don't overestimate your power to resist a temptation. After all, we don't want the Devil to take us by surprise. He never sleeps. He goes about seeking whom he may devour, as Peter wrote in his First Letter (5:8).

What's the moral?

No one's so honied and wholesome that he can't be deviled for dinner. And at dinner, or so the Gospels would have us believe, the Devil's the guest from Hell.

Yes, temptations are often useful to the human race, whether they come in small packages or large. But how can this be? They bring us low, purge, scourge, and school us in the fire; that's to say, they scare the living daylights out of us.

All the Saints have passed barefoot over the coals and in the process still made some spiritual progress. Alas, those who can't withstand temptations become the shipwrecked, cast adrift forever.

Yes, there's a moral.

There's no religious order so lofty or monastery so remote that the Unwanted Visitor can't slip in and make some mischief.

Over time Humankind hasn't been able to defend itself success-fully from the assaults of all temptations. Our common experience tells us that. And the reason why? The source of our temptations has already invaded us; that's to say, we were born in concupiscence, and in concupiscence we thrive. Sad to say, we didn't need the Letter of James to remind us of that (1:14).

We do have some success in the fight. But as one temptation or tribulation is dispatched, another soon takes its place. We'll always have something to whack away at, it seems, for aren't we still paying the price for pummeling our Primal Felicity?

Many seek to flee temptations altogether. Alas, the escape route is clogged, and the refugee is destined to succumb!

Advancing to the rear, then, isn't the answer. We can't hope to conquer that way. But through spiritual cunning—that's to say, through Patience and True Humility—we become the stronger, and the tempters have to try the harder.

If a wildly successful plant—that's to say, a temptation—causes you pain, you'll probably take the pruning knife and trim it back. Do that, and it'll return the hardier. Pull out its root, however, and it's gone forever. You'll feel better, and your spiritual garden will recover its charm.

You have some other implements, rarely used. Patience and Endurance Paul would include in that number, as he did in Colossians (1:11). It may take a little while, but with these and the help of God, you'll triumph amid the tulips. Callousness and Petulance, broken tools both. What's the common wisdom? *Impatiens* can't be hurried by impatience!

In times of temptation, and if you're the tempted, accept all the advice you can get. If someone else is the tempted, don't deal harshly with him. Give him all the consolation he can handle.

Like a ship unmoored, the soul is set adrift by temptation. Like a ship without a tiller, the soul is tossed about the waves. Like a mariner without a chart, the soul is tempted every which way. Like a seaman who has a chart but can't make head or tail out of it, the soul is at the mercy of the sea.

Fire proves iron—that's the kind of point Jesus son of Sirach liked to make (31:26)—and temptation fires the just man.

Often we don't know what we can do until temptation opens us up to what we are.

Stand sentinel in the intellect we must, before temptation strikes. Engage the Enemy at the earliest possible moment. In the chapel. In the dining hall. At the gate. On the road. In the field.

To this very point a certain ancient Roman writer, Ovid, the amatory poet, had this wheeze: "If you want to stop, stop at the start. Have the antidote ready before you drink the poison. Otherwise you'll be dead before the saving draft can reach the lips" (*Remedies for Love* 2.91–92).

That's how temptation works. A simple thought enters the mind. A vivid imagination goes to work. After that it's a nudge, a wink, and a nod.

Right from the start you should resist strongly. When you don't, the Enemy bearing evils tiptoes in unawares and wins the day. And so it is every day. The slower your response, the quicker the Devil's step.

The temptations you have to undergo are graver at the beginning of your spiritual life than at the end. However you look at it, they're all mud. For one person it's a wallow all his life. For another, it's just an occasional splatter.

Whatever the grand total, we notice one thing. Our temptations have been customized. No two are alike. That explains why each one fits perfectly. The Divine Designer, in association with Weights & Measures Supernatural, has seen to that. That explains also why we can shed each and every temptation that's laid upon us. The Designer fully expects us to. Another garment awaits the Elect.

Therefore, we shouldn't despair when we're tempted. We should pray more fervently to God. After all, He thinks us worthy of help in every tribulation.

According to Paul in First Corinthians, who should know, "God will give us resources enough" (10:13) so that we can overcome.

Therefore, let's humble our souls, huddle ourselves, under the hand of God in every trial and tribulation, as the story of Judith encourages us to do (8:17). Why? "He'll help the humble in spirit," the Evangelist Luke has promised (1:52). And at every temptation that's overcome, He'll sound the trumpet.

In trials and tribulations the perfection of Humankind is hammered out. I give you one example—Virtue. The better it's hidden, the more light it gives off, or so the common spiritual wisdom goes. But if the virtuous can't recognize a temptation when it kisses them on the cheek, what good is all the devotion and fervor? For these poor souls, though, there's still hope. If they patiently sustain themselves in time of adversity, then they'll continue to inch along the spiritual path.

Some seem to be protected from the great temptations of life and yet are overwhelmed by the nit-picking of daily routine. But there's another way of looking at it. They're humbled, hobbled, by their poor, shabby response to the small temptations. Hence, they're not so overconfident about their ability to handle the large ones.

14
RUSH TO JUDGMENT

Turn your eyes on yourself. Stop judging the faults of others. Why? You snoop about long and hard in the lives of others, and all you come up with is a thimbleful. In the process you leave much wreckage behind even where you found no fault.

Make an inventory of your own faults and negligences, and you'll come up with a basketful. Yes, it's a matter of the heart, our heart, and we're always in a terrible judgmental state.

But have you noticed? When others commit faults, we harden our hearts against them, excusing little because they should know better. But when we commit the very same faults, we soften our hearts, excusing much because of the wonderfulness of ourselves.

It's a matter of common sense. Resist the rush to judgment. You know it's wrong, and it wouldn't happen so often if God were truly the sole object of your gaze.

But there's no doubt we suffer damage. Something lurks on the inside. Something trips us up on the outside. Unbeknownst to themselves, many people are self-seekers; that's to say, it's themselves they're chasing, and they don't even know it. They seem happy enough when things are going their own way. But when they aren't, they run and sit in a corner and cry big tears. How can this happen? Well, with so many of us thinking and holding so many different opinions, there's bound to be a disagreement now and then; and no one, not even the friendly and the civil, the religious and the devout, are exempt from hurt feelings.

Old habits die hard. That's practical wisdom, and so is this: Nobody trusts farther than he can see.

Here's some spiritual wisdom. Rely on Jesus Christ as your Lord and Master. If you don't, but rely rather on your own ability to logick your way through life, then you won't be nominated for the *Homo Illuminatus* award.

God sees Himself as creator and sees us as creatures. To that end He wants us to climb above mere human reason. He wants to light our love with the Divine Torch.

15

CHARITABLE WORKS

A bad deed should never be done, no, not for anything in the world, not even for the love of God or another human being.

A good deed sometimes has to be squeezed into the daily routine, especially when it's for the advantage of the poor.

The *opus interruptum* in question would seem to be lost forever, but it isn't; it's been converted to a better work.

A deed done without charity has no spiritual value. Paul pro-pounded that in his First to the Corinthians (13:3).

A deed done with charity, however small or insignificant it may be, is a thoroughly fruitful work.

The way God weighs in, it's not what the deed is; humongous doesn't count. It's the motive, how the deed is done. Done for the love of Jesus Christ is by far the best.

He does much who loves much. He does much who does a thing well. He does a thing well who serves his community more than him-self.

Carnality often mummers as Charity. Human Nature, Selfishness, Retribution, Convenience, they too hide behind the same holy mask, attempting to crash the Final Party.

The one who has True and Perfect Charity can't find himself in the mirror. He desires only that the glory of God flare out in all things. He envies no one; he has no pet peeves, no private toys; he doesn't rejoice in himself alone.

On the contrary, he wants to be blessed in God rather than pos-sess all things without God; again, Paul's First to the Corinthians (13:4). He attributes nothing to anyone, but refers everything to God. He sees all things fluting fountainlike from God. He sees all Saints on the far side of Judgment picnicking in the Heavenly Orchard.

Charity it is, then, the love for Jesus Christ.

From a spark of this True Charity, you'd have more than enough light to see that all earthly things—pressed down, filled to overflow-ing, beyond all measure, out of all proportion, plentifully, prodigally, extravagantly, superfluously, redundantly, excessively—mount up to nothing at all.

16

PUTTING UP WITH PUTTING DOWN

Some things you just aren't strong enough to change either in yourself or others. What can you do but patiently endure until God orders otherwise? Yes, this is a trial, and it's meant to prove your virtue under fire. Without experience in long-suffering, such merits as you have won't amount to a hill of beans.

What you might want to do is ask God for more annoyance rather than less. Perhaps then He'll think it worth His while to come to your aid. In the meantime bear up and be benign.

Once someone has been admonished a couple of times, he becomes anxious. Don't mess with him. Instead, commit yourself totally to God. Pray to God that His will and honor will appear in Him and all His servants. But how can He do this? Well, He's converted bad wine into good on at least one festive occasion!

Strive to be patient by putting up with the defects of others. Why? Because you've saddled onto others the infirmities that are dragging you down.

If you can't express approval of others, how can you possibly expect them to return approval to you?

We're quick to want others to appear polished, but why is it that we're so slow to hammer out our own dents?

We want others to be held to the letter of the law. Ourselves? We want to swan around barely observing the spirit of the law.

Worse, the uncontrollable behavior of others has spread through the populace like a plague. Better, our own errant behavior has swept over the lowlands like a flood. Clearly the latter is to be preferred to the former.

We want those others to be surrounded with strictures. We want our own behavior to know no boundaries.

Rare it is that we put ourselves on a par with our neighbor, allowing him the same amount of slack as we've come to expect ourselves.

If all the world and all the worldlings were perfect, what glory could we give to God! After all, the source of our spiritual progress is all those neighbors who are annoying us to death.

God has ordained it, and Paul has written to the Galatians (6:2). We should learn "to carry the burdens of another."

No one's without a defect, no one's without a burden, no one's sufficient unto himself, no one's wise enough to represent himself. Pauline wisdom to the Galatians (6:2) and Second Corinthians (3:5)!

We should carry each other, console each other, help, instruct, admonish each other. That's the sort of wisdom found in Proverbs (3:7), Colossians (3:13), and First Thessalonians (5:11).

The more virtue you have, the more adversity you'll encounter. Confrontations result. They shake a man up, but at the same time they reveal just what kind of man he is.

17

MONASTIC LIFE

The first thing about monastic life? You have to live in peace and harmony with others. To do that you have to discipline yourself in a thousand ways.

It's not a small thing to live in a religious community. It's not an easy thing to converse for a lifetime without a quarrel and to persevere faithfully all the way to death, as the Last Book of the New Testament encourages us to do (2:10). Blessed is he who lived well within the walls and came to a felicitous end!

If you want to survive and make progress inside the walls, you have to consider yourself an exile and wanderer outside the walls. That's what the Author of the Letter to the Hebrews encouraged the Jews in the Diaspora to think (11:13).

If you want to live the life of a monk, then you have to live the life of Christ. Not an easy thing to do. The World'll think you're a clown.

That's what Paul wrote to the First Corinthians centuries ago (4:10), and as we've come to know, his point was very well made.

The habit and the tonsure help precious little in the making of a monk. A complete change of life and a program of mortification are what make the Devout a monk.

If questions about God or salvation persist, the monk'll find nothing but tribulation and pain.

Serenity is hard to maintain, but thinking oneself the least and the lowliest does help a little.

You entered the monastery to serve, not to rule. You've been called to long suffer and long labor, not to lounge around and tell long stories. With these hard tasks Humankind is proved like gold in the furnace.

Inside the walls no one can survive unless he's wished from the bottom of his heart to flatten himself in front of God.

18

FATHERS OF THE DESERT

Keep vivid in your memory the many splendid exploits of the Holy Fathers of the desert. In their lives true religious perfection has shone out like a flaming beacon on a hill. Sad to say, what we've been able to accomplish in our own modest lives adds up to a guttering candle.

As Saints and friends of Christ, they've served the Lord in famine and drought, coldness and nakedness, labor and fatigue, vigils and fasts, holy prayers and meditations, persecutions and derisions.

Oh, how they suffered, the Apostles, the Martyrs, the Confessors, the Virgins, and all the rest who followed close upon the footsteps of Christ! They did the evangelical thing, at least as described by John (12:25), dispossessing their souls in this world that they might possess them in the next.

Oh, how isolated and dedicated was the life the Holy Fathers led in the desert! Their temptations were long and lurid, but they managed to endure. The Enemy harassed them suddenly and frequently. Just as sudden and frequent were the prayers they shot to Heaven.

Their abstinences were rugged, but they managed to swallow their hunger. Crazed was their desire for spiritual progress! Feverish was their battle against what seemed the overwhelming supremacy of their vices!

Through it all they held fast to God. Through the day they worked hard and prayed quietly to survive their harsh life; through the night they prayed, even in their sleep, their snores rising like incense to the Lord."

Every hour of work seemed too long; every hour of prayer, too short. Making time to eat was impossible. The sweetness of contemplation was irresistible.

All wealth, title, and honor, every friend and relative, they renounced. Nothing that smacked of the World did they want to have.

The necessities of life they scarcely touched. The pangs in their stomachs they begrudgingly satisfied.

And so poor were they in the things of this world, but rich, so very rich, in graces and virtues! They were ravaged on the outside, but on the inside they were refreshed with Grace and Divine Consolation.

The Fathers of the desert were aliens in their own world, but close family friends with God. In their own eyes self-esteem had no value, and hence they dressed like castaways. But in the eyes of God they were precious, chosen ones, and further haberdashery was far from their minds.

They stood in True Humility; they lived in Simple Obedience; they walked in Charity and Patience. And so daily they progressed in spirit and obtained great grace in God's presence. They've been given as examples to all Religious and ought to rouse us to more spiritual progress.

Standing in opposition to them are the Tepids, milling around every which way, affirming and denying, mummering and murmuring, whispering the rest of the world to a spiritual standstill.

Religious orders, when they were founded, were quite remarkable gardens. Hotbeds of fervor they were. Their prayers were awash with devotion. Their virtue was pruned and precise. Discipline, sometimes harsh and heavy-handed, took root. Under the rule of their Founder, and indeed under the inspiration of the Founder of Founders, Reverence and Obedience walked hand-in-hand down the garden paths.

These truly holy and perfect men poured out their lives in the strenuous fight against the World. The footprints they left behind are visible to this day.

Odd thing, though. Today's monk, who's anything but exceptional when compared to the monk of old, seems to be the exception to the rule; that's to say, he's thought to be observant and doesn't rock the boat, but there's not a great deal else that he does.

Ah, the laziness and sloppiness of the religious life today! What worldly winds could have cooled the fervor of our white-hot forge! Whatever happened to Motivation and Enthusiasm? They're nowhere to be seen! Is it any wonder, then, that the desire to live the religious life has decreased?

Once so awake during the nocturnal watch, now you're found snoring on the battlement. Is this any way to live the religious life? And you of all people! You've had the privilege of meeting many of the devout Religious in your own community in the generation just passed!

19

SPIRITUAL EXERCISES

The life of a good monk must be seen as strong in all the virtues. But often what Humanity sees is only the spit and polish; that's to say, in some respects the interior life lags behind the exterior life. Therefore, the good monk should appear to the rest of the world not as he really is, but as he wishes he were. Nonetheless, one's interior life is always to be evaluated on a higher scale than one's exterior life.

The reason for all this is that our Inspector General is God, whom we ought to reverence in all our pomps and poops. We never leave His sight. Wherever we go, we should walk, step smartly, march with the Angels.

Every day we ought to renew our commitment and excite ourselves to fervor. We should recapture the excitement of that first day of our conversion.

To that end we should say: "Help me, Lord God, in good commitment and holy service, and grant that I may begin this day as though it were my birthday in the Lord, for what I've done up to now is more the work of a mole than a monk."

The course of our spiritual progress has already been charted by our religious commitment. That's to say, the monk of goodwill has to progress with all possible diligence toward the ultimate goal.

The monk who lives out his commitment bravely often fails. The monk who lives out his commitment slapdashedly rarely succeeds. Make no mistake about it! A slippage in religious commitment, regardless of who makes it and however slight it is, causes damage to the fabric of all monasticism.

The religious commitment of the just monk depends more on the grace of God than on his own wisdom. He always relies on his vows no matter what the labor he puts his hand to. Man proposes, but God disposes, as the Book of Proverbs has it (16:9). And as a sad prophet has happily noted, "A man's path isn't always a product of his own planning"; do look at Jeremiah (10:23).

If a scheduled spiritual exercise is omitted for a good reason—say, so that you can hide an act of charity or help a needy brother—it can easily be rescheduled. If, however, the reason it's left undone is soul weariness or just plain negligence, that's enough to make it culpable in itself, and it may be considered injurious to spiritual progress.

Try though we do, we know we're going to fall short in many ways. But that's no excuse. Let's try again and as hard as we can.

To protect against occurrences like these, we have to take some positive steps. If we don't, they'll continue to trip us up. Scrutinize our Externals and Internals, that's what we have to do, and make whatever realignments are necessary. Why? Because properly paved, both speed the journey toward perfection.

You can't keep yourself in a continuous state of recollection in the monastic life. You know that already, but know also that recollect you must.

When?

Not less than once a day.

Morning or evening?

In the morning make a plan; in the evening, check how you did, that's to say, what and how you did in word, deed, and thought.

Why?

More often than you'd like to think, you've offended God and neighbor in one manner or another.

No droopy drawers here! Cinch up that cincture! Be a monk and face the diabolical onslaught head on! That's what Paul exhorted the Ephesians to do (6:11–17).

Rein in your gluttony, and you'll find it easier to bridle every other inclination of the flesh.

Never drop your guard. Read or write or pray or meditate, but whatever you do, busy yourself at all times with some form of labor for the community.

When it comes to corporal austerities, forget what everybody else does. Use your head. Sting, don't wound. No more. No less.

Personal prayers inside the walls shouldn't be paraded around outside the walls. The reason for that is simple. When you pray by yourself, you can hurt only yourself; that's to say, no damage is done to others.

As for your own spiritual life, don't become a pig about it, too lazy to come to chapel, yet strong enough to wallow through your own peculiosities.

The community's regular spiritual exercises, participate in them wholeheartedly and single-mindedly. Beyond that—and God forbid there's any time left over!—you can pray yourselves silly. Let devotion be your guide.

All spiritual exercises are suitable for all monks. Sadly, not all these exercises are equally profitable to each monk. Happily, no two monks have the same taste.

As the year passes, the many varietals of spiritual exercise are always welcomed by a monastic community. Some are good on feasts; others, on ferials. Temptation requires one sort; peace and quiet, quite another. And so on, from the times of spiritual sadness, when the dry tears sting, to the sweet weepiness of True Spiritual Joy.

Any day is a hard day to renew our spiritual exercises, but when the principal feast days roll around, it all seems so easy. And the Saints, they're waiting to help if only they're asked; they only pretend they're deaf.

From one feast day to the next, we ought to make resolutions as if they'll be our last. But how can we do this? We could imagine we're about to take wing from this world to a perch in the next.

And so we should make these times devout times, preparing ourselves carefully, passing our time prayerfully, and guarding our every observance of the Holy Rule more strictly. What's the rush? In no time we'll be brought before the Final Bar, attempting to cash in on our life of spiritual labor.

If we mistook the time of departure, let's put the blame on ourselves. From our point of view, we weren't all that well enough prepared; from God's point of view, we weren't yet ready for glory. Paul described that state in his Letter to the Romans (8:18). As for the next date of departure, who knows?

Whenever it is, let's strive to prepare better for the trip out there. "Blessed is the servant," wrote the Evangelists Luke (12:37, 42), "who, when his Lord came, was found awake. Amen I say to you, all God's goods will be put under this servant's watchful eye."

20

SOLITUDE & SILENCE

Plan to take some time off, and give some thought to what you'd do with that time; hopefully, you'll spend part of it reviewing God's favors to you in the past. What else?

Lock up ye olde curiosity shoppe. Devote more time to reading your spiritual books than your survival manuals. Withdraw from casual conversations and leisurely pursuits. Don't contract for new ventures, and don't gossip about old ones.

After you've done all these, you'll find more than enough time to undertake a program of meditation. Most of the Saints did just that—avoided collaborative projects whenever they could, choosing instead to spend some private time with God.

Seneca, that old pagan philosopher and playwright, had it right so many centuries ago. When he went out with the intelligentsia or hung around with entertainers, he returned home utterly talked out and terribly hoarse, or so he said in one of his letters (7). Quite often we have the same experience when we horse around with our friends and associates for hours, even days, on end.

What's the remedy for a talkathon? It's easier to cut out the conversation altogether than it is to cut it down to size. What's the point? It's easier to stay at home alone than to stroll about the rialto with an entourage. What's certain? Whoever wants to arrive at interiority and spirituality has to leave the crowd behind and spend some time with Jesus. The Evangelists Mark (6:31) and Luke (5:16) wrote as much.

What's the general wisdom? Nobody's comfortable in public unless he's spent a good deal of time in the quiet of his home. Nobody speaks with assurance who hasn't learned to hold his tongue. Nobody's a success as general who hasn't already survived as soldier. Nobody respects decrees who hasn't already obeyed writs.

If you want to feel secure, then you have to have a good conscience. Paul made that clear in his Second Letter to the Corinthians (1:12). And that's how the Saints did it. Virtue and Grace shone from their very faces, but Fear of God ran deep in their very veins; even then they were subject to fits of spiritual anxiety and secular stress. As for the depraved, what security they do feel in their being rises from a swamp of pride and presumption.

Is there a moral?

On the outside you may appear modest as a monk or holy as a hermit; but on the inside, at least while you're on this earth, you're seething and frothing and feeling anything but secure.

More often than they might suspect, people of reputation have been in grave danger and didn't know it. They're good people, but they've extended their self-confidence beyond its natural limit. From this one could draw the conclusion that it's helpful to be tempted from time to time. One might even say that to be tempted to the point of endurance could help deflate interior desolations and deflect exterior consolations.

Who doesn't seek transitory joy? Who doesn't occupy himself with the World? We all do. But the one who has a good conscience, severs all tentacles to attachment, meditates on divine and salutary things—he's the one who places his whole hope in God. He's the one who sails his boats on a sea of calm.

No one can ascend to Heavenly Consolation. That's because there's no sure stair. One solid step, though, is our heart's True Sorrow. And where else can this sorrow be found but in one's cubicle. There you can shut out the hubbub of the World. "In your cubicles, on your cots, work out your sorrowful contrition," said the Psalmist (4:4). More often than not, you'll find in your cell what you lost in the streets.

A cell that's much prayed in is a pleasant spot. A cell that's rarely prayed in is a forbidding place. That makes sense, doesn't it? In the first blush of your conversion you cultivated the solitude of your cell, and guarded against all invasions of your quietude. Now you find it warming, welcoming, like an old dog or an old shoe.

In quiet and silence the faithful soul makes progress, the hidden meanings of the Scriptures become clear, and the eyes weep with devotion every night. Even as one learns to grow still, one draws closer to the Creator and farther from the hurly-burly of the World. As one divests oneself of one set of friends and acquaintances, one's visited by another, God and his Holy Angels.

Two courses of action. Better, to lie still in one's cubicle and worry about one's spiritual welfare. Worse, to roam the streets a wonder-worker for others to the neglect of one's own spiritual life.

Laudable it is for the Religious to go to market only rarely. Laudable too is that, even when he does go, he refrains from meeting the eyes of others; from his very mien they know that he lives in another world.

Why do you want to go out and see what you really shouldn't need to see?

"The World passes, as does its concupiscence," wrote John the Evangelist in his First Letter (2:17).

Our sensual desires promise us a promenade, but deliver us only a dragonnade.

A sprightly step in the forenoon turns into a draggled tail in the afternoon.

All-nighters of roister-doistery lead only to mornings of hugger-muggery, that's to say, of sickness and sadness.

Need I ask?

Every carnal joy begins with a caress, or so the Proverb goes (23:31–32), but in the end curls up into a furry ball and dies.

I ask the question again.

What can you see outside the monastery walls that you can't see inside?

Behold Heaven and Earth and all the elements; from these all things are made.

What can you see on the outside that will survive the sun? That was the sort of question the Ancient Preacher in Ecclesiastes asked (2:11). What's your answer? Perhaps you can find satisfaction somewhere out there, but truth to tell, you still can't reach out to touch it. If you were to see all the things in all the world crammed into one still life, no matter how large the canvas, you'd still be no better off.

"Raise your eyes to God in the highest," said the Psalmist (123:1). Pray for your own sins and negligences. Forgive the vain things vain people have done to you.

Look to the precepts God gave you. "Shut the door behind you," wrote the Evangelist Matthew (6:6). Call Jesus, your Beloved Friend, to join you. Remain with Him in your cell. Why? You won't find peace like this anywhere else in the world.

If you hadn't gone outside the walls, you wouldn't have heard the disturbing rumors; better for you to have stayed inside in blissful ignorance. From which it follows that you may delight in hearing the latest news on the strand, but you'll surely have to deal with the terrible dislocation that results.

21
SCRUPLES OF THE HEART

If you genuinely want to make spiritual progress, then fear two things, or so the Book of Proverbs has suggested (19:23). Life with God. Life without God.

Discipline your senses. Don't let them dance you at the end of a string.

It's always a dry season until you give way to the sorrowing of the heart. Only then will the drops of devotion come.

Heart-felt sorrow opens many a door. Deep-down compulsion slams the door in your face every time.

We may stumble onto happiness, but, remember, we're exiles and the world is alive with peril.

You laugh at the defects of the world, but your own spiritual defects you shrug off. Yet they bedevil your soul, and what do you do about it? You laugh. Nobody laughs in public these days, except you. You laugh uproariously, but the joke's on you. It's the other way around. Your peccadillos are laughing at you when you should be weeping uncontrollably where no one can see.

What's missing is the fear of God and a working conscience.

Joy or Liberty can't be true and good if we don't feel the pain of reformation in our souls.

Happy the monk who can scatter his distractions and collect himself into holy sorrowing of the heart!

Happy the monk who can shield his snow-white conscience from bilious gray pigeons! That's to say, from the droppings of his own inordinate affections.

Face it! When it comes to manliness, it takes a good habit to whip a bad habit. If you don't care a fig for the World, the World won't care a farthing for you.

Don't inundate yourself with the affairs of the low and unlovely, and don't insinuate yourself into the affairs of the high and mighty. Remember, you're a member of a holy company dedicated to spiritual progress. Hence, keep a steely eye on yourself. Upbraid yourself, when necessary.

If you cast a knowing wink at the World and the World doesn't return the wink, don't tear up, don't waste a single tear of your own.

Give serious thought to this possibility. You may not have the right stuff to be a servant of God and live the devout life.

After all, we don't have many consolations in this sort of life; at least as Flesh counts them. That's what our experience tells us. And rarer still, at least as the Soul counts them, are the Divine Consolations. There's got to be a reason, and it's sin. We just don't seek the sorrowing of the heart hard enough. The least we could do is throw our vanities to the wind.

Are you worth Divine Consolation? Face it, all you're worth is a bundle of snakes!

When you are contrite to the point of perfection, the face you present to the world is never cheerful, always chary.

The good person has more than enough to be sorrowful for, to weep for.

No matter how you look at it—and your neighbor will confirm it—no one lives on this earth without tribulation.

The more you eye the condition of your own soul, the more openly you weep. The causes of just sorrow and internal contrition are our sins and the vices that lead to our sins. And isn't it true that we spend so much time on earthly grapplings that we have almost no time to give to celestial contemplations?

Death is approaching more quickly than life's unfolding. Think about that now, and put more shoulder into your reformation of life.

We're on the near side of death now, but on the far side await the pains of Hell or Purgatory. Weigh that in your heart, and maybe now you'll be willing to undertake the laborious program of reform, readying yourself for the Final Rigor.

Why is it that considerations like these don't hit the target? Why are we so blind to the blandishments bandied about us? Are we as lazy and loutish as that?

What spirit is left in that wretched body of yours? A whistle? A whimper? A whisper? Pray, therefore, humbly to the Lord that He give you the spirit of contrition. Say as the Psalmist said (80:5), "With the bread of tears satisfy my hunger, Lord, and with a measure of tears satisfy my thirst."

22

MISERIES OF THIS LIFE

Wherever you are, whatever you turn to, you're in a wretched state, unless you turn to God.

So you don't succeed in everything you do? What's the big fuss?

What monk gets everything he wants? Not I, not you, not anyone else on the face of this earth. Not even a king or a pope. All worldlings must wade through the gutters of tribulation and anguish. If anyone fares better, then he's in a good position to suffer rather more for God's sake.

"Look, there goes a man who's got a good life!" That's what the feeble-minded say. "He's got a lot of money, a big house, friends in high places!"

But there's another way.

Look to the Celestial, and you'll see that the Temporal doesn't amount to a great deal.

Possessions are here one day, gone the next. If you're overly possessive, then your mind plays a trick. Everyone you meet is plotting to swipe them.

Ten of everything? Having ten settees won't make your bottom ten times happier. One of everything will do.

Misery, if you want the true definition of the word, is just living on this earth.

The more you attend to the sweetness of spiritual things, the more you realize how bitter the human experience is.

That's because you feel more dearly and see more clearly the defects of human corruption. To eat, drink, watch, sleep, relax, labor, and be subject to all the bodily functions, to have to do all these things, that's the truly great misery. That's the great affliction, one has to conclude. Free from sin, and free for Heaven—that's the freedom to pray for.

The bag of bones we have to lug around this world is a rackety load. The Psalmist knew (25:17). Hence, his heart-rending cry, "Grasp my body with one hand, O Lord, and with the other rip my heart from it!"

How unhappy are those who don't know their own misery! How unhappier still are those who know this miserable and corruptible life, but also love it! Why? They've embraced this misery even when it's brought them only the barest necessities. Laborers and beggars they are! But they'd still rather hang out on this earth than give a thought about the kingdom of God.

The wisdom of the flesh—that's all some people know. Insane of mind and soul, they laze about the loam and think they're in Heaven.

When their end comes, these wretched folk will surely realize that their love for the things of this earth is low-down, even loathsome.

The Saints of God, on the other hand, and the Devouts, all friends of Christ, paid no attention to their carnal desires and what passed for pleasure in their time. They focused only on their eternal desires. They ogled only the Perennials and Invisibles; the Visibles they ignored lest they drag them down to the lower depths. Don't, dear friend, lose confidence in making spiritual progress. There's still time, still opportunity.

Why do you postpone your plan? Arise this instant, and begin to pray. Now's the time to do something—that's what Paul asked the Corinthians, in his Second Letter, to do (6:2)—to stand up and fight, to make the necessary changes.

When you're doing badly and your head aches, you think it's the end of the world. If it is, fine. But if it isn't, there's time to do something worthwhile. It's necessary to go through fire and water, before the warmth returns to the coolth.

No pain, no gain—at least as far as vice is concerned. As long as you beg off because your body might bruise, you can't be without sin or live without tedium and pain. We'd like to have a respite from all the misery, but we can't. We've lost our innocence through sin. In the same Fell Swoop we also lost our True Beatitude.

Is there no hope? Well, there's always Patience, which the Letter to the Hebrews tries to offer (10:36). We must hold on to it, as we wait for the mercy of God. How long will that be? Until this iniquity that passes for life has ebbed and this mortality has been wrung from our soul; that's Paul's best surmise in that same letter to the Corinthians (2 Cor. 5:4).

Our porcelain's perfect, or so we think, but that's when the brown veins come a-creeping.

Today we confess our sins, but tomorrow we commit more of the same. Now we propose to be on the lookout; yet after an hour we do what we promised we wouldn't.

Deservedly, therefore, we should humble ourselves.

But how can we do that?

We should go into a corner and not think of the wonderfulness of ourselves.

Why? you ask for the thousandth time.

We all develop veins, yes, but we also manage to fall off the shelf.

Which is another way of saying the obvious. All too soon what we've acquired with hard labor, and with additional help from Grace, can be lost in a nonce through negligence.

If we get up in the morning with a grouch and drag ourselves through the day, what'll we have done by nightfall?

Peace and Security—those are the virtues singled out by Paul, Silvanus, and Timothy in their First Letter to the Thessalonians (5:3). We have to pretend we have them, but why won't we work to get them? Why do we want just to lie down and go back to sleep?

In our conversation, why isn't there a hint, just a whiff, of True Sanctity? Perhaps we should go back to school, pretend we're novices again, and listen to all those tedious instructions about how to change our behavior.

Perhaps then there'd be hope we could make some changes now and progress a little farther down the road to spiritual perfection in the future.

23
STRUGGLING

Sooner than you think, Death will come to call. While you can, look over your shoulder to see how you've been doing.

Terrible tigers one day, dust kittens the next! Do look at First Maccabees (2:63).

Whenever a Devout's out of eyesight, he's out of mind-set.

Oh, the blobbiness and blabbiness of the human heart! It meditates only on the present and makes no provision for the future!

In everything you think and do, you ought to conduct yourself as though you were going to die tomorrow.

If you have a good conscience, there's not much to fear. Hide, yes, but not from Death; it's your sins you should take cover from.

But what if there's no tomorrow and you aren't ready today? And in the unlikely event that there is a tomorrow, what then?

A long life is good to have, but how does it compare to a changed life? Let me put that another way. Is there really a connection between length of life and amount of change for the better? Often just the opposite is true. The longer you live, the more guilt you rack up. One day—just imagine one day—of your life devoted to spiritual change! If you could find just one such day in your life, you'd be better off than the rest of Humankind.

Many monks reflect on the fact that years have passed since their conversion. But I'd contest that what they underwent so long ago was a real conversion. Why? The fruit of that change is barely visible to the naked eye today.

A short life has its fears, but a long life has its dangers.

Always keep before your eyes the hour of your own death, and daily prepare yourself for the moment of death. That would please Jesus son of Sirach (7:36). Do this, and happiness will be yours.

Often you've been present when a monk dies. Just drink that scene in, in the full knowledge that you'll soon be making this very same journey. Jesus son of Sirach promised that (38:22), and, of course, he too has fulfilled his own promise.

When morning comes, think to yourself that night will never come. When night falls, dare not to promise yourself another dawn.

My point is—and I do have a point—hold yourself in readiness, as the Gospel of Luke urges (21:36), and don't miss a beat. Why? We all know people who've died before they said a prayer or changed their life.

When Death knocks, surprise him. Invite him in and ask what took him so long—the tea's been getting cold.

Much the same thing the Evangelist Luke wrote about in his twelfth chapter, verse 40, but he phrased it a different way. Yes, there'll be knock at the door. And yes, the Son of Man will come as surely as Death. Problem is, we still don't know when to put the kettle on. Nor did Matthew in his own Gospel (24:44). Readiness is all.

How happy and prudent is the person whose life's lived up to his eulogy! What steps did he take to attain such perfection? Complete contempt for the World and everything in it. Fervent desire to make spiritual progress. Love of discipline. Labor of penitence. Promptness of obedience. Abnegation of self. Bearing up under every adversity for the love of Christ. Having become expert in all these virtues, he can feel confident that he'll die a good death.

While you have your health, you can do many good things. But once sickness comes, I don't know what you'll be able to do.

Few are able to turn sickness to their spiritual advantage. Or so I've been able to observe.

As for those poor pilgrims who think that making the rounds of all the Martyrs' shrines will improve their own chances at death, they're just deluding themselves.

Friends and neighbors are nice, but don't put your confidence in them for long, and certainly don't expect them to stand in for you at the Final Bar. Why? Because they'll forget you more quickly than you'd guess.

Now's the time for you to do something about it. Do provide for yourself, and do set aside a bit of the good for the future.

Worry about yourself, yes, and do it now. Why? Who'll worry about you in the future?

The present moment is precious, as the Apostle Paul said in his Second Letter to the Corinthians. Now is "the day of salvation; now, the perfect time" (6:2).

Oh, what an outrage it is! You live your life without a plan. You fill your day with indifferent acts. Don't you realize what's at stake? It's your eternal life!

Just one day more, just one hour more, to change your life for the better—that's what you'll petition the Almighty for sometime soon, someday soon. And what you want to know from me today is whether your request'll be honored. Well, I really don't know.

Just the thought of death is paralyzing, dearest friend, and there's nothing you can do about it.

All you can do is build up your strength, your spiritual strength—that's what you'll need in the Final Hour. Then you'll rejoice, not recoil, at the thought of death.

Now's the time, when you've got your physical strength, to stop living with the World and start living with Jesus Christ—that was Paul's advice to the Romans (6:8), to condemn everything in the World and forge ahead for Christ.

To face death with confidence, you must commit your creaking corpus to a grueling program of penance.

Ahhh, what a *Dummkopf!* You think you'll live a long life when you don't know if you can survive till the end of the day! Lots of people have had the same thought, but now they're no longer with us, swept off the face of the earth before they had a chance at a second thought.

How many have died recently—isn't that often the subject of casual conversation? This one's been stabbed; that one's been drowned. So-and-so's had a great fall and broken his thick neck.

What's-his-name's choked to death on his dinner. You-know-who began his game, but someone else had to finish it!

Fire, war, plague, robbery—killers all!

So it may be said, and it's true in several senses, death is the end of all of us. Did we really need the Ancient Preacher in Ecclesiastes (7:20) to tell us this?

What is life after all? It's like a cloud formed by the wind into a puff, sang the Psalmist (144:4), and yet by the very same wind wheezed away in all directions.

Death will surely come, but who'll remember you after death? And who'll pray for you?

Do it, dear soul; just do it now. You don't know when you'll die. And when you do drop dead, you don't know what'll happen right after.

Once you've made the time, gather around you only immortal riches, or so the Gospel of Luke exhorted (12:33). Think of nothing else but your own salvation. Take care only for the things of God.

Also use the time you have left to make some new friends for yourself: the Saints of God. Venerate them and imitate their lives. Then, when it's time to leave your wretched hut, as Luke would say (16:9), "They'll welcome you into their tents."

While you're on this earth, abandon your citizenship, but preserve your status as a wanderer who knows no home but a hostel. That's how the First Letter of the Apostle Peter summed it up (2:11).

Pay no attention to the commerce of this world.

Keep your affections unencumbered and always raised to God. Why? You know why. You don't have here a lasting dwelling place, warned the Letter to the Hebrews (13:14).

To that Heavenly Domicile, then, direct your daily prayers and tearful practices. If you don't, what will happen to your spirit after death? One thing is sure. It won't deserve to pass happily through to the Lord. Amen.

24
JUDGMENT & PUNISHMENT

Put everything into final perspective. You live and work in this century, but the judgment, the Final Appraisal, of who you truly are will come at the end of time. Yes, you'll stand before the Judge of judges, as Paul promised the Romans (14:10), you and everyone else who's lived on the face of the earth.

Look smart. This Judge can't be hoodwinked—that's what Job found out (31:14). He can't be softened up with a bribe. He knows a bad alibi when He hears one. All He has to do is render a just verdict, and He can do that in no time flat.

O thrice miserable and thoroughly insipid sinner, just what do you think you're doing? What'll you respond to the God who knows no tremble, but all your evil? You'll turn to jelly, that's what you'll do. Why now, you start to shiver and to shake when someone just makes a face at you!

On the Day of Judgment you'll need to bring papers, proof of all the stuff you did. Why? Well, you'll have to defend yourself; no defense counsel here. Each defendant'll be presented with a detailed indictment. Examine it closely. Not an error on the list!

All that's in the indefinite future. Today your labor can bear fruit, plums and pomegranates. Your spiritual pain can bear fruit too, elephant tears, waterfalls of sorrows. Fortunately, they can be considered purgative and, happily, in an amount equal to your guilt.

Purgatory's a lot like the life of a patient monk on earth.

He bears up under the terrible weight of injustice. He worries more about the man who hit him in the mush than the bloody nose he sustained. He prays for the contrarians who always seem to be buzzing about. He indulges the bad behavior of others; and yet he's slow to seek indulgence for his own shortcomings.

He's quicker to pardon a mugger than the mugger to pummel him. Such violence as he may engage in is directed only toward himself as he vainly tries to whip his flesh into spiritual submission.

Purge your sins, excise your vices—that's the message of Purgatory. And better now than later, in the hairy hands of another.

One more thing, and I wish it weren't so, but in all of this there's just one continuing and complicating factor. It's that flaming love we have for the flesh!

What else will that Fire of fires devour but your sins?

As for now, you make a serious mistake when you spare yourself the spiritual rigors. Follow the flesh, an easier path now, but it's the harder one down the line. In fact, keep going as you are, and you'll just be piling up the kindling for your own pyre.

But fire isn't the only grief. Each sin has its own particular punishment. The Lazy will be prickled with pointy tips. The Gluttonous will be choked with the glutinous. The Lustful will burn like pitch and stink like sulfur. And for their own particular grief, the Envious will be set to howl like rabid dogs at midnight.

In Hell every vice'll have its own excruciating punishment. For example, the Prideful will be flustered with confusion. The Greedy will be bent over like famine victims.

One hour in this hellhole will produce more pain than a hundred years of penitential practice.

There, there's no rest for the Wicked, no consolation for the Condemned. At least here on earth, there's some respite from the spiritual rigors—one doesn't have to fast forever—and some consolation from one's spiritual friends.

The Day of Judgment is approaching at a gallop. So now's the time to look to your life. Do daily sorrow for your sins, and the Blessed above will greet you at the terminus of time.

As the Great Solomon said in his book of Wisdom, "The just will stand in great constancy against those who pinned them down" and oppressed them (5:1).

At the Final Bar you who subject yourselves to the judgments of Humankind will be able to stand up and look the Final Judge in the eye. Then the Poor and the Humble will come into new boldness, and the Proud will face fear for the first time.

In Heaven everything will be turned upside down.

The one who gave up everything to follow Christ—a dreadful mistake in the eyes of the World, as Paul found out, to his own discomfort, and passed the word on in his First Letter to the Corinthians (4:10)—will be considered wise. The one who endured every trial and tribulation will be pleasantly surprised when he's called patient. As the Psalmist has sung, "Every iniquity will be nailed to the wall once and for all" (107:42).

Every religious person will rejoice, and every irreligious person will recoil. The cheeks of those who've never shown cheek to others will have a heavenly glow. The cheapest attire will become the rage, and designer raiment will be left on the rack. The pauper's hovel will attract visitors while weeds will overrun the magnate's manse. Patience will overpower Force. Obedience will outwit Cunning.

In Heaven there'll be many rewards. Clear Conscience will rejoice over Learned Philosophy. Contempt of Riches will weigh in over Earthly Goods. Devout Prayer'll be more consoling than Delicious Food. Guarded Silence will out-talk Excessive Conversation. Holy Works will have more value than Pretty Words. Strict Life and Hard Penance will be more than a match for Silkness and Softness.

School yourself in how to suffer a little now so that you'll know how to suffer a lot later on.

Practice now what you'll have to put into practice then.

If you can sustain so little pain in your regular spiritual regimen now, how will you be able to suffer eternal torments then?

If just a handful of penitential practices gives you the hives now, what will Gehenna do?

Face up to it. You just can't have two joys. Either regale yourself in this world, or rule with Christ in the next. Pick one.

Suppose you lived every day up to your hip, up to your lip even, in honors and pleasures. What good would they do if you dropped dead this instant? Not a whit! That's why I say, everything is vanity, except to love God and serve Him alone.

But what good do love and service do? Well, you who love God from your whole heart have nothing to fear, neither death nor punishment nor judgment nor Hell. That's why perfect love makes so much sense; that's to say, it makes access to God a sure thing.

Summing it up, then, love alone should be enough to call you back from the brink of spiritual disaster; but if it isn't, then fear of Gehenna should do the trick.

What's the trick? To stay good for as long as you can.

Sad to say, whoever postpones his commitment to God won't have the strength to stay good for very long. What then? No matter which way he traipses through the forest, or so Paul wrote in his First Letter to Timothy (6:9), he won't be able to outstep the Devil's outlandish snares.

25

HEAVENLY CHANGES

"Be vigilant" and diligent in the service of God, if I may borrow a caution from the Last Book of the New Testament (3:2).

Ask yourself frequently, Why did I leave the World behind and come to the monastery? To live for God, that's why. Next step? To pray to God.

So hit the road in hot pursuit of spiritual progress. It won't take long before you see the *reward* of your labors, if I may use Paul's precise word when expressing a similar sentiment in First Corinthians (3:8). The fear and pain that has held you in its grip for so long will begin to ease up.

All of which means, labor for a bit now, and you'll find great rest, even perpetual joy, in the end.

Remain faithful and fervent along the way, and without a doubt God'll be faithful and generous to you when the time comes. That's how Jesus son of Sirach put it in his book of Wisdom (51:30).

Don't ever doubt that you'll reach the palm of victory; but don't think you can take Confidence a prisoner along the way; that'd be a tactical blunder; you'd be tempted to think you could sail around the world without a sail.

When someone's nervous, he's fearful one day, hopeful the next. In a moment of great spiritual pain, or so the story goes, one such Devout fled to a church, where he flopped in front of an altar.

"If only I could've known then what I know now," he prayed, "I'd have saved myself a lot of grief!"

He knew his prayer'd be answered, but he didn't know when.

"If you did know, what would you do?" came the Divine Response immediately. "That's what you should do now. Once you start down this pathway, you'll begin to feel better about the long-term future."

Consoled and comforted, he committed himself to the Divine Will and rose from the cold stone floor.

As the day passed, his nervousness did indeed begin to disappear. But more than that had changed. He no longer was trying to satisfy his curiosity about the future. Rather, as Paul urged the Romans (12:1), he spent his time trying to figure out how to turn the present to his spiritual advantage.

"Hope in the Lord, and do good things," sang the Psalmist; "plough the fields, and they'll feed you wealthily" (37:3).

What makes us shrink from spiritual progress and fervent change? One thing only. The horrific difficulty of keeping the pressure on. Which is another way of saying that, over time, the good person can be subject to battle fatigue.

Who makes progress in the virtues? The one who takes the manly way out; that's to say, isolates the things that are wrong with himself and methodically destroys them one by one.

When he conquers the Enemy and mortifies his spirit, he makes progress down the spiritual path and deposits more grace in his Heavenly Account.

Each of us has to general his own spiritual battles, right down to dealing death to his own vices.

Who'll win the spiritual race? The wild, unbridled man, with a bundle of prickly passions under his saddle, but with a good nature overall? Or the well-bridled fellow who strives for virtue but at his own well-modulated gait?

If you want to accelerate your spiritual progress, two things'll help. First, spot what human nature draws you to and, using violence if necessary, haul yourself with all deliberate speed in the opposite direction. Second, inventory your virtues and concentrate your efforts in filling in the gaps.

One clue. If self-analysis has never been one of your strong suits, don't despair. Note down the *nil admirari*'s in others and avoid the same sorts of things. Let that be your own personal agenda for the future.

Make spiritual hay wherever you go.

If and when you see or hear examples of good behavior, make haste to imitate them. On the other hand, if you run into something immovable, pick up your feet and fly.

If you make a wrong turn, do make up the ground you lost with all deliberate haste.

As you see the faults of the World, know that through that very same peephole the eyes of the World are ogling you.

What a pleasure it is to happen upon a community of fervent and devout brothers, sang the Psalmist (133:1), well-seasoned fellows who've grown easy over the years with the disciplined life!

What a troubling and demoralizing experience it is to bump into brothers in another religious house who are walking about aimlessly, not doing the daily exercises that are so much a part of their vocation!

How devastating it is to neglect the monastic vocation for an occupation that has no true home in the monastery!

Recall your shaggy life as a monk and compare it to the image of the Crucified. You'd do well to be ashamed. You've been in the monastery long enough to know the life of Jesus Christ inside out, and yet you've striven so little to conform your life to His. Why is that? How can that be?

Whoever pours over the Most Holy Life and Passion of the Lord with intensity and devotion will find in it everything he needs to get ahead. At last he can discontinue his perennial search; he's found the person of Jesus Christ, the subject of all holy quests.

If only the Crucified Jesus would come into our hearts! He'd teach us all we need to know.

The fervent Religious does tolerably well in the monastery, and that makes his superior's life an easier one.

The negligent and tepid Religious, though, undergoes one tribulation after another and ends up claustrophobic to boot! Consolation's the reason. He can't find it inside the walls, and he's prohibited from seeking it outside the walls.

The Religious who's left discipline behind leaves himself wide open to gravest ruin.

The Religious who plays fast and loose with the monastic life'll always find himself in a bind. That's because laxness and looseness, lateness and loutishness, no matter how attractive they may seem or feel at the time, are never benign.

How come there are so many monks who've lived fairly satisfied lives under the discipline of the cloister? They rarely leave the monastery grounds, they live without much external event to speak of, eat like paupers, dress uncomfortably, labor much, speak little, watch long hours, arise early, prolong their prayer time, read frequently, and keep a guard on themselves with every discipline.

Carthusians, Cistercians, and a rainbow of other religious orders—they rise every night to psalm the Lord. So it's matins and lauds, and the whole of monasticism has already begun to sing "Joy to the Lord!" Why, then, are you always the last one to straggle into the chapel and take your place in the choir? Sham bells *in excelsis!*

Just one thing I wish for monasticism. To praise our Lord God with our whole heart and voice! Nothing else. Just think, never to have to eat, or drink, or sleep again! Then we could praise the Lord without interruption and devote ourselves to spiritual studies without fainting or farting!

We'd be a happier lot, you and I, doing any one of these than having to stop every now and then to attend to our corporal needs. Would that there were no such things as baths or bowel movements!

Just suppose there were only sweetmeats of the spirit, a platter of them on the sideboard at the Heavenly Banquet. The taste? Out of this world! Though offered to us more frequently than we think, these nibblings often go unnibbled. Why is that?

When you stop seeking consolation from created things below, you start receiving godly wisdom from above. But how'll you know the transformation is taking place? You'll no longer rejoice in greatness or weep about insignificance. Instead, you'll place yourself wholly and confidently in God.

God is all in all, as Paul wrote to the Colossians (3:11). He loses nothing, He lets nothing perish. For Him every created thing lives and obeys His every wink without His ever having to miss a wink.

Some thumbnails and nutshells.

Everything comes to an end, and time lost is gone forever.

Without Solicitude and Diligence you'll never acquire Virtue.

Grow tepid, and you'll begin to behave badly.

Give yourself to fervor, and you'll feel the great weight lift, all due to the grace of God and the love of virtue.

The fervent and diligent monk is ready for any and every thing, whatever, to rip.

The rigors of the soul vastly outsweat the labors of the body.

Whoever stubs his toe on small vices will take a header on large defects.

You'll enjoy the evening only if you spent the day making progress.

Vigilate. Actuate. Remonstrate.

Whatever bothers you about others, don't neglect in yourself.

As for spiritual progress, that should be painfully obvious by now. You get out of it only what you put into it.

Amen to that!

BOOK TWO

✠ ✠ ✠

The Interior Life

✠ ✠ ✠

Where It Is
&
How to Find It

1

THE CONVERSATION WITHIN

"The Kingdom of God is within," said the Lord in Luke (17:21). Therefore, turn your back on this wretched world, as the prophet Joel cried out (2:12). Grab hold of your heart and stand facing the Lord. Do that, wrote the Evangelist Matthew (11:29), and your soul'll find peace.

The outside world? You know where that's at already. But as to the whereabouts of the inside world, do you have a clue? No matter. The Kingdom of God'll find you. How? The "Peace and Joy in the Holy Spirit," as Paul wrote to the Romans (14:17), comes only to the pious; that's to say, only to those who invite Him.

Clear out the rubbish within, then, and prepare a cool, bare place. Christ'll come and take up residence. He'll furnish it with "all of his glory," as the Psalmist has sung in the Latin Bible (45:14), and make it a warm, chatsworthy spot. Visit Him whenever you like. Feel at home there. It's your own True Home at last. Who would've believed?

O Faithful Soul, prepare your heart for this committed Friend of yours. Make it a worthwhile retreat so that He'll come visit and visit again. How? By keeping His word, as the Evangelist John put it (14:23). Do that, and He'll establish quite a respectable presence under your very roof.

Give Christ some space, therefore, and bar the door to the rest of your crowd. Why? When you have Christ, you have everything, as Paul phrased it in First Corinthians (1:5). He'll take care of your needs; you'll never want for a thing.

The rest of Humankind? Forget about that reckless rabble! They're deflatable, defatigable. Christ, however, speaking in John (12:35), remains a friend, firm and fast forever.

Even if you need people to do for you or just to be friends with, don't put any great confidence in them; they try, of course, but eventually they trip up. Which is another way of saying, don't shed a tear if they behave badly in public. One day they're slapping you on the back, and the next, they're stabbing you in the back. Rudderless, their skiffs are battered to smithereens on the gusty *Nordsee*.

Of course, we all need friends, or there's no way we can survive. But invest your friendship in God, as the Proverb has it (3:5). Let Him be your friend in good times and bad. He'll respond in your behalf when the going gets rough; when things smooth out, He'll look to your best interests. Why's this so? Because He knows, and He'll teach you to know, that on this earth you don't have "a city that lasts," as the Letter to the Hebrews described it (13:14). Yet trudge you must. The beds are hard; the pillows, rocks; so Paul warned the Hebrews (11:13). No rest for the weary. No, no comfort until you've made room for Christ in your life.

Why do you look for a comfortable rendezvous on this earth when your heart's True Home isn't really here? "Heaven ought to be your home," reads Paul's Second Letter to the Corinthians (5:2). Earth, therefore, ought to be viewed as a hostile hostelry, as the Wisdom of Solomon had it (5:9). What I mean to say is, all things pass away, and you with them. See, then, that you don't hang around too long. Why? The danger's that you'll be sucked under and die.

Let your rumination rise to the Most High, as Paul wrote to the First Thessalonians (5:17). Let your meditation seek Christ. But if your gaze rises too high for your nose and it begins to bleed, then lower your gaze and let your eyes rest on the Passion of Christ and His Holy Wounds. Flee to Jesus and let your eyes tend to His welts and wounds. When the world's falling apart, you'll feel great comfort there; there you'll recover the reputation your rivals stole from you; you'll bear up under the blizzard of verbal abuse.

When Christ walked among us, He suffered because of us. The neglect reached its climax at the time of the Great Necessity. The

friends and acquaintances with whom He enjoyed *euphoria* left Him
behind alone to suffer *opprobria*.

Which raises some reasonable questions.

Christ was willing to be assaulted and despised, and yet you have
the nerve to moan and to wail just because something untoward happened to you?

Christ had accusers and detractors, and yet you want to have only
friends and benefactors?

How can your patience be crowned with prosperity if it's never
been crushed by adversity?

How'll you ever be a friend of Christ's if you're going to cry out
every time you stub your toe?

What's the answer? Face up to it. If you want to rule with Christ,
then, as Paul put it to Timothy (2:12), you're going to have to suck it
in and wade through the same muck as Christ.

If you ever have the chance to visit the heart of Jesus, you'll feel
the love glowing in His hearth. No longer would you care about such
petty things as convenience or inconvenience. Instead, you'd rejoice
over the woeful *opprobria* that were laid on Him. Truth to tell, Jesus
could and does get mad, but oftentimes He doesn't. He just allows
Humankind to make a fool of itself.

What's the moral?

Whoever loves Jesus and Truth—that's to say, the truly internal
soul who's disciplined his rumbustious affections—can turn to God
whenever he wants, rise above himself in spirit, and refresh himself
at his leisure.

The person who trusts his own taste at the banquet of life, and not
the finicky palates of the theological gourmets—he's the one who's
truly wise; that's how the prophet Isaiah would describe him (54:13).
His knowledge comes more from God than man.

The Devout who knows from within how to walk and from without how to think doesn't require much space. Nor does he expect
scheduled times to do his devotions.

The internal man can recollect himself as quickly as need be. That's because he hasn't filled his shelves with baubles and bibelots.

External labor doesn't maim a monk, nor does an occupation that's deemed necessary for his community. No, he doesn't hesitate to make adjustments from time to time when survival's the issue.

Whoever's well disposed and well ordered within doesn't cause the wonderful or horrible things that Humankind does.

As the details of a transaction tend to absorb one's attention, one must be on guard lest they appear in prayer as impediments and distractions.

If you'd disciplined yourself right from the start, as Paul wrote to the Romans (8:28), everything would've turned out all right, at least with regard to your own spiritual progress. But apparently you didn't. How do I know? So many things still displease you, drive you to distraction, sadden, even madden you. Why? You're not completely dead to yourself; that's to say, you haven't really drawn the line between yourself and all the trinkets and trifles of this world. After all, nothing so soils or embroils the human heart as a reckless love of created things.

What's the moral?

Stand up to it! Put your foot down! Refuse all worldly consolations! Only then can you get a clear vision of Heaven. Only then can you celebrate what little spiritual progress you've made to date.

2

HUMBLE SUBMISSION

High Society may be for you or against you—again, Paul to the Romans (8:31)—but don't hang your life on such a supercilious judgment. Just take care that the Supernatural is with you in everything you do; in other words, keep a good conscience.

In return, God'll defend you well, and He'll steer you clear of oncoming perversities. But just in case you swerve unawares, know that there's no trick to extricating you from the ditch. God's faithful and quick; He knows the when and the how; at least according to the Acts of the Apostles (1:7). His *modus operandi?* He rescues, and He sweeps up after. You know you're in good hands.

But what if others discover your defects and throw them in your face? Well, that's humility. And if you suffer that exquisite pain in silence, it'll lead to, of all things, greater humility.

Yes, there are rascals who spend their days standing on the corner watching all the world go by. And yes, they're waiting for just such an oaf as yourself to trip up on your own defects. One moment you're humble, and the next? Well, you've given the ruffians a good laugh.

Anyone humbled in this way God shields from further harm, dusts him off, patches him up. This is the sort of person He takes a liking to, according to Second Corinthians (7:6), and enriches with spiritual generosity according to First Peter (5:5) and James (4:6). He raises him from the street and lifts him up to Glory. Into his ear, or so the Gospel of Matthew intimates (11:25), He whispers the most extraordinary things, even asking him if he'd like to be friends.

What's the result of this sudden humility? Whenever the person trips, he falls, but the bloodied nose no longer shakes his peace of mind. That's because his standing is not with the rowdies on the next corner, but with the Angels in the next world.

Now that's how God looks at it, but the view from your promontory—if indeed there is one—is entirely different. Supposedly, you've made all this spiritual progress, but that's no reason to puff yourself up. Know that, compared with the rest of Humankind, none of whose spiritual condition you've any true knowledge of, you're still a very flat and uninspired fellow.

3
THE TRULY UNTROUBLED

Not so fast! You have to hold your own peace first. Then others will come to admire it and want to do the same. Why? Well, the truly peaceful person seems more perceptive than the well-educated person in this regard. For example, he often sees the passionate person mixing the good with the bad and swallowing the unholy concoction whole. On the other hand, just as often he sees himself turning everything into good.

The truly untroubled spirit is suspicious of nothing. But every shadow makes the nervous, the contentious dance with St. Vitus; he's jumpy, and he makes everyone else jumpy. He says what he shouldn't, and just as often he neglects to do what he should. He holds others to a high standard of behavior, but in public behaves himself rather badly.

The moral?

First and last, worry yourself into virtue, and at the same time don't worry about how others are doing.

You're quick to offer excuses for your own erratic behavior, but why are you slow to accept the excuses of others? Wouldn't it be more just to accuse yourself and excuse your brother? If you want to be carried yourself, or so Paul wrote to the Ephesians (4:2) and Galatians (6:2), then you'll have to carry someone else.

Well, if you must know, you're a long way from Charity and Humility, and you've got no one to be angry with or upset about but yourself.

What's the moral?

It's no great thing to converse with your regular circle of friends. In fact, it's rather pleasant, spending time with those who feel the same way about the same things. But to be able to live with the adverse and the perverse, the disorganized and the undisciplined, the people who just plain hate your guts, is a great grace. It's also the only laudable—and indeed the only manly—thing to do.

There are those who hold themselves in peace and also make peace with others, as Paul described to the Romans (12:18).

Others there are who have no peace in themselves and make no peace with others. The former's a grave condition of soul; the latter, a graveyard situation if ever there was one.

And there are those who retain peace in themselves and strive to bring others to peace.

Nonetheless, our total peace in this miserable life must be placed more in thinking humble things than in not thinking naughty things.

Whoever knows how to suffer well will end up achieving a sense of peace. He's the victor over himself and the lord of the world, a friend of Christ's and an heir to Heaven.

4
PURITY & SIMPLICITY

It takes two wings to get you off the ground, or so said the Great Bernard in his *Consideration* of mental prayer (5.3); that's to say, it takes Simplicity and Purity. Simplicity you should be able to find under Intention. Purity resides in Affection; yes, the soul has affections. Simplicity leads to God; Purity, to general understanding and enjoyment.

No good action will get in your spiritual way if the raucous affections of your soul are under your control. If you intend to seek nothing else than the good favor of God and the goodwill of your neighbor, your heart'll be free as a bird's. If your heart is right, then every creature great and small is a mirror of life and a book of doctrine. And that from the wormy to the pachydermy: each one of them reflects something of the goodness of God.

Here's some common wisdom on the subject of Purity.

If you're good and pure on the inside, then you'll see everything on the outside without impediment and seize it well.

The pure of heart sees clearly through to Heaven and Hell.

As each one lives interiorly, so he'll judge exteriorly.

If there's joy in the world, the person with the pure heart surely possesses it.

If there's tribulation and anxiety anywhere in the world, or so Paul surmised to the Romans (2:9), who knows more about it than the gentleperson whose conscience is continually assailed by evil?

As an iron thrust into the fire loses its rust and heats to a glowing whole, so Humankind turning itself completely to God emerges from its torpor and is transmuted into a new Humanity.

Humanity quickly loses interest in the spiritual life. At moments like this, people don't want to lift a finger to help themselves; they freely accept all the handouts they can get.

But when they increase their efforts in behalf of the spiritual life, an odd thing happens. They stand up straight and begin to walk it virilely on the *Via Domini*. There's one sure sign of this. What they once thought important, they now can hardly remember.

5

THINKING ABOUT ONESELF

We'd like to believe that everything we think and say is right, but we can't. That's because we don't have grace enough or sense enough. Of course, there's a wit in each of us, but even this is dimmed through negligence. What we really fail to notice is that we're losing our interior vision. How do we know?

When we act so badly, and the excuses we cook up are so abysmal!

When we explode with passion and think, no, I'm not angry, I'm just defending the faith.

When we peck at the peccadillos of others, and our own whoppers we let pass unchallenged, as the Evangelist Matthew has pointed out (7:3)!

When we ponder what we'll put up with from others, but pay little attention to how much others'll have to put up with from us!

Is there a moral anywhere in this?

Whoever wants his own actions to be tolerably received would do well not to judge the behavior of others so intolerably.

Whoever has an interior life should put the spiritual care of himself before the care of others. That's to say, he should look to himself alone and say nothing smart-alecky about the spiritual condition of others.

You'll never be internal and devout until you hold your tongue about others. If speak you must, then let loose on your own wretched spiritual condition.

If you focus entirely on your relationship to God, precious little of the hubbub of the World will be able to penetrate your recollection.

When you have that vacant stare in your eye, you might well ask yourself, before someone else does, just where are you?

When you've run through everything the World has to offer, why, if I may echo Matthew (16:26), do you seem to have advanced to the rear?

The moral?

If you want True Peace and True Union, then you just have to postpone everything else and attend to your own case.

You'll make spiritual progress only if you drag your torso away from every temporal festival. You'll lose spiritual ground when you put a value on each temporal thing. All of which means, you can keep nothing as your own, nothing big, nothing small, nothing nice, nothing new; that's to say, nothing except God and everything that smacks of God.

But all those lovely creaturely consolations that came your way, what about them? Forget about them! The soul that loves God loathes everything that isn't God. God Eternal, God Immense, "filling all the space," as Jeremiah phrased it (23:24); the soul's solace, the heart's True Joy.

6
A GOOD CONSCIENCE

The glory of a good man? asked Paul in Second Corinthians (1:12). A good conscience.

Have a good conscience, and it'll show.

The good conscience can carry a heavy load; again, from Paul in the same letter to the Corinthians (7:4); even when things go wrong, it has a smile on its face.

The bad conscience frowns, frets, fidgets.

How sweet it is when your head hits the pillow at night, expostulated John in his First Letter (3:12), and your conscience isn't nagging you to death!

Good people don't feel happy unless they're doing good things.

Bad people never have a good day, never have a moment's rest. That's because, as the prophet Isaiah suggested (48:22), "There's no peace for the once and future pious, says the Lord."

According to the prophet Micah (3:11), the impious are always chatting us up. "Who says we're not peaceful?" "Is the sky falling?" "Who'd dare lay a finger on us?"

Don't believe them! The gorge of God will rise suddenly, swallow them up, grind them down, then spit them out. Don't worry! urges the Psalmist (146:4). They'll feel the Hellhound's breath soon enough.

To boast in the Lord is one thing, but to boast when one is toast, that's quite another. For to boast in the Lord is, at least according to Galatians (6:14), to toast the cross of the Lord.

Fleeting is the sort of glory that's given and taken by Humanity.

Melancholy is the constant companion of Worldly Glory.

The glory of the Good lies in their consciences; it isn't something that burbles from their mouths.

The person who desires Eternal Glory isn't distracted by the glitter of time.

If you still feel you must have some sliver of glory on this earth, then you've missed the point. To embrace eternity you must rid yourself of all temporality.

Who cares whether praise or blame is raining on your soul when tranquillity is puddling in your heart?

If your conscience is clean, then you can rest easy. Praise won't make you better; blame won't make you worse. This is what you are, and God's the witness to that.

If you're your own interior gardener, you won't care a fig what the World says about your virtuous vines.

"When they look at you, they see your face; but when God looks at you, He sees your heart"; or so wrote the author of First Kings, or First Samuel, as it's called in the Latin Bible (16:7).

A human judge looks at facts, but the Divine Judge weighs intentions.

Do good always and always focus on where you are in the spiritual scheme of things—that's the sign of great purity and inner confidence.

Anyone who doesn't require worldly validation for his own existence has already committed himself wholly to God. Much the same sentiment Paul wrote in his Second Letter to the Corinthians. "The person to be commended isn't the one who's nominated himself, but the one God's had His eye on for some time" (10:18).

What should the status of internal man be? To walk with God on the inward path, as the prophet Micah would say (6:8), and not to be waylaid on the outward path by some brusque, bruising affection.

7

THE LOVE OF JESUS

Happy's the one who understands that to love Jesus is to ignore himself.

You have to leave behind your self, whom you love dearly, for Someone who loves you wholly and wishes you to love Him completely.

The love of one creature for another is a frail structure; the love of Jesus is a permanent abode.

Clinging for dear life to a created thing is fatalistic. Clinging to Jesus is futuristic. Love Him and keep Him as your friend.

When everyone else leaves you high and dry, He won't. Nor will He allow you to perish at the Final Bar.

The moral?

Whether you like it or not, sooner or later you and all your old crowd'll have to come to a parting of the ways.

In life and in death you should keep yourself in the presence of Jesus. Commit yourself to Him always. Why? When all else fails, He alone'll be left to help you, and what's more, He won't allow your earthly friends to trample on the friendship. What He plans to do is furnish your heart and leave behind a fairly comfortable chair for Himself.

If you've pretty well cleaned out your heart of all the creaturely trash, then, according to John (15:4), Jesus will make His move.

You'll find whatever affection you've placed in Humankind moribund; but that's never the case with Jesus.

The moral?

As the Evangelist Matthew put it (11:7), don't confide in or rely upon the waverly reed. As the Prophet Isaiah so aptly put it (40:6), "All flesh is grass, all glory is flower"; their season, as we surely know, is always cut short.

Yes, you look at the external person every day, but if that's the sole object of your gaze, then you're easily deceived. Seek your solace and profit in others, and you'll find it a losing proposition.

Seek Jesus in everything, and you'll find Him there. If, however, you seek only yourself in human affairs, then that's what you'll find, and what a risk that is to your eternal welfare!

The moral?

Ignoring Jesus does more to harm Humanity than all the tornados and volcanos and hurricanos in the history of the world.

8
FRIENDSHIP WITH JESUS

When Jesus is here, everything's good and nothing's hard. But when He's gone, everything seems to lumber.

When we don't hear His voice, we quickly grow numb. But when we hear His voice in the next room, we're atingle again.

Remember that passage in the Gospel of John (11:28) where Mary Magdalene was crying? When Martha said to her, "The Master's here and asking for you," didn't she leave her tears behind and rush out to greet Him?

It's a happy moment when Jesus calls us from tears to joy! Without Him it's amazing how everything goes awry! And to long for someone, something, instead of Jesus—this is a loss, a greater loss than if you'd destroyed the world.

Jesus alone excepted, what can the World confer on you, and why would you want it? To be without Jesus is harsh, even hellish, but to be with Him, according to Romans (8:31), is paradise, sweet paradise. When He's with you, He makes your enemies think twice.

Finding Jesus is a little like stumbling onto hidden treasure; that's to say, the Good beyond all good. Losing Jesus is a lot like misplacing all that treasure; that's to say, forgetting where you found God in the first place.

Surely there's a moral in here somewhere.

Pitifully poor is the person who lives without Jesus, and extravagantly rich is the one who's well with Jesus.

It takes a lot of practice to carry on a conversation with Jesus, and a fair amount of knowledge to keep up with Him. But do look Him in the eye, yet be respectful. Listen closely, and He'll have no trouble talking with you.

The one thing, though, that'll make Jesus yawn, then excuse Himself, is your sitting Him down to tell Him all about the wonderfulness of each and every one of your seemingly endless material possessions. Your chitter-chatter will simply drive Him away; then you'll be friendless.

Without friends no one can survive, and if Jesus isn't first among your friends, you'll be, if I may paraphrase John (6:68), a desolate duck.

The moral?

To confide in and enjoy the company of some other person when you can have Jesus as your friend—that's a very foolhardy thing. The choice is yours, of course, and no matter whom you choose, you're going to make someone hopping mad. So who's it going to be, the World or Jesus? Of all the things you hold dear, let Jesus be your choice, your One True Friend.

Jesus should be loved for who He is—everyone knows that. And because He's who He is, everyone else should also be loved. Only Jesus Christ is in this singular position of being loved and yet letting others love each other.

He alone, Good and Faithful Fellow that He is, is found to be pre-eminent among friends. Because of Him and in Him you associate with a variety of people, friends as well as enemies. In behalf of all these He must be beseeched that they may come to know and love Him.

As for yourself, never desire to be singled out for praise or love. That, according to Jeremiah (10:6), is for God alone, who has no one like Himself.

Two mistakes your heart makes. Don't wish that someone like yourself should monopolize your thoughts and conversations; and don't occupy yourself with the care and attention of a friend like yourself.

One recommendation your heart should follow. Just let Jesus come visit you and every other good human being.

Dust up and empty out that place within, and don't leave behind any fur balls. Strip bare your soul, and purify your heart first; then you'll have some time to see how sweet the Lord is.

Truth to tell, you won't arrive at this blessed state until, atiptoe and akimbo, you're drawn to it by Prevenient Grace (see John 6:24).

Everything having been cleared out and freed up, you're finally alone with the Alone.

When the grace of God comes, then Humanity has the potency, as the Schoolmen would say, to do all things. When it goes, Humanity is left limp as a lash. In an instance like this, you shouldn't become dejected or desperate. Rather, you should stand up straight for the will of God and suffer all the slings and arrows for the praise of Jesus Christ.

The moral?

After winter, the spring. After night, the day. After storm, the calm.

9

THE LOSS OF SOLACE

When you're in the presence of Divine Solace, it's no big deal to turn your back on human solace. But it's a big deal to have no solace whatsoever, either human or divine. A bigger deal still is willingly to sustain exile of the heart for the honor of God. Biggest deal of all is not to seek yourself in any one thing and not to look for any one merit in return.

What's better than having Hilarity and Devotion accompanied by Advenient Grace? Everybody desires this hour. Borne by the grace of

God, you ride sweetly enough in the saddle, and lightly too; it's the Omnipotent who's bearing your brunt, and the Great Leader who's walking the reins.

We know what solace is, and sometimes we even experience it. But for a human being to be stripped of all solace? That's what happened to holy deacon Lawrence, who with his chaplain was martyred in the third century—marvels both even in their own age. Everything the World held up as desirable he despised. For the love of Christ, he even endured the martyrdom, a few days before his own, of the great high priest at the time, Pope Sixtus II, whom he dearly loved. And so Lawrence could have chosen personal comfort, but instead, for the love of the Creator, he chose Divine Pleasure.

The moral?

One day too you'll be called upon to leave behind a close friend for the love of God. And don't behave badly when you find yourself abandoned by a friend who's chosen God over you. In the end we'll all be separated from each other.

You must fight against yourself—that you know. But it takes long bouts over long periods before you begin to win consistently enough to train your whole affection on God.

When you face off against yourself, you're easily suckered into human consolations. But the true lover of Christ and unswerving pursuivant of virtues is succored by Divine Consolations. That's to say, he doesn't fall for the sticky, sugary kind, nor does he seek to wallow in the sleek, cool sweetness. What he does do for Christ is seek rugged spiritual exercise and harsh physical labor.

When God gives spiritual consolation, accept it with good grace. Just know that it's His doing, not yours. Don't blow your horn, don't prance about, don't carry on like a clown. Just be all the more humble for the gift. If anything, be even more cautious in all your actions. Why? The hour of consolation will pass and soon be followed by temptation.

When consolation's taken away, don't climb out on the ledge, don't throw a noose over the branch. Just wait with Humility and Patience for the Celestial Visitation to come again. Why? God has it in His power to visit upon you even more consolation.

The moral?

This teetering and tottering in the life of prayer is well documented. The great Saints and the ancient Prophets were tormented by it and, much to our edification, learned to survive it.

When consolation came, the Psalmist sang out in his thirtieth, "I was so full of it, there was nothing I couldn't do" (6). When consolation left, he changed his tune, "You've turned your face away from me, and driven me out of my mind" (7).

In these ups and downs, the Psalmist never despaired. Rather, he pressed his wretched case in prayer. "To you, O Lord, I complain, and flat in front of you I pound my fists into the turf" (8).

Finally, he reported the fruit of his prayer, singing out for all the world. "The Lord heard me and felt sorry for me; He took me by the hand" (10).

But in what way? "You've turned my mournful wails into squeals of delight, surrounded me with gifts" (11).

It happened that way in the lives of the great Saints, so why won't it happen to us poor paupers? We shouldn't despair if we find ourselves sometimes in fervor, sometimes in frigor. Why? Because the Spirit ebbs and flows according to the Divine Pleasure. Whence the blessed Job who, more than once the victim of Divine Whimsy, was moved to say, "You visited him at the same time every day, but you tempted him without warning" (7:18).

What can I hope for when I'm deserted by Grace? Whom should I confide in when I'm left to wallow in my own poverty of spirit? There's always the mercy of God and the hope of Heavenly Grace. There are some other good people around, some fellow Devouts, some faithful friends, some holy books, some illustrated tomes, some chants and hymns whose sweetness lingers. All of these help a little, tell a little. But at a solemn time like this there's no better remedy than suffering, self-abnegation, and, ultimately and inevitably, unconditional surrender to what is, evidently, the will of God.

I've never found a dedicated soul who, at least once in a while, didn't lose a little grace, who didn't sense a diminution in fervor.

A holy person may experience rapture or illumination, but even as he does so, he knows that it's at horrific expense to his spiritual life; that's to say, as surely as temptation has left, it'll come again.

In other words, there's no one worthy of spiritual experience, whether high or deep, who hasn't been exercised somehow by tribulation for God's sake.

Yes, there's a moral.

Temptation is generally thought to herald the arrival of consolation. Just remember, to those who've been severely tried by temptation, Heavenly Consolation is already on the way. "From the tree of life," wrote John in his Revelation (2:7), "the victor can have his pick of the fruit."

Divine Consolation, or so the spiritual wisdom has it, is conferred on Humankind in order to make it stronger when it has to beat off attacks. Temptation surely follows consolation, so that we won't blubber about the virtuosity of our own virtues. Remember, the Devil doesn't sleep, nor has our flesh lost its itch, at least up to this point. Remember also, don't let your guard down; don't stop preparing for the battle. Why? Because your enemies are massing on the right and on the left. That's decent enough in the daytime, but what's positively indecent is that, while you sleep, they continue their preparations throughout the night.

10

GRATITUDE FOR GRACE

Why do you demand your beauty rest—another echo from the Book of Job (5:7)—when you were born for hard labor? Set yourself up more for long-suffering than short-suffering, more for toting the cross than admiring it.

What character from the secular world wouldn't gladly accept consolations if he could have them on demand? After all, they exceed in delectation and duration all the delicacies of the World and all the pleasures of the Flesh. The former taste out of this world, but only for a while; then they begin to cloy. As for the latter, trying to prolong a pleasure—isn't that just about the most pitiful of human exercises?

What's the moral?

Truly, spiritual desserts alone are the real thing, whipped up from virtues into frosted layers of pure thoughts. But however mouth-watering they are, no one can enjoy them for long. Why? Because the time for temptation is never far off.

Consolation would visit us more often if we didn't put up so many roadblocks. Two bumptious examples: Braggart Spirituality and Bogus Confidence.

God does well by giving the grace of consolation.

We do ill when we attribute the whole gracious phenomenon to our own efforts. In a situation like this, the graces can't flow; our pipes are clogged. That's because we're ungrateful to the Fountainhead of All Grace, from whom we receive all these Heavenly Gifts and to whom we should return all thanks.

What's the moral?

Grace is always available for the asking. Trouble is, not everyone asks.

Sometimes, to feed the humble pigeon, God robs the proud puffin.

Yes, consolation's a good thing, but not all consolations are good. We're succored by some, but suckered by others.

I don't want the sort that takes contrition away from me. And the same could be said of contemplation. I don't want the kind that leads me to pride.

Is there a snare here? Of course there is.

Not everything that's high is holy; nor every sweet, good; nor every desire, pure; nor every dear thing, something that tickles God's fancy.

How then can we tell the Good from the good?

The grace that makes me more humble, more careful, that's the True Grace, the grace that truly helps me leave my worldliness behind.

Having gone to the School of Grace, then, and severed all ties to worldliness, we won't have the audacity to beat our breasts like drums and trumpet our goodness abroad. Rather, we'll mouth our *maximas culpas* and bare our poor souls at home.

What's the moral?

Give to God what belongs to Him, Matthew has advised (22:21), and take note of what's yours.

Give thanks to God for grace. But your faults and the punishment that's due them you'll have to bear yourself.

Keep placing yourself on the lowest rung—if I may be pardoned a little laddering in the Lord—and the highest rung will soon be yours. Why? Because the highest stands on the shoulders of the lowest. Luke said something similar (14:10).

The Saints who stand high in God's esteem are the same blokes who lie low in their own esteem. The more they grovel, if I may put it crudely, the more they'll revel.

Founded and grounded in God, they can't be proud. Full of Truth and Heavenly Glory, they lose their taste for earthly glory. They ascribe totally to God whatever good comes their way. They seek glory—not the kind that's from human beings, but the kind of glory that's from God alone; the Evangelist John has said much the same (5:44).

The moral?

Devouts desire God to be praised in Himself and all His Saints above all else, and they direct all their efforts toward that very goal.

We should be grateful for the small gifts, and soon we'll be found worthy of larger ones. A word of advice. Unwrap the tiniest one with the same sense of glee as the humongous one. And if a truly disgusting thing is found inside, count it a special gift.

Always consider the dignity of the donor, and no gift'll ever seem too small, too cheap. Need I say it? It's not the largeness of the gift; it's the largesse of the giver.

What I'm trying to say is, if God should give pain and suffering, count them as gifts too. Why? it seems to me I hear you ask. Because what He gives and what He allows are for your own salvation.

Anyone who wants to keep the blessings of God coming should be grateful for the grace just given and patient for the grace yet to come. In the latter instance, you should pray that the grace may return. If you don't prostrate yourself before the Divine Tribunal toward that end, I can't help adding, it may not return. As always, you should be open and humble.

11

SHUNNERS OF THE CROSS

At this point in history Jesus is surrounded with flocks wherever He is, but all's not well.

Many are happy to make the trip to the Heavenly Kingdom, but few there are who'll cart and haul that cross of His. Many enjoy the sweet sentiments He utters, but few, the tart words He sometimes has to say. Many'll wolf down the food with the Famous Man, as Jesus son of Sirach put it in his Book of Wisdom (6:10), but few'll join Him in the fasts. They're all there in the good times, but few'll take on the tough tasks He inevitably asks.

Yes, many like to be seen breaking bread with Jesus but, as Matthew has described (20:22), they're nowhere to be found when the passion cup is passed. Many are wowed by His miracles; few are wooed by His cross. Many just love chatting with Jesus so long as He isn't rude about their not embracing His rood.

What's the moral?

Many praise Jesus and bless Him as long as the good times roll. But when He absents Himself for a few moments or just goes off for a while to pray, they become bellicose, then lachrymose, then comatose.

We should love Jesus for His own sweet sake, and not because of any magic He'll do in our behalf. And so when the bad times rock, we'll bless Him as though the good times'd never left. Even if He'll never want to give us consolation again, we'll still praise Him and thank Him for what He once did.

Here are some questions for us.

How can the love of Jesus, pure as it is, have no particular price tag, no terrestrial taint?

Can't those who spend all their time hunting down consolations be called mercenaries?

Aren't those who think of nothing but their own comfort and profit hoarders of stuff rather than lovers of Christ?

Can anyone be found who wants to serve God without counting the cost?

Some considerations.

Rare is the person who's so spiritual that he's denuded himself of every material thing!

Is there anyone who's truly poor in spirit and bereft of every creaturely thing?

Can any of us be discovered whose interior life is like the Proverbial "gift of great price from a foreign land" (31:10)?

If a Devout gave all his substance, that's good, but it isn't everything.

If his penitential practices were punishing and public, that's good too, but he still has a long way to go.

If he understands all knowledge, that's fine, but there's so much more to know. In this connection one might look at First Corinthians (13:1).

Even if he has great virtue and indeed flaming devotion, it's still a long way to Purgatory.

Why?

For he has one step farther to go and, at least according to Luke (10:42), it's the most important step of all.

What's that?

That he leave behind not only all created things, but also his self. That's to say, dump his selfish pride by the side of the road. Empty out his petty pockets. And when he's done all this, which he knows has yet to be done, then and only then will he come to the realization that of himself he's nothing.

One day we may come to think we're rather skilled in the service of the Lord. Some of our peers may even encourage us to think we're slick. But even if there's some truth to it, we should still describe ourselves as just another clumsy oaf.

"When you've done everything that's required of you, repeat after me," Revealed Truth has spoken in the Gospel of Luke, "we're truly the bumbling and stumbling servants" (17:10).

We have to be truly poor in body and spirit before we can say with the Psalmist, "Yes, I'm a leper, and a pauper too" (25:16). Nevertheless, no one's richer or stronger than the person who knows how to leave his material self and all his trash behind and place himself on the rutted, deeply rutted, road to Humbletown.

12

WAY OF THE CROSS

"Hard saying, all this stuff about Jesus!" wrote the Evangelist John in his Gospel (6:61).

"For just once in your life forget yourself, lose yourself, leave yourself behind!" wrote the Evangelist Matthew in his Gospel (16:24). "Go on, get on with it. Pick up that cross and follow Jesus."

Yes, hard sayings these, and harder still, they're not going to go away.

Hardest of all will be the words of the Final Sentence, as it's recorded in Matthew (25:41). "Yes, you ended up as moral felons, malefactors and maledictors, and yes, you'll depart from this place of judgment for the Eternal Bonfire, where you'll spend the rest of your supernatural life!"

These words, if I may echo the Psalmist (112:7), will go unheard by those who already follow the word of the Cross, as Paul put it so felicitously to the First Corinthians (1:18).

When the Lord comes to pass the Final Judgment, the finger of God will draw the sign of a cross across the Heavenly Vault.

At the Endtime all who'd planked themselves down on their own crosses during their own lifetimes, at least according to Romans (8:29), will be able to approach Christ the Judge with good humor and happy tread.

New Devouts facing the Cross for the first time often toss their victuals right on the spot. They see only death and destruction, theirs and their friends', and they tend to faint dead away. But why? The Way of the Cross, or so the Great Bernard has it in his *Second Sermon for the Feast of St. Andrew,* is the most direct route to the Kingdom of Heaven. But apparently, for a queasy Devout, that's not much of a reason. So let me list, in no particular order, a few of the good things that may be found in the Cross.

Life in this world and life in the next.

Sanctuary from enemies, natural as well as supernatural.

Health of mind, joy of spirit, sweetness of breath.

Sanctity at its most attractive.

Hope of eternal life and faith in salvation.

Do any of these make a difference in your attitude toward the Cross? They should. And that's why I'm going to say to you now, in the words of the Evangelist Matthew (16:24), "Take up the cross, your cross, and begin to follow Jesus." The destination? According to Matthew (25:46), the Heavenly City.

It's not that hard, you know. Jesus has already cut the path with

His own cross. Just follow His steps, one by one, one after the other, and you're on your way.

The cross He carried, according to the Evangelist John (19:17), was the one He died on for you. He wants you to carry on and, eventually, to die on your own cross as He did on His. If you die as He did, at least according to Romans (6:8), so you'll rise as He did and enjoy the fruits of the Long Haul.

The moral?

If you share His ghastly if ghostly pain, you'll share His glorious gain.

Behold everything's the Cross! That's to say, the Way of the Cross and the daily task of dying to self. Whether you like it or not, that's the secret of life and genuine peace of mind and soul.

Read the map, ask for directions, but you won't find a more smoothly surfaced, bandit-free road than the Way of the Cross.

Put your own welfare first, and you'll still find you have to suffer in this world, whether you want to or not. Which is another way of saying, no matter which way you turn, you'll always confront the Cross.

What's the moral?

Inevitably, pain'll come to your limbs, and your soul'll be stretched to the breaking point, but in the end you'll be able to bear up pretty well under the stress.

When God stops bothering you, it's your neighbor's turn, and he'll torment you till he gives you the hives. And the latter's usually worse than the former.

Try what remedies or potions you want, but your skin'll continue to weep. You'll just have to bear up until God sends blessed relief. Why's this so? God wants you to learn to do without, to endure tribulation without consolation.

No one feels the Passion of Christ so deeply in his heart as the one who's committed himself to the same holy path as his Fair Lord.

What's the moral?

The Cross is always waiting. No matter which way you turn in the dark, it's there. Run where you will. Flee toward a safe street, search for a safe house, and the Cross'll follow. Blithely, it'll be there to greet you when you arrive.

What's the moral?

Change your ways, give yourself a fresh coat of paint, convert yourself. Do all this, and you'll find the Cross before it finds you.

Internal Peace and Perpetual Crown—that's who you want to come, but when? They'll come when they will come. In the meantime, as always, patience.

Carry the Cross willingly, and it'll carry you all the way to Sufferings' End.

Soon? you ask. Not on this earth, I reply.

Some reasonable advice.

Trudge and grudge the Cross in your heart, and you'll just make it heavier for yourself.

Shake the Cross off, and I know you'll try, but you can't get rid of it.

If by some extraordinary circumstance you're able to get that Cross off your back, guess what? You'll stumble onto another—and indeed a heavier one—almost immediately.

The moral?

Flee the Cross, and it only gets worse.

Sometimes novices are cunning. They think they can evade the Cross and still remain in good odor. How addled can one get! No other mortal has been able to live without cross and stress. Jesus Christ Himself, our Fair Lord, never spent an hour on this earth without feeling the pain of His Passion. Why? Luke had an explanation. "It was necessary," he said in his Gospel (24:46, 26), "that Christ suffer so that He could rise from the dead and enter into His glory." Seems plain enough to me.

So why are you new novices, so swift of mind and yet so slow of spirit, spending so much time devising evasive actions? Why aren't you out there now on the Way of the Cross with the jubilarians? Christ had to travel it. So did we. And so do you!

If the life of Christ means anything at all, it means the cross of martyrs. Yet you New Devout novices seek out a life of quiet amusement in the monastery. What a mistake! What a colossal mistake if you seek anything but suffering tribulations! Why? you ask for the hundredth time. Because, as Job moaned for the hundredth time (14:1), all of life on this planet earth is full of misery and wretchedness. That's to say, everything bears the sign of the Cross.

The moral?

If your cross gets heavier as you go along, know that you're making a modicum of spiritual progress. But if, after some hours, it weighs about the same, look down. Why? You're standing still.

Sometimes there's a soul who enjoys his multiple afflictions; that's to say, the more he suffers on his own cross, the lighter his load seems to become. Every ripple of pain he converts to his spiritual advantage. As much as his flesh is torn with the thorn of affliction, his spirit is stiffened with grace.

I've seen it happen—although I'd never encourage it—that an afflicted soul has received so much consolation from his suffering that he never wants the suffering to end; if anything, he wants it increased because it's from and for God. When I see this happen—and thank God it happens rarely—I realize that it's neither virtue nor virility that keeps him going; it's the grace of Christ.

The moral?

When you're repelled by the grubbiness of the Cross, you should swallow hard, then step up, grab hold with your bare hands, and embrace that holy piece of timber.

Carrying the Cross—it's not the sort of thing a novice wants to get mixed up with. That, and some other unpleasantnesses.

Embracing the Cross. Castigating the flesh. Subjecting oneself to servitude. Fleeing honors. Enduring disgrace with a smile. Despising oneself, and desiring to be despised by others. Suffering the tortures of the Damned. Desiring nothing that smacks of prosperity on this side of the Final Veil.

Soberly reflect on yourself as others see you—that should sober you up. You'll quickly see that you're not a pretty sight. All these rigorous practices are beyond your natural powers. What should you do? Confide in the Lord, and He'll send you reinforcements from Heaven. The result? You should be able to hold your ground against the assaults of the World and the Flesh. As for that Hound of Hell, that old war dog of a Devil, you really won't have to fear him as an enemy. Armed with the shield of faith and wearing the emblem of the Cross, you'll still find him a threat, but no more so than a warm puppy shitting in your lap.

Position yourself as a good and faithful servant of Jesus Christ. Wear the cross of your Lord proudly both for your own good and out of a love for the Crucifix as a symbol.

Prepare yourself to withstand a whole range of adversities and inconveniences in this wretched campaign. Why all the fuss and bother? Because the miseries never end, at least in this life; you'll find them wherever you lay your head.

All these evils and pains you suffer for Christ there's really no earthly remedy for.

No matter how bitter the draft of the Lord tastes, down it without making a face, says Matthew (20:23); that's to say, if you want to be a friend of His and fight the good fight beside Him, says John (13:8). Accept what few consolations He has to offer under these battle conditions.

What more do you have to do? It's enough to put yourself in harm's way. Hold your ground against the repeated onslaughts of adversity and consider each attack a great honor. Why? Because "the present sufferings," even if you were man enough to handle them without Christ's help, "can't be compared with the future glories"; at least that's what Paul said to the Romans (8:18).

When you reach that point in the fray when you and Jesus are fighting as one, the bitter turns to sweet; victory's in the air; the Hellhound turns to a lap dog; it's Paradise right before your very eyes.

But when you lose sight of Jesus in the din and smoke of battle, then your wounds weigh heavily upon you, fear invades your vitals, and tribulation tracks you down.

If you're where you're supposed to be on the battlefield—that's to say, where the suffering and the dying are—then the tide begins to turn. That's to say, amid the scourge of war, you'll find a ray of inner peace.

Even if you were rapt all the way to Third Heaven—Paul described the phenomenon in the Second Letter to the Corinthians (12:2)— you still wouldn't be able to escape the wounds of war.

"I haven't told him yet," Luke quoted Jesus as saying in Acts (9:16), "how much he'll have to bear for My name's sake." Apparently, a great deal of suffering remains to be done.

What's the moral?

Suffering—that's what a soldier of Christ signs up for; that, and to love Jesus and serve Him forever.

Do you have the stuff to do as Acts suggests (5:41), that's to say, suffer for the name of Jesus? I don't really think so. But, fortunately for you, He thinks so. And so do the Saints; they think such behavior would magnify the Lord. And so do your neighbors on earth; they might just follow your good example.

Why do I raise the question? Everyone, it seems, wants to slow the spiritual life down. Few, sad to say, want to endure the grunt and the grind of the Cross.

What's the moral?

By rights, considering the Goal of goals, you deserve to suffer a little for Jesus, so why do you squawk at the prospect? Many of your peers in the world are already straining their groins to achieve grubbier goals.

If I may paraphrase and condense a line from Romans (6:8), as you die to self, so you'll live to God—that's for certain.

No one really likes being stiffed for Christ, but once that happens, one can begin to make a habit of it.

Joining Christ in His suffering has some value not only in the next world, but also in this one.

Which would you rather choose, to suffer nasty desolations for Christ or just to mess about with recreational consolations? I hope you choose the former.

You're a little like Christ, but a lot like the Saints; in either instance, you're a living reproach to the laggard.

It isn't the levities you enjoy that inch you forward in the spiritual life; it's the gravities you suffer.

Is there anything better than suffering for the salvation of Humankind? If there were, Christ would have shown us by word or example. For veterans as well as recruits, therefore, Jesus makes it perfectly clear that the Cross must be carried. "If anyone wants to come after Me," He was quoted as saying in the Gospels of Matthew (16:24), Mark (8:34), and Luke (9:23), "let him lean into the cross and follow Me."

How shall I end this chapter, this book?

For all who've taken the time to read and to think about what's been read, there's this one inescapable conclusion, and I put it in the words of Luke as he remembered the words of Jesus in the Acts of the Apostles (14:22): "Yes, on earth for the sake of Christ you gave up your pleasure, and now the Kingdom of Heaven awaits your pleasure."

BOOK THREE

✠ ✠ ✠

Internal Consolation

✠ ✠ ✠

*How Jesus Describes It
&
How the Soul Experiences It*

1

CHATSWORTH

"Let me hear what the Lord God is saying in me!"

That was the cry of the Psalmist (85:8). But just as piercing are my own humble cries, My Holy Friend.

As the boy Samuel found out to his joy, and as the author of First Samuel noted, blessed is the soul that hears the Lord jabbering and chattering within (1 Sam. 3:9).

Let me see if I can recall the particulars. Let's continue our chatsworth, O Lord. That's to say, let's pick up our conversation where it left off, at Chatsworth, our secret rendezvous, the little room within my soul that can be reached only inside my cell.

Blessed are the ears that pick up the Godly Whispering, if I may borrow an expression from 1 Kings (19:12), and at the same time block out the Worldly Whisperer!

Blessed are the ears that listen, not to Untruth mouthing off out in the street, but to Truth instructing inside the monastery!

Blessed are the eyes that blink in distress at the world outside, but stare unblinkingly at the world inside!

Blessed are those who get beyond the entrance of the interior life and strive daily to grasp what's hidden in Deepest Heaven!

Blessed are those who make time for the God of the ages and at the same time cut themselves off from all the distractions of the age!

O my soul, take note of these beatitudes and bar the gates before your sensuality charges in! Only then can you hear what your Lord God's saying in you.

LORD

"I'm your salvation!" That's what the Psalmist wanted the Lord to say (35:3). And that's what I, your Beloved Lord, am saying to you, My dear friend. I'm your peace, I'm your life, and what's more, I've many things to say to you.

First, be on your best behavior when we have our chats, and you'll soon learn to enjoy them.

Second, let the eely Transitories slip—grasp the eternal things only.

Third, they're sweet, they're nice, all those petty yet pretty Temporalities, but they'll drag you under the bushes every time.

Fourth, all those creatures in the world, what help would they be if you were deserted by the Creator?

To sum up, dear friend of Mine, unclench your fists, and let everything you have fly out of your hands. Clean yourself up nicely and stay faithful to your Creator. Then you'll begin to behold Beatitude.

2

SPEAKING WITHOUT WORDS

DEVOUT

How should I pray, O Lord? There are so many ways.

Like the Psalmist? "I'm Your servant" too, and I cry out. "Give me mind enough to know what You're talking about," as the Psalmist sang (119:125). Or, "Draw my heart closer so that I'll hear Your words better," as the Psalmist sang (78:1).

Like the Deuteronomist? "Do flutter your utterances as the dew droppeth," sang Moses in prayer with the Israelites before they crossed the Jordan into Canaan (32:2).

Like the Exodist? "Do speak to us, and we'll listen!" exclaimed the sons of Israel to the Great Moses long, long ago. "Don't let the Lord talk to us, for fear that we'll die at the sound of His voice" (20:19).

Like Samuel, the great prophet who ruled Israel so long ago? "Speak, O Lord, that Your servant may hear" (1 Sam. 3:10).

Yes, yes, O Lord, that's the way I want to pray. That's the way Samuel prayed when he was a young boy; that's to say, with all humility and yet with some hilarity.

"Speak, O Lord, that Your servant may hear."

By the bye, my Distant if Divine Friend, it isn't Moses I want to converse with, nor any of the other Prophets. No, Inspirer and Illuminator of all Prophets, it's You I want to talk with. You don't need their help to tell me what I need to know; they, on the other hand, can't utter a word without Your help.

The Prophets can certainly mouth the words of prophecy, or so I've been given to understand, but they don't confer the spirit. Their pronunciation may be beautiful, remarkably so, like the sound of silver tinkling, but without Your inspiration their words wouldn't set my heart on fire. Their enunciation may be perfect, each letter receiving a single stress, but You, O Lord, stress the meaning.

The Prophets give voice to the mysteries, but You make clear the meaning. They promulgate Your commands, but You help their observance. They show the way, but You walk with those on the way. They instruct crowds, but You tutor hearts. They provide the humidity; You, the fecundity; Paul wrote something similar in First Corinthians (3:7).

To sum up then, the Prophets just shout the words, but the crowd gets the gist from You.

I know You have a list of "won'ts," my Willful Friend, but I have this list of "don'ts."

Don't send Moses to speak to me; it's You, O Lord God, Eternal Truth, that I want to hear, and it's You I want to listen to.

Don't let me die before my tree's borne fruit!

Don't let me hear the truth preached abroad and not put it into action within.

Don't let me come before the Final Judge having heard the word and not done anything about it, having learned it but not loved it, even believed it but not observed it.

And so I return to where I began, crying out with the boy Samuel. "Speak, Lord, that Your servant may hear" (3:10). Why? "You have the words of eternal life," as Peter pleaded with the Lord in the Gospel of John (6:68).

Speak to me, console me, correct me, my Lord and Friend, and may glory galore be Yours for evermore!

3

HEARING WITH HUMILITY

LORD

I hear your words, My dear Devout; now you hear Mine. You'll find them not only suasive, but also persuasive. In fact, they exceed in wisdom all the accumulated knowledge of Philosophy since the world began.

My particular words for you today are "spirit and life." My Beloved Disciple recorded them in his Gospel (6:63), but Humanity can't seem to make any sense out of them. Important words, they shouldn't be exegeted smugly, if I may allude to that hoary Preacher of Ecclesiastes (9:17), but listened to respectfully. That's to say, they should be received with all humility and yet with great affection.

DEVOUT

Humility and affection? Sounds like trouble for me, O Lord, the sort one finds in psalmistries and prophecies.

"Blessed is he whom You've brought up, O Lord, and taught about Your law," as the Psalmist prayed (94:12–13); "may he not be swamped by the troubles!"

And may he not ramble about the earth like the ravaged Daughters of Zion in Isaiah (3:26)!

LORD

Don't worry about the Prophets, My dear friend. I was their tutor from the beginning, as the Author of the Letter to the Hebrews correctly has it (1:1–2), and I haven't stopped talking since. Funny thing, though. Nowadays, when I begin to speak, people feel their deafness coming on.

They'd rather hear the World than the Word of God; they'd rather tickle the fancies of the flesh than tackle the fancy of God.

Something's wrong here.

The World promises a lot of pretty small stuff, much of it perishable, and guards the warehouse aggressively. But when I promise Highest Quality and Lasting Value, the mortal heart begins to cringe.

The World and its managers have no trouble commanding performance, but I have difficulty in finding just a few good people who'll follow My commandments.

"Run red with bloody shame, O Sidon, says the sea"; that's what the oracle about the destruction of Tyre and Sidon, those doleful cities, said in Isaiah (23:4).

But I, the Lord and Tailor of the Universe, have a question.

Why do I always seem to come out on the short end?

For a small benefice you'll run a mile, but for Eternal Life you won't lift a single sandal. For a tinny toy people'll haggle for the lowest price. But why does just one coin seem to make so much difference? So the hagglers linger over the litigation until their faces turn red. And what's truly astonishing is that, for a vain premise or a small promise, they're not afraid to work themselves silly day and night.

What a shame it is! For Incommutable Good, Inestimable Reward, Incomparable Honor, Interminable Glory, Humanity's slow to break a sweat.

Blush with the common beet, you sluggish and querulous soul, and answer Me these!

Why are there people out there more prepared for perdition than you are for Eternal Life?

Why do they rejoice more in Vanity than you in Verity?

Why are their hopes always coming up short, and yet, for all their foolishness, they never seem sad?

Why is that? What's wrong with My promises? Nothing that I can see.

First, they don't lumber anyone.

Second, they don't dismiss as dolts the persons who put confidence in Me.

Third, I give what I promise; I fulfill what I order.

Fourth, My only condition is that a person remain faithful to Me till the end. Not exactly a bad condition when you remember I'm the Rigorous Examiner of all Devouts and the Rewarder of all good folk everywhere.

Now, before you forget, some things to remember.

Write My words in your heart and familiarize yourself with them. Why? In time of temptation you'll have to put them into play.

What you don't understand when you read, you'll learn on the Days of Visitation, that's to say, when I visit My chosen people on the Day of Temptation and the Day of Consolation.

Every day I read two lessons to My friends. First, to encourage them to decrease their vices; second, to exhort them to increase their virtues.

Whoever "hears My words and spurns them has picked his own judge on the Last Day," I've said in the Gospel of John (12:48); and an unsympathetic judge at that.

DEVOUT

Why do You scarify me, Lord and God of all I own? You make me tremble so, yet I must dare to speak with You! That's how the Great Abraham haggled with God the Father in Genesis (18:27), quivering and quavering, and that's how I'm going to haggle with You now, my Outraged if Outspoken Friend. I'm just Your average pauperous, verminous servant—much more poor and contemptible than I dare to say and You seem to know.

Not that I need to remind You, O Lord, but just in case You've forgotten, remember I'm *nothing*, as the Great Paul described himself to the Second Corinthians (12:11). I have nothing, and I have the strength for nothing.

You alone, on the other hand, are good, just, holy. You have the strength for everything, cried Job to the Lord God My Father (42:2). You surpass everything. You fill everything; that's to say, except perhaps the holey and unholy sinner.

"Remember Your mercies," cried the Psalmist to the Lord God My Father (25:6), and so do I. Fill my heart with Your grace "if You want Your works to work," as the Wisdom of Solomon so wisely has it (14:5).

How can I put up with this wretched life unless Your mercy and grace comfort me? "Don't turn Your face from me"—that was the Psalmist's great fear (143:7), and it's also mine. Don't prolong the times between Your visits. Don't take Your consolation away lest, as the Psalmist cried (143:6; 63:1), "my soul appear to You as hard, cracked earth crying out for rain."

O Lord, "Teach me to do Your will," as the whipped and beaten Psalmist pled (143:10). Teach me how to walk with dignity in Your presence and how to talk with wisdom in our chatsworth. You know who I am. You've known before I was born into the world, even before the world came into being.

4

TRUTH & HUMILITY

LORD
Dear friend, you need to do two things.

First, "Walk with Me," as My Father in Heaven told the decrepit Abraham in Genesis, "and let Truth come with us" (12:1).

Second, "Seek Me always in the sincerity of your heart," as the Wisdom of Solomon said right at the beginning (1:1).

Do these two things, and you'll be well protected from the bandit horde.

Truth'll free you—as I said to the Jews who believed in Me, and as the Beloved Disciple recorded in his Gospel (8:32)—from the seductions and detractions of those who hunt you down.

Yes, Truth has freed you already; and when you're truly free, you don't care what epithets the vain world slings at you.

DEVOUT

Well, my Demanding if Divine Friend, that's easy for You to say, but hard for me to do. Yes, I'll try. "Do let Your Truth teach me," as the Psalmist begged (25:5). Do let it guard and save me all the way to Salvation's End. Do let it rid me of the pimples and pustules that plague my love. Then and only then will I walk with You in great freedom of heart.

LORD

Yes, My humble friend, I'll teach you some true things, that's to say, what's right and pleasing to Me, if I may paraphrase the words of the beloved John in his First Letter (3:22).

First, think of your sins with great displeasure and grief.

Second, don't think that you'll amount to something just because you've done a few good deeds. On the contrary, you're a sinner subjected to, and indeed smothered by, your many swarming passions.

Third, left to your own devices, you always take a header.

Fourth, at the first sign of trouble, you wobble, then you fall down. You get tied up into knots, then you melt away in tears.

Fifth, you don't have a lot to boast about, but you do have a lot to bring yourself down a peg with. Yes, that's true. And if I may put it delicately, you're rather more infirm than you'd like to admit. And who better to say it than I?

DEVOUT

Well, my Feisty if Fearful Friend, that's a low blow, if there ever was one, I must say, taking advantage of a friend.

LORD

Admit it, I'm right!

DEVOUT

Even if You are right!

LORD

I'm only saying it for your own good!

DEVOUT

Well, I think You've done quite enough good for one day!

LORD

I seem to have gotten off on the wrong foot, My dearest friend. Let Me start again with some quiet words of advice.

Of all the things you do, rank none above the other. Nothing sizable, nothing likable, nothing pricey, nothing dicey, let none of these appear worthy of remark.

Consider nothing exalted, laudable, desirable, except what has immortal trappings. Above all, let Eternal Truth be the only thing that gives you pleasure. And let nothing be so upsetting to you as your own cheapness. That's to say, may you fear, blame, flee nothing so much as your own vices and sins; they ought to be more distressing to you than all the insects of the world.

Like Tobit, some people pretend they're sincere (3:5). Motivated by a certain curiosity and arrogance, they strut about in My presence, trying to sniff out My secrets, only to snuff out God's plans. Their time would be better spent, I think, tending their own spiritual lives and salvation.

But more often than I'd like to admit, it's these very same people who put Me into an adversarial position. Is it any wonder, then, that, goaded on by a grizzly pride and curiosity, they've wandered into a forest of towering temptations?

"Fear the judgments of God," said the Psalmist (119:120), and with good reason.

Tremble at the wrath of the Omnipotent, as Second Maccabees has it (7:38)!

Don't take the works of the Most High and scatter them all over the landscape.

Scrutinize the iniquities you've committed in quantity, and remember all the good works you could've done in their place.

Some of you carry your devotion in books, others in images; still others put their devotion in miracles and metaphors. "My name crosses their lips when they pray," wrote the Prophet Isaiah, "but there's no room for Me in their hearts" (29:13).

Some have their intellects in hand and their affections under control, and at the same time they seem to pant for eternal things. They listen to the issues of this world with some seriousness, and they pay rather less attention to the necessities of nature. But they do feel "the Spirit of Truth speaking within," as Matthew put it in his Gospel (10:20). That's to say, the voice they hear within teaches them to despise the Terrestrials and love the Celestials, to pay no attention to the World, to desire Heaven night and day.

5

THE EFFECT OF DIVINE LOVE

DEVOUT

Pray I must, my Lordly Friend, but what should I pray?

Bless You, Heavenly Father, Father of my Lord Jesus Christ, for remembering me, pauper that I am?

O Father of mercies and God of consolations, as Paul began his Second Letter to the Corinthians (1:3), I give You thanks, unworthy as I am of Your every consolation?

I bless You always, and I glorify You, with Your Only Begotten Son and the Holy Spirit, the Paraclete, for ever and ever?

O Lord God, my Holy Loving Friend, when You come into my heart, You make my blood dance?

"You're my glory," thrummed the Psalmist (3:3) and "the exaltation of my heart" (119:111)?

You're my hope and—thrumming again—"my refuge in the day of my tribulation" (59:16)?

I ask again, O Lord, what should I pray?

At this point in my life, I find myself not only a little long in the tooth, but also a little short in the hoof; that's to say, a little short of breath in the pursuit of Love and Virtue. I've no one to turn to. You're the only One who can help me.

Don't be surprised, then, when I ask You to visit me more often. I need to know more about the holy disciplines. Will they free my body from the itch, cure my heart from the worm?

Cleanse me on the inside, scrub me on the outside, and I'll be ready enough to love, strong enough to suffer, stable enough to persevere.

LORD

Love's a great thing, My monastic, monotheistic friend, altogether a great good. "It makes every burden light," as Matthew has recorded My saying in his Gospel (11:30), and manages to carry every load, no matter how slip-sliding it may be. What's more, it makes every tart and bitter thing taste sweet and juicy.

My love is noble and provides the energy for doing great things; it encourages the desiring of even greater things. Love wants to rise, doesn't want to be tied down. Love wants to walk free, not to be told where to go. But sadly, it loses its sense of direction. That's to say, it can't sustain anything in time of consolation; it succumbs in time of desolation.

There's nothing sweeter than Love; nothing stronger, higher, broader, happier, fuller, better in Heaven and on Earth. That's because Love is born of God, as the Beloved John has written in his First Letter (4:7), and can't rest except in God, who's above all created things.

Some wonderful effects of Love.

First, he who knows how to love runs and rejoices; he's a free man and has no restraints.

Second, he gives everything and in return receives everything; in a manner of speaking, he may be said to have everything. That's because he rests in the Great One, who has everything and from whom every good fountain flows.

Third, he doesn't look for gifts for himself, but love turns him into the giver of all goods.

Fourth, Love isn't measured out in small packets; more often than not, it spills all over.

Fifth, Love isn't seen as a load, doesn't have a reputation as a chore; it's more in the area of motivation than in the exercise of strength.

Sixth, Love doesn't rise out of impossibility; that's because it comes out of possibility and permission.

All things considered, whoever knows how to love has the strength for everything, fills to overflowing, causes every effect. The one who hasn't learned to love merely flops to the floor in a heap.

Some more effects of Love.

Love stands the night watch, yet sleeps with one eye open. Exhausted, it nonetheless doesn't nod off. Shoved, it shoves back. Terrified, it doesn't pass the terror down the line, but like a flickering flame, a smoking torch, it flares up and burns brighter than before.

If you know how to love, then you can make out the words of this riotous shout. It's a burning affection of the soul clamoring in the ears of the Lord, echoing the Song of Songs (2:16): "Mine? You're all mine! Yours? I'm all Yours!"

WORD OF THE WEEK

The Subject: God ordains certain men to hell on purpose

Isaiah 64:8 - *O Lord, thou art our Father; we are the clay; and thou our potter; and we all are the work of thy hand.*

> work - Hebrew: Maaseh-an action (good or bad); product; transaction; business

Romans 9:20-23 - *Who art thou that repliest against God? Shall the thing formed say to him that formed it, why hast thou made me thus? Hath not the potter the power over the clay of the same lump, to make one vessel unto honour and another unto dishonour -- What if God willing to show his wrath, and to make his power known, endured with much long suffering the vessels of wrath fitted to destruction: And that he might make known the riches of his glory on the vessels of mercy, which he hath afore prepared unto glory.*

> fitted - Greek: katartizo - to complete thoroughly; fit; frame; arrange; prepare. Thayer says this word speaks of men whose souls God has so constituted that they cannot escape destruction; their mind is fixed that they frame themselves.

Men get angry to think that we serve a God that can do as it pleases him. They actually think that an almighty God thinks the way they think and that he could not possibly form-fit a vessel to hell merely to show his wrath and power. Paul said he does. Men have difficulty perceiving a God that predestinates men (Rom. 8:29) on whom he desires to show his grace (unmerited favor) and mercy, that he may shower them throughout eternity with the riches of his glory. We like to believe that we must give him permission; if he is to operate in our hearts and minds. The Lord said, "My thoughts are not your thoughts, neither are your ways my ways. As the heavens are higher than the earth, so are my ways higher than your ways and my thoughts than your thoughts (Isaiah 55:8,9)". Our God is in the heavens: he hath done whatsoever he hath pleased (Psalms 115:3). He doeth whatsoever pleaseth him (Eccl 8:3). Thou, O Lord hast done as it pleased thee (Jonah 1:14). Whatsoever the Lord pleased, that did he in heaven, and earth, and in the seas, and in all deep places (Psalms 135:6). He does all his pleasure (Isa. 46:10; Isa. 44:24-28; Eph. 1:5,9; Philippians 2:13). It is Jesus that holds the keys to death and hell (Rev. 1:18), not Satan. God will intentionally cast these evil vessels of wrath into hell and lock them up for eternity because it is not his pleasure to draw them to him (John 6:44). This doctrine angers men, though it is taught throughout the pages of God's Holy Book. Men do not have a Biblical view of the living God when they think he is not in control of all things including the minds and hearts of all men. God is not only love to the vessels of mercy, but he is a consuming fire (Deut 4:24) upon the vessels of wrath fitted to destruction. We do not serve a God who is Superman that can only shake mountains, implode blackholes, and explode quasars. The God of the universe can harden and soften the hearts of men at will (Rom 9:18; Ezek. 36:26). He giveth not account of any of his matters (Job 33:13).

GRACE AND TRUTH MINISTRIES

P.O. Box 1109 Hendersonville, TN 37077
Jim Brown - Bible Teacher - 824-8502

Radio Broadcast – Sat. Morn. 8am 1300 AM Dial WNQM
TV – Mon. & Sat 10pm, Wed. & Fri. 12am Channel 176;
Tues. & Thurs. 5pm Channel 3; Thurs. 11am Channel 49

Join us for fellowship at 394 West Main Street on
Sunday Mornings @ 11:00am, Sunday Evenings @ 7:00pm,
Wednesday Evenings @ 7:00pm
Or
Watch us live via U-Stream on the web at
www.graceandtruth.net

Drown me in Love, my Lord, that I may learn how smooth and swimming it is to love. Love has me in its grasp, sending me to the heights with fervor and wonder I didn't know I had within me.

Let me follow You on high, my Beloved Lord, "canting the canticle of love," as Isaiah put it (5:1). Let my soul, beside itself with love, weary itself in Your praise! Let me love You more than myself! Let me love myself because You loved me first! Let me love everyone else who truly loves You! That sounds like a lot, but it's only what the law of Love, of which You're the Chiefest Illumination, tells me I have to do.

Love's swift, sincere, pious, joyous, pleasant, brave, patient, long-suffering, virile, and selfless, as Paul wrote in his First Letter to the Corinthians (13:4–7).

Love's selfless; that's to say, when you pursue only your own interests, you may be said to have fallen out of love.

Love's mindful of others, humble, honorable; not soft, not giddy, not messing around with the meaningless tasks of this world.

Love's sober, chaste, not given to flights of fancy, quiet, and has all the senses under control.

In tatters, like a waif or a wastrel, Love nonetheless can approach a prelate with confident step.

Love's devoted and thankful to God, trusting and hoping in Him, even though it's been a long time between consolations. That's to say, Love and Pain go hand in hand throughout life.

You may think you know something about Love, but if you aren't prepared to suffer for or stand by the Loved One, then you aren't worthy to be called a lover.

Any lover worth his word should freely embrace the hard and the harsh for the Loved One, and at the same time he shouldn't allow himself to be distracted by Contraries or Contretemps.

6
PROVING A LOVER TRUE

LORD

Dear soul, up to this point in our friendly chatsworth, with lots of give and take on both sides—and I hope you won't take offense—but I think I can safely say, you're not what I'd call—and I want you to know that I speak only as a friend—a *vigorous* or *prudent* lover.

DEVOUT

What, my Distraught if Divine Friend, have I ever said or done that'd provoke You to make such a disgusting and decidedly unfriendly remark?

LORD

What are friends for?

DEVOUT

If that was meant to be a friendly remark, it's no wonder You have so few friends!

LORD

When just a jot or tittle of contrariety alights on your nose, what do you do? You could swat it, you know; you could use it to your spiritual progress. But no, you just leave it there, and nervously look around in the vain hope that nobody's watching.

The *vigorous* lover, on the other hand, meets temptations head on and doesn't fall for the sweet-talking Enemy, whose only weapons are his flashing teeth and forked tongue.

Now don't be upset, My dear friend. This is just My way of saying, you're no more My favorite when the good times roll and no less My favorite when the hard times rock.

Take My handkerchief, please, and stop that sniveling!

The *prudent* lover, please notice, doesn't consider the gift of the Loved One so much as the love of the Giver. He pays more attention to the amount of affection than the cost of the gift. And he places all gifts under the Loved One's lock and key. Look at the *noble* lover too. He doesn't fuss so much about the gift as he does about Me.

I know there are times, My imprudent and sometimes impudent friend, when you feel that I'm far from your heart; and the same from the Saints. Just know that I'm not offended. Know also that good affection and sweet, of which you have a taste every now and then, is the effect of Present Grace; and in a sense it's a foretaste of the Heavenly Country.

All of which is another way of saying, don't rely too much on such consolation; it comes and it goes. However, to respond with force to the Enemy's incursions and to spurn the Devil's clever interpretation of what's happening along the boundaries of the soul—both are outstanding signs of great virtue and merit decorations.

Know that the Ancient Enemy tries his damnedest to impede desire in the good soul. He also tries to draw him away from a variety of particulars. For example, the cult of the Saints. The pious memory of My Passion. A practical checklist of sins. An honor guard for the heart. A firm purpose of progressing in Virtue.

Many evil thoughts the Enemy forces upon the devout soul, trying to wear him down by the horror of it all and distracting him from praying and reading the Scriptures.

Humble Confession displeases the Enemy; Holy Communion enrages him.

Don't believe the Enemy. Ignore what he says. And mind where you walk; he's spread his traps along your usual paths.

Thoughts may come your way, loathsome and lithesome, but don't blame them on yourself. Blame them on the Enemy, and save your best for him. Epithets and expletives like the following.

Avaunt, Unclean Spirit!

Blush, you matted, clotted thug!

It's you who fill my ears with such horrid unhearable stuff!

"Depart from me, you seducer and traducer" (Matt. 4:10)!

You won't have any part of me!

"The Lord'll be with me, great warrior that He is" (Jer. 20:11), and you'll stand before Him in a state of complete confusion!

I prefer to undergo every pain, even to die, than to think like you! Avast! Don't say it! Bite your tongue! (Mark 4:39).

I'll not listen to you any more! I mean it! Just try—one more time, one hundred more times!—to molest me and see what happens!

"O Lord, my illumination, my salvation, whom shall I fear?" (Psalm 27:1).

"Even if the armies of my Enemy are tenting around me, my heart'll not quiver" (Psalm 27:3).

"O Lord, come to my help, come to my rescue!" (Psalm 19:14).

"Do battle as though you were a good soldier," wrote Paul to Timothy the second time (2:3). And if your fragility takes a tumble, make a second effort, a new start. Rearrange your pack. Reinforcements are coming; that's to say, additional grace is on the way.

Watch where you step. Complacency and Pride are squirreled everywhere, blinding the unsuspecting as they advance. The Proud are the first casualties, but for you Caution and Humility are the watchwords. All of which is another way of saying, proceed with care, but stay level with the ground.

7
GRACE UNDER HUMILITY

LORD

My dear Devout, is there a good way to put the grace of devotion to work? Of course, there is. You hide it. That's to say, don't flaunt it; don't meander around it; don't maunder over it.

A better way to handle the situation is to render yourself undeserving. How? Just imagine that the Gracious Gift is delivered to the wrong person. Namely, you.

This affection of the soul, this consolation, mustn't be clung to too tenaciously, for it can very quickly be changed to its contrary.

When in grace, think how wretched you are; but when out of grace, think how utterly destitute you must be!

Odd thing about the grace of consolation. Not much spiritual progress is made when it's present. But when it's absent, you do cover rather more ground. How? By dutifully enduring the slippage of consolation; that's to say, by not dozing off during scheduled prayer, not allowing the rest of your *ordo diei* to fall apart. Just because you feel spiritually dry or mentally anxious, that's no reason to disintegrate. Just do what you think ought to be done and only what you're able to do.

Many Devouts, when Success doesn't come up and buss them on the bum, immediately become nervous. That's to say, they sit down and cross their legs in a way that'd make the Great Arsenius blush. That's to say, they cross their legs at the knee and drum their fingers on the table.

As the Old Jeremiah has said (10:23), not everyone can choose the road he travels. But God always has the power to give and console when He wants, how much He wants, and to whom He wants. He has only one rule: does it please Him, or doesn't it?

Certain Devouts have thrown caution to the wind; that's to say, wanting to fulfill their expectations, yet unwilling to acknowledge their limitations, they've destroyed themselves. The grace of devotion made them do it! Or so they said.

Trouble was, they followed the urging of their heart and neglected the judgment of their reason. Because they presumed the grace was greater than God actually gave, they quickly lost that grace. Instantly, they were thrown down, made destitute, the lowest of the low.

They'd built themselves a quiet little nest in Heaven, but now they were pulverized and pauperized. Once they flew, but now their wings were clipped. If there were any hope for them at all, it would be under My wings, as the Psalmist had it (91:4).

The Devouts who at this point are new and inexperienced in the way of the Lord should pay special attention to this. Why? They can easily be deceived or knocked about in the rugged course of the spiritual life. To avoid much of this roister-doistery, they should take advantage of the experience of the discreet old Devouts in their community.

When these young Devouts follow their own heads in this regard, they come to regard the elder Devouts as old trouts. That's a perilous path to follow, especially if they've made up their minds to trust no one older than themselves.

Rare it is for those "who think they know it all," as Paul characterized them to the Romans (11:25), to allow themselves to be ruled by others.

A tale of two Devouts. One may have a modest education and carry it off with great humility and yet with some hilarity. Another may be a walking encyclopedia spouting the wisdom of the West to a world with wax in its ears. Pick one.

It's better to have little to be proud of than to pride yourself over a lot.

You're not all that wise when you give yourself too much joy. Actually, that joy is rather smaller than you think, and losing it is the last thing you want to do. But obviously, you're oblivious of your Pristine Destitution and the chaste fear of the Lord that should have resulted.

You're never so virtuous that in times of crisis you don't find your faith in Me profoundly shaken.

No one wants to feel too hemmed in during peacetime, but in time of war, you'd welcome restrictions; without them you don't know where you are or where the fear is coming from.

Remain humble and modest always. Rein in that runaway spirit of yours, and you won't fall into danger so easily.

Good counsel has it that you should meditate at noonday about what your future'll be at midnight.

Even in this prayer, remember that the light will return. It's that light I withhold every now and then as a caution to you and a glory to Me.

The temptational process has its uses.

First, it's better to greet Temptation as an old friend than to meet it as a stranger.

Second, merits aren't accumulated by the number of visions and consolations you have.

Third, your skill in interpreting the Scriptures has little to do with your spiritual progress.

Fourth, a young man's exalted social station in the outside world certainly has absolutely nothing to do with his capacity for spiritual progress in the inside world.

Fifth, if you are truly humbled and really charitable, if you always seek the honor of God—that has everything to do with your spiritual progress.

Sixth, if you think yourself an ant, and really despise your antics, and don't antagonize others, and prefer to be squished under foot than crowned king of the world—then that's something to be truly proud of.

8

THE LOWEST DEPTHS

DEVOUT

You're hogging the conversation, my Garrulous if Gracious Friend, the way I hog the fire in winter! Do let me get a word in edgeways. The Great Abraham again, in Genesis again (18:27): "Let me speak to My Lord when I'm dust and ash!"

If that isn't just the perfect description of myself about to pray! Of course, I could puff myself up a little, but then You'd get mad. You'd stand against me, line up my iniquities, and use them as witnesses against me! How could I contradict them? You'd have me then. But what would happen to me?

I'd vilify myself and reduce myself to nothing. I'd give up all claim to reputation. I'd pestle myself to death, or at least into dust. All this, and still Your grace'd favor me. Still Your light'd illumine my heart.

But still all wouldn't be well. Everything about me that seemed so good, You'd drown like kittens. And in the very puddles made by my nothingness. That done, You'd show me to myself, what I am, what I was, where I've arrived, because, as the Psalmist has said in the Latin Bible, "I'm nothing, and I know nothing" (72:22).

If, however, You take even a quick look at me, a sidelong glance maybe, I take on new strength, new joy. Wow! Raised up, revived, embraced. A feather, yes, but also a dead weight. Let me go, O Lord, and I'll plummet to the Lowest Depths at my slowest speed.

Your love does this, preventing me from falling and raising me up once I've fallen, guarding me from grave dangers and yet rescuing me from all scrapes.

Love of self—that was the dagger that did me in. But seeking You and loving You, I found not only You, but also myself. Then something happened. From that mutual love, I slid down the slippery slope again, bottoming out in the deepest wells. That's because You, O Sweetest Lord, You do for me far beyond what I could earn and above what I could ever dare hope or ask.

Blessed are You, my God. That's the prayer of one who's all unworthy of Your blessings. Even to the ingrates and apostates Your infinite goodness never ceases doing good. Turn us around till we face You again, that again we may be thankful, dutiful, prayerful. What else can we say, except, with Isaiah, that "You're our only salvation" (33:2) and, with the Psalmist, our only "virtue and strength" (46:1).

9

GOD, THE ULTIMATE END

LORD

Dearest son and friend of Mine, do Me one favor. Put some finality into your life. That's to say, make Me your supreme and ultimate end, and you'll mingle with the Blessed.

In the past, you haven't always done that. More often than I like to say, your affection has centered on yourself and other creatures. So your affection will have to be cauterized. Why? Seek yourself in something, and immediately you collapse and give up. Therefore, you should refer everything to Me. I'm the One who gave everything.

Individual graces—consider them as drips from the Divine Tap, drops from the Heavenly Basin, and give Me full credit for them; that's to say, in the Divine Plan all things have to be recirculated to their origin.

The tintinnabulous and the timid, the rich and the poor, all drink the Living Water from Me. Those who serve Me as though they were slaves—that's to say, spontaneously and freely—will, according to John, "receive grace after grace" (1:16).

Whoever wants to make hay without Me or delight in some good not known to Me won't be rooted in True Joy, nor will his heart expand. Rather, his spiritual progress'll be obstructed and restricted in a multiplicity of ways.

How do you get out of this mess, My poor friend? First, ascribe nothing good to yourself. Then don't attribute virtue to any other human being. Last, give God everything, without whom Humankind has nothing.

So what's so hard about this? After all, I gave everything I had; I want you to do the same. And I insist—nay, I require—that you thank Me for it.

When Virtue strides into the room, Vainglory vanishes. When Heavenly Grace and True Charity sweep into the room, Virid Envy turns up her nose, High Anxiety has a fit, Particular Friendship is beside himself. We all know why. Grace and Charity have this way of clearing the floor of cranks and releasing all the warmths of the soul.

If you get My drift, you'll rejoice in Me alone, hope in Me alone. "No one's good," Luke has quoted Me as saying, "except God alone" (18:19). God must be praised above all things and blessed in all things.

10

SHAPING UP IN A SHABBY WORLD

DEVOUT

My turn at last, my Loquacious if Lofty Friend.

"How multitudinous are Your sweetnesses, O Lord, which You've hoarded for those who fear You!" That was the shout of the Psalmist (31:19), and it's my shout too.

But what are You to those who love? And to those who serve You with their whole heart? You're the sweetness of contemplation—who can describe it?—that You bestow generously on those who love You.

To this point, in the most generous way possible, You've shown me the sweetness of Your charity. How do I know? You've made me into something better than I was, what I'm not, and when I've strayed far afield, You found me and led me back. Hence it is that I serve You now. What's more? You've laid down the one condition, that I should love You. No big deal! I do that already. Although not very well, as You are so fond of pointing out.

O Fountain of Perpetual Love! What may I say about You? How can I forget You after You kept me on Your list of friends, even after I pined away and died the spiritual death. Your response to Your servant at that unhappy time was extravagant, an act of friendship, making my every hope a mercy, and my every merit a grace.

"What can I give You in return for that grace?" I ask with the Psalmist (116:12). Not everyone's received it. Not everyone's been called to leave everything behind, renounce the World, enter the monastic life.

At this point—and, before You say it, O Lord, I do have a point—may I ask a stupid question? What's so great about serving You? We're already under all obligation to serve You; yes, the whole of Humankind. So pardon me if I don't think it's such a great new idea.

What's really great, though—and this is an argument You seemed to have missed—is that You picked a pauper and a pooper like me for Your monastery and put me in the company of Your beloved monks. Now that's astounding! That's astonishing!

Look at all this earthly clutter of mine! It's Yours too, as the First Book of Chronicles has it (29:14), at least according to the terms of our present agreement, and I use bits and bobs of it to serve You. But that's the wrong end to approach it from. You serve me more than I serve You.

Just take a look at Heaven and Earth. You created them for the use of Humankind. They're right here in front of our eyes, and every day they do just what You've ordered them to do. And this is just the beginning. "You've ordered the Angels to minister to Humankind," as the Psalmist has it (91:11).

Transcending all of this transcendence is Your deigning to serve Humanity and promising to give Yourself to us.

All those thousands of gifts You've given me, what can I give in return? I know. I'll serve You all the days of my life! Better, I'll serve You just one day of my life, but I'll make it a day of perfect service!

Ah, my Lord and Gracious Friend, "You're worth the perfect service, and all the honor and eternal praise that go with it," as the twenty-four elders in Revelation sang to the Spirit on the throne (4:11).

As for me, poor servant that I am, I've vowed to serve You with every fiber of my being, to praise You without ever stinting. That's my wish. That's my desire. And You know what I like best? Whenever I come undone, You kindly see to my mending.

Great honor? To serve You!

Great glory? To condemn everything else because of You.

Like me, those who on the spur of the moment enlisted in Your Most Holy Service have a great grace. That's to say, we who ditched every carnal delight now discover the most delightful consolation of the Holy Spirit.

We who ignored the World's broad highways and followed Your pointy sign down the narrow dirt road, as Matthew quoted You (7:14), are having a fairly pleasant journey.

How sweet is the service of the Lord!

Yes, my Lordly if sometimes Leery Friend, we like to think the monastery a great and happy place, and we hope You think the same. And yes, religious service has a lot to recommend it. As You say, it does indeed promote Freedom and Holiness. And it does render Humankind equal to Angels, satisfactory to God, unwelcome to Demons, and commendable to all faithful! It's a life one can learn to love and embrace for a lifetime. A service promising the *Summum Bonum*. With the *Gaudium Perenne* to boot!

11
DECELERATING DESIRES

LORD

My son and friend, you've learned many things up to this point, but, I must say, some of them you haven't learned well enough.

DEVOUT

And what might these be, my Disarming if Dismaying Friend?

LORD

One thing you should concentrate on is desire, in fact, your alarming number of desires. You should make them conform to My pleasure.

That's to say, you shouldn't prefer your own will to Mine, as the Great Matthew recorded in the Lord's Prayer in his Gospel (6:10); you should fall all over yourself to put My will first in your life. Why?

Desires, I've noticed, often rouse you to act before you think. That's nice, but I think you should consider whether you're acting for our mutually agreed upon alliance or just for your own dalliance. If, however, I'm the overt cause, you'll be happy enough, no matter how much I bang you about. But if you have some covert initiative, something you don't want to reveal to Me, watch your step. It will trip you up and weigh you down.

A few things to beware of.

First, don't lean too much on these subcutaneous, subterranean desires of yours. Consult Me first. If you don't, it will make you suffer a lot later. One hint. A desire may please you at first, but it doesn't satisfy for long. It can only lead you to another, seemingly better, supposedly greater desire, which itself is just another one in an endless chain of self-devouring desires that can only lead you to spiritual ruin.

Second, not every Friendly Affection has to be seized immediately. There can be an interval. Examine it closely. Use restraint. You don't want to distract your mind from your goodly and indeed godly studies simply because a Friendly Affection suddenly presents itself.

Third, not every Unfriendly Affection must be fled from right away. Again, let there be an interval. Instantaneous and negative reaction may result more in Vitus than Virtue. The last thing you want to do is engender scandal in those who look up to you. Worse, you'll arouse those who look down upon you; they'll whirl you about until you finally fly apart.

Fourth, sometimes you have to use physical violence, that's to say, to mount an assault against the Sensitive Appetite. The Flesh'll make demands. Counter them; demand unconditional surrender—that was the way the pugnacious Paul handled the problem, or so he said in his First Letter to the Corinthians (9:27).

Trouble erupts when the Flesh is unwilling to respond to the wishes of the Spirit. Alas, the Flesh has to be broken and bridled until it's willing to do everything that's required of it. That's to say, until it learns to be content with few things, delight in simple things, and overlook annoying things.

12
PATIENCE & CONCUPISCENCE

DEVOUT

Lord God, what You're telling me is that if I can't have peace, then I have to make do, like the Author of the Letter to the Hebrews (10:36), that's to say, have patience. If for no other reason than that so many things go wrong in life. I know; I keep whistling in the dark like the Psalmist (31:10). But try though I do to keep the peace in my own life, war and the panic of war blow it to Hell.

LORD

Isn't that always the way, My son and friend? But I still want you to seek peace. Question is, what kind of peace? Peace without pain, without temptation, without catastrophe? That's not the peace I'm talking about!

You, My beloved, you've been able to find some measure of peace and tranquillity amid a variety of tribulations. Just by being patient in each one, you've shown your spiritual mettle.

If you have little capacity for suffering, how then will you sustain the fire of Purgatory?

When it comes to two evils, always choose the lesser. In the case of Purgatory, either you can endure the fiery punishments after death or you can tolerate the burning evils that beset you now. If the latter, then do it right; that's to say, do it for God's sake and without blowing your top.

Do you think the people of this age escape all suffering? Poll the most refined of Pleasurers, and you'll find that they too howl when skulled or skunked.

DEVOUT

Of course, they will. I know that. But they have so many pleasurable distractions, and they lose themselves in so many whimsical mazes, that when confronted with distress, they hardly notice.

LORD

That's as may be, but consider this, My shrewd Devout. The Pleasurers of this world may have whatever they want now, but will they have it forever? No, only "as long as smoke will last," if I may reply with the Psalmist (37:20). That's the fate of every Midas since time began.

Know there's no recordist of past joys, no lasting list of things that brought us pleasure. "As the smoke vanishes," sang the Psalmist in another place (68:2).

Even at the high point of their lives, the wealthy've never spent a night without bitterness, boredom, or fear. The very things that brought them delight during the day haunted them throughout the night. But what did they expect? They went out of their way to find good bad companions. Take Delectation and Delight, for example. They seemed fanciful creatures at first, what with a myriad of murmurings and mummerings, but off with the masks, and there stood Bitterness and Consternation with scented breaths and missing teeth.

Oh, how brief, false, wild, base these so-called pleasures are! You'd think the Pleasurers would've understood this, but apparently they didn't. Their judgment was impaired, perhaps by boozing, perhaps by bamboozling. In this regard they were no better than the dumb animals, as the Apostle Jude might have put it (v. 10); they grazed their way through life, eating what they should have and also what they shouldn't have, till they brought on themselves an early death.

Two Scriptures for you, My soulful friend.

"Don't trail after your concupiscences," as Jesus son of Sirach put it (18:30), "and swerve while you can from the headlong flight of your own will."

"Delight in the Lord," if I may sing with the Psalmist (37:4), "and He'll grant you the petitions of your heart."

If you want to be entertained and consoled by Me, then you can. Merely hold in contempt all worldly things and cut off all sickly delectations. Then My blessing will be yours, to be followed by copious consolation.

Withdraw yourself, therefore, from every solace known to creatures, and you'll find in Me no sweeter, no stronger consolation.

That won't happen right away in the spiritual life, as you, My friend, already know; at least not without some spiritual sadness and fatigue. The ingrained habits of a lifetime will stand in the way, as the Great Augustine acknowledged in his *Confessions* (8.11). They too can be overcome, but only by a better habit, which, alas for the New Devout, will be hard to do.

The Flesh will murmur and demur at first, but the fervor of the Spirit will bridle it.

The Ancient Serpent that Genesis spoke of in chapter 3 and the Great Dragon of Revelation in chapter 12 will chat you up, of course, but they'll only make things worse. Prayer is useful in this regard. It'll make them stop, stare, then slither away. To prevent their returning anytime soon, do keep yourself occupied.

13
OBEDIENCE TO CHRIST
LORD

Some thoughts.

The Devout who snatches another's obedience will also grab his grace.

The Devout who squirrels away some personal possessions loses his right to communal property.

The Devout who gives himself to his superior, but does it hesitantly, begrudgingly—well, that's a sign that his own flesh hasn't learned to obey itself; that's to say, having gurgitated, it often has to regurgitate.

Learn, therefore, to quickly submit yourself to your superior; that's to say, if you finally want to get your flesh under control.

The exterior Enemy is more quickly overcome than you'd first imagine, especially if your interior life hasn't been a total loss.

A worse, more pestiferous Enemy of the soul lurks, if all were known. It's you yourself, what with your spirit and flesh in total disarray.

If you want to prevail against your flesh and blood, then you have to take back full possession of yourself.

Up to this very point in your personal history you've yet to do this. And it's not so surprising. Your love for yourself exceeds all reasonable standards of quantity and quality; that's to say, there's too much of it, and you've spread it too broadly. No wonder you're afraid to resign yourself fully to the will of others!

But what's the big deal here? You who are dust and nothing but dust—you subjected yourself to Me because God asked you to, and you know what? People applauded! But I, Lord and Tailor of the Universe—I created everything, and I did it out of nothing, if you can imagine that. What's more, I humbly subjected Myself to Humankind because you asked Me to, but what credit, what respect, did I get? I even made Myself lowest of the low, flattest of the flat, and why would I do that? So that you could use My humility as a weapon against your own pride.

The moral? It's from the Great Bernard's homily for the Feast of the Annunciation (8): "Dustman, dust thyself! Refuse Collector, collect thyself? Proud Flesh, prostrate thyself under the feet of the passing crowd!"

Some recommendations.

Light a torch under yourself.

Don't let pride eat away at you like a tumor.

Be an obedient child, and accept the mud from the feet in front of you as you trudge with the adults on the highway of life. That would avoid the wrath of the Psalmist's Lord (18:42)!

Why do you wail about, you silly fool? That's a sentiment I plucked from the Letter of the Great James (2:20).

What have you got to say, you sinful sot, against those who take you to task?

You've offended God so many times, and so many times you've merited Hell. I speak with the voice of the Great Ezekiel when I say, "My eye has spared you" (20:17). I'm echoing the Great Saul to the Great David in First Samuel when I say, "Your soul is precious in my sight" (26:21). You should learn to recognize My love and be grateful for My little gifts.

Give yourself always to True Subjection and Humility and patiently bear up when the contempt you deserve is heaped upon you.

14

HIDDEN JUDGMENTS, INFLATED GOODS

DEVOUT

A turn at last, my Long-winded if Lofty-minded Friend. I got lost somewhere in Your rhetoric. Now tell me if I have You right.

Roll Your thunderous judgments over me, O Lord! Shiver my timbers with fear and trembling! Scarify my soul!

I stand astounded, as the words of Job come tumbling into my mind. "The heavens aren't clean in Your sight" (15:15).

But "if You found depravity among the Angels" (4:18) and You didn't spare them, what will become of me?

"They've fallen like stars from the Heavens," wrote John in Revelation (6:13).

I've read all those passages in Second Peter (2:4), Job (4:18), Revelation (6:13), Psalms (78:25), and Luke (15:16). In them the Angels, some of the best and brightest who lauded You to the highest, fell to the lowest.

And so it is, then, that some of the Notables of our land who used to receive the Bread of Angels have fallen afoul of You, O Lord. Now they delight in the swill of the swell-fed, if forbidden, pig. If that's what happened to them, what do I, a simple man of dust, a collector of garbage, have to look forward to?

No sanctity, O Lord, if You withdraw Your hand.

No wisdom, O Lord, if You stop governing the universe.

No fortitude, O Lord, if You stop conserving.

No chastity, O Lord, if You don't protect it.

No self-control, O Lord, if Your sacred vigilance is absent; the Psalmist knew that the Lord guarded the city, not the sentinels (127:1).

"Leave us behind, O Lord, and we'll be swamped and die"—the Disciples shouted that to You when the storm rose, or so Matthew reported (8:25). Stay with us, and we rise to the surface and live.

We're up and down, but we're confirmed through You. Hot, we grow cool. Cold, we grow warm. Yes, You're our fuel, our fervor, forever.

Here are a few somethings about nothings; that's to say, a few thoughts of my own.

Toad I must be, O Lord, and toad I must remain. Why? Because I toed the mark and failed. Of course, I could have toadied up to You, Lord God of all amphibians, but even in this I failed.

Think it nothing when something good is associated with my name!

O Lord, I cannot sound the depths of Your profoundest judgments, as the Psalmist called them (36:6). Lured by the deep, I dove. All I could see was nothing, and worse than nothing.

My God, You're the Inconsiderable Consideration, the Impassable Archipelago! In traversing Your vastness I leave not a trace or wake!

What can I do to prevent my pride from being discovered?

Where can I discover the confidence I thought I had?

Your judgments have sopped up all this idiotic gloriation of mine, leaving not a stain behind.

What does all the Flesh in the world amount to in Your sight, O Lord? That's the sort of question the Great Paul asked the First Corinthians (1:29). Not a great deal, I should think. As the Prophet Isaiah asked it, "Can the pot glory more than the potter who made it?" (29:16). I think not, but what precisely does this mean? I think I can give some examples of the pot and potter from my own monastic experience.

A Devout wants to be his own chief praiser and appraiser, but why, when his heart's already been verified by God?

A Devout is toasted by the whole world for all of his wonderful qualities, but why, when he's already been credentialed by Truth herself?

A Devout is moved to tears by a choir of voices chanting his praises, but why, when he's already confirmed his hope in God?

These silly Devouts who speak such nonsense, take a close look at them; they're nothing to write home about. Their verbiage fails even as their voices fade. But "the truth of the Lord," as the Psalmist has sung, "remains in tune for ever and ever" (117:2).

15
STAND & PRAY

LORD

My dearest son, may this be your continual prayer.

Lord, if You're pleased with what I pray for, please let it happen; that's how James put it (4:15).

Lord, if You're pleased to find some honor for Yourself in my prayer, please let it happen in Your Holy Name.

Lord, if You're pleased to find some spiritual advantage in my prayer, please let it happen to Your honor.

But, Lord, if what I pray for is harmful to me and not at all helpful to the salvation of my soul, please, please save me from my prayers.

As I've already taught you, My friend and son, not every desire comes from the Holy Spirit, not even if it seems in general to be right and good for Humankind.

Yes, it's difficult to judge for true whether the spirit that moves one to pray for this or that is a good one or a bad one or whether it just comes from one's own self-centeredness.

Alas, toward the end of their lives, many come to see that all along they've been deceived by the Bad Spirit. Which is so sad! At the beginning of their spiritual lives they seemed to have been motivated only by the Spirit of Good.

Therefore, whatever desirable comes into the mind must be longed for first, then prayed for, but always with fear of God and humility of heart. Especially must you be resigned to whatever the outcome. That's to say, the prayer must be totally committed to Me and prayed this way.

O Lord, You know what's good and bad, what's better and worse, what's best and worst—may my prayer be as You wish it to be.

Give what You want, and how much You want, and when You want.

Do with me as You know how.

Pick what's more pleasing, more honoring.

Put me where You want, and deal freely with me in all things.

My reins are in Your hand—put me through my paces, as the amatory Ovid might have put it.

Mark You, I'm Your full-time servant now, prepared for all exigencies. My life's not for me any longer; it's for You to do with it as You want, as the Psalmist has sung (119:125). Wouldn't that be nice, O Lord, if I could ever really pull it off!

Here's a prayer for making God happy.

Grant me Your grace, Kindest Jesus, that it may come with me, work with me, persevere with me until the end of End.

Grant that I may always desire and wish this one thing, what fits You more closely and pleases You more dearly.

May Your will be mine always—may my will follow Yours in perfect harmony.

Two things I crave. Enable me to will and to nill the way You do. Disable me from willing and nilling the ways You don't.

Grant that I may die in all things that have to do with the World.

Grant that I may grow accustomed to being despised and unknown in the age in which I live, as You did in Yours.

Above all other desirables, grant that I not take our friendship for granted; rather, as the Great Augustine suggested in his *Confessions* (1.1), to rest in it and quiet my heart in You.

You are my heart's True Peace. Without You all this is too hard, too harsh, if I may echo Augustine again (6.16).

In this peace, which is Yourself, the One Great and Eternal Good, if I may bejumble the Psalmist's verse (4:8), I sleep and take my rest. Amen.

16

TRUE SOLACE IN CONSOLATION ALONE

DEVOUT

Whatever I want and think with regard to solace, to comfort, I don't expect to find it here in this life, but in the next. Even if I could have every earthly solace and enjoy all earthly delight, one thing's certain: they wouldn't last for long.

Whence, O Soul, don't expect to find full solace, perfect refreshment, until and unless it's in God, whom we've come to know as Consoler of the Poor and Protector of the Low.

Wait a while, my Soul. Expect the Divine Promise, yes, and then you'll have more than you can handle in Heaven. Drool over these things on Earth, and you'll let loose—that's to say, you'll lose—the Eternals and Celestials. Use Temporals that are around you, yes, but desire Eternals that are yet to come. Temporals offer no True Satisfaction. That's because your creation isn't totally suited to enjoyment of that kind.

Even if you had the whole world in your pocket, you wouldn't feel particularly happy or especially blessed. But in God, who created everything, your True Beatitude and Felicity will surely be found.

That's not how the Stupids, sotted and sodden with the things of this world, approach and appraise it. But that's exactly how the Spiritually-minded and Clean-hearted, whose chatsworth is already in the clouds, as Paul and Timothy described it to the Philippians (3:20), interpret it in the interval between now and then; that's to say, between this life and the next.

The One True Solace—that's what Truth has detected within. The Devout brings his friend Jesus with him wherever he goes, chatting him up along the way. "Keep up with me, Lord Jesus! I mean to keep a mean pace."

Let this be my consolation, to freely wish to do without every human solace. And if, as a result of my wish, consolation is nowhere to be found, I'll gladly settle for Your good favor and approval. In this regard I could quote the Psalmist (103:9). "You won't be hounding and harassing me for long, O Lord! You won't be shouting and scaring me out of my wits for ever!"

17

ENTIRELY TOO CASUAL

LORD

With Me or without Me, I know what'll help. You see, you think as a mere hominoid. Which means you have many human feelings as well as some animal urges. It's as simple as that.

DEVOUT

O Lord, of course what You say is true, but I'm having trouble believing it. Be that as it may. Your solicitude in my behalf has been greater than mine in my own behalf. For a Devout like me seems entirely too casual when he doesn't forward to You all his own solicitude; that's the sort of advice Peter offered in his First Letter (5:7).

O Lord, while my will is aimed at and locked firm in You, do for me what You feel and think best. For whatever You do for me can't be anything but good. If You want me to be blanketed in darkness, my blessing to You. If bathed in lightness, my blessing to You also. If You think me worth a quick hug, blessings on Your house. If You think I deserve a swift kick, more blessings on Your house. All of which is to say, whatever the holy day or holly day, may my blessings festoon Your hallowed halls!

LORD

My friend, you have to stand up on your own two legs before you can walk with Me. You have to be as prompt to suffer as to enjoy. You ought to be pocketless and pauperous as interchangeably as industrious and prosperous.

DEVOUT

Lord, I suffer willingly for Your sake whatever You want to lay on me. I wish to accept from Your hand—I don't care what the sequence— good to bad or bad to good, and so on with the sweet and the bitter- sweet, the happy and the sad, and to give thanks for all the things that happen to me.

Guard me from every sin, and neither Death nor Hell will be a stranger to me. In the meantime don't cast me into eternity, as the Psalmist feared would happen to him (77:7); and don't delete me from the Book of Life; that's the terrible threat, one of many, in Revelation (3:5). Whatever the tribulation laid upon me, it may hurt me now but won't affect me in the long run.

18

TEMPORAL MISERIES

LORD

My son, I descended from Heaven for the purpose of your salvation; and My Beloved Disciple recorded it in his Gospel (3:17). I took on your miseries, drawn not by necessity but charity. Why? So that you could learn patience and consider it a not unworthy task to tote some of your temporal miseries yourself. As for Myself, from the hour of My coming to the moment of My leaving, I managed to bear the pain, but just.

Alas, I've not had much success with affairs on earth. Everybody seems to complain about Me. Confusion and *opprobrium* I've tried to meet with a smile. For My gifts I've received ingratitude; for My mir- acles, blasphemies; for My doctrines, censures.

DEVOUT

Lord, I know Your suffering in this life was meant to fulfill the Edict of Your Heavenly Father. Because of that, I, a wretched little sinner, should suffer too, shouldering my corruptible life on the road to Salvation City.

Although the present life is felt to be onerous, it does have a meritorious, and indeed a merry, aspect to it. Your Holy Example and the footprints of the Saints have led the way, and because of that, the trudge is made the more bearable even for the weakest among us.

That's not to say the Old Testament didn't offer some hope and consolation in this regard. But in those holy pages the Gate of Heaven appeared to be closed. Did it really matter? So few took pains to seek the Kingdom of Heaven, and those that did often found the road to Heaven heavily fogged.

Somehow, though, the Just and their friends made it through to the gate, that brazen barrier, but there they had to wait before they could enter. First, O Lord, You had to pay the entrance fee, that's to say, expunge the debt of debts by dying the death of deaths.

How can I thank You enough! To show me and all the faithful the right and good way to Your Eternal Kingdom was a gamble on Your part, and as happened, it turned into a gambol on our part. Yes, Your life is our way, and through holy patience we walk toward You, who are our Crown.

But I have to ask, who on earth would follow You if You hadn't already charted the path and acted as guide? We'd still be milling around on earth if we hadn't had Your astonishing model of spiritual behavior before us.

Up to the time of Your arrival, You know, Humankind was neither hot nor cold about this Heavenly Enterprise. Of course, there were signs along the way, from the Old Dispensation as well as the New (John 12:37). And aren't these the great illuminations that John spoke of (8:12)? Without them—which is to say, without You, O Lord—wouldn't we still be stumbling around in the dark instead of staggering up toward the light?

19
TOLERATING INJURIES

LORD

These questions you're asking, My silly friend, they're the wrong ones. The right one—and there is indeed a right one—goes something like this. "If the Lord and Tailor of the Universe had to suffer and die, and if the legions of His saintly followers had to suffer, many of them to the point of martyrdom, then, at the very least, won't I have to suffer too?"

The answer is, of course, yes, but as for your so-called sufferings to date, I just might paraphrase the Letter to the Hebrews (12:4). "You've suffered all right, and you've made a great squawk about it, but I don't see one single drop of your precious red blood on the pavement!"

DEVOUT

I want to thank You, my Cruel if Creative Friend, for pointing this out, but I'd say in my defense that I had several very excellent reasons.

LORD

But you always have reasons—excuses, really—and they're always dog-eared and flea-bitten!

DEVOUT

Flea-bitten they may be, my Once and Future Friend, but they're mine own!

LORD

Whatever you may have suffered to date, My dear Devout, is but a jot, a tittle, a smidge, a skosh, especially when compared to those over the centuries who've been battered so much, tempted so relentlessly, troubled so grievously, twisted and tortured in so many hard and horrid ways.

Therefore, you should take another look at the rather grand sufferings of others. Why? That you might learn to bear your own rather grandiose discomfits. To you they seem mountains; to Me, they're molehills. How could this happen? Your impatience has magnified them out of all proportion. Nevertheless, whether the aching of your soul is small or large, be a good patient; strive to endure them all.

There's an advantage to you bettering your attitude toward battering and getting battered. You'll begin to appear sagacious and meritorious not only to yourself, but also to others.

There's another advantage. No doubt suffering lays a terrible load on a person, but the proper spiritual attitude lightens the load. That'll be especially true in your case, what with your having so carelessly prepared your mind and body up to this point. That's to say, any adjustment on your part is bound to be an improvement.

DEVOUT

There You go again, my Fine Fisher of Friends!

LORD

Don't say it, My dear Devout!

DEVOUT

You've just smacked me in the face with a herring!

LORD

No, I didn't!

DEVOUT

Well, that's how it felt to me!

LORD

Well, that's just another of your endless excuses! As if you haven't said them all already.

"He hit me first, and I just don't have the strength to suffer another blow. I think I must be in the wrong walk of life."

As if I haven't heard it all already.

"That person brought a serious charge against me, and harried me with all sorts of horrid stuff I couldn't possibly think up myself! I can't accept that, and from him all people! Is that the sort of miserable suffering I'm supposed to put up with, O Lord and Tailor of the Universe?"

What vapid and insipid thoughts! First, it doesn't do justice to the virtue of patience or—ahem—to the Person who rewards all patience. Second, all it does is focus attention on you and the garbage that person dumped on you.

One's not really getting serious about suffering if he can dictate just how much and at whose hand. Another, though, is indeed serious about it when he pays no attention to the person wielding the lash. He doesn't care whether it's his superior, his peer, or his inferior; it can be a good and holy man with knotted cords or just a vulgarian or barbarian with a whip.

As much and as often as the Devout encounters rough skating or tough sledding, he gratefully accepts it all as coming from the hand of God; he even counts it not as a loss, but as a substantial gain. How? Nothing in the presence of God, however minuscule, however majuscule, as long as it's a step taken for God, can be transacted without an increase in merit.

Suffering it is then. If you want to have the victory, ready yourself for battle. If you truly want the crown of patience, wrote Paul in his Second Letter to Timothy (2:5), then engage the Enemy.

But what if you change your mind and don't want to suffer? Then you're in the wrong line of work.

But if you truly want to be a Devout, then you'll have to fight manfully, endure vigorously. Without huffing and puffing there's no movement along the road to peace. Without slugging it out there's no decisive victory.

DEVOUT

Make possible through grace, O Lord, what seems so impossible through nature. Isn't that what You promised You'd do when the people of Jerusalem asked who'd be saved? Luke wrote that You did (18:27).

You know what little I can put up with and how quickly I give up, even when it's only a tiny adversity that rears its timorous head. What I should really do is consider every tribulation as a token of

affection from You. After all, to suffer a little physically and spiritually is not exactly unhealthy for the soul.

20

CONFESSING INFIRMITY

DEVOUT

"Against my better judgment I'll confess my injustice," sang the
Psalmist (32:5). And I too shall confess my infirmity, O Lord. Often
it's a small thing that jogs me off my stride; it makes me so mad at
first, and then I grow sad. To remedy that, I resolve to act more ener-
genitcally in the future. But a modest temptation comes along, and
I'm completely thrown for a loss. Something trivial trips me, and I
end up on my face. Just when I recover and think myself safe again—
the moment when I least expect it—the briefest wisp whispers me
away.

Therefore, O Lord, about my humility and fragility, there's nothing new for You to know.

Have mercy on me. "Rescue me," as the Psalmist has had to cry
out on more than one occasion, "before I'm sucked up by the mire"
(69:14).

This thrashing about in the muck has got to stop! Yes, it embar-
rasses me to have to confess once again that I've made no progress.
But when it comes to putting up a front against the passions, I'm still
so nervous and cowardly. It isn't as though I open the floodgates to
them, but the leakage in the dikes is so persistent and pervasive that
it's driving me crazy.

All of which is another way of saying, do lecture me about my
infirmity. I need to know, because these foul fantasies are seeping in
more quickly than they're draining out.

O Warrior God of Israel, Shepherd King of the faithful souls,
would that You'd look at the labor and pain in me, Your slavish

Devout, and assist me in everything I put my mind to. Fortify me with oak and Heavenly Fortitude lest the Old Man the New Testament spoke of—that wretched Flesh not yet fully subjected to the whims of the spirit—be strong enough to tumble me in the hay. Against that one it'll certainly be necessary to do battle as long as there's breath in my wretched life.

Alas, what kind of a life is this where tribulations abound, where everything underfoot is game for the Enemy's snares? What is it when one tribulation ebbs and another flows? What is it when one conflict has been in full throttle for some time and yet, before it's had a chance to choke, others spring up on the horizon? Is it a world without hope?

How can life be loved? It has so many bittersweet things about it, so many calamities and miseries. And how can life be called *life* when it's generated so many deaths and diseases? Even so, a wretched life, or so many people are inclined to think, is better than no life at all.

The World is frequently blamed when something goes hideously wrong. But for many it isn't easily left behind; the concupiscences of the flesh still cling for dear life to the diseased soul.

Some things about the World aren't so attractive; but others apparently still have some allure. Itching flesh, ogling eyes, luxuriant living; that's as John put it in his First Letter (2:16). But wherever these are found, pangs and throbs are surely present, turning the World into a playground of hatred and unrest.

Depraved Delight, sad to say, has had no such trouble distracting a mind dedicated to the things of this world. Vixen that she is, she's even had the cheek to tell the chickens not to worry. Nor should the rest of Humankind, she says, now that she's got everything under her personal control!

Well, I'm chuffed! How could this have happened? It could happen only because that poor damaged damsel has neither seen nor tasted the spiritual amenities, that's to say, God in Heaven and God on Earth.

Devouts, I'm rather happy to say, wholeheartedly and whole-mindedly condemn the World and strive to live for God under holy discipline. Hence, they're no strangers to the Divine Sweetness promised to all genuine renouncers of the World. These last see quite clearly just how the World has made the Serious Error and, because of it, has disintegrated in a variety of splashy ways.

21
RESTING IN GOD

DEVOUT

Take flight, my Soul, and circle creation until you find a perch. Not just any perch. Certainly not one with a view. A place for a rest is what I need. A perch with the Lord would be best. That's where the Saints are pillowed, or so I've been given to understand. To that end I've composed these little prayers.

IN SEARCH OF A PERCH

Grant me, Sweet Jesus, Loving Friend, rest, not in the rest of creation, but in You. That's to say, not in beatitude or pulchritude, glory or honor, science or subtlety, richness or artistry, jig or dance, fame or praise, consecration or consolation, hope or promise, merit or desire, beneficence or munificence, joy or jubilation, Angels or Archangels or any other Heavenly Militia, or indeed any of the other Visibles or Invisibles. That's simply to say, grant me rest only in Your company.

WITHOUT GOD, OTHER GOODS ARE NOTHING

More than once over the eons, my Timeless if Timely Lord and God, You've been pronounced overall best of show. The tallest and strongest. The most self-sufficient and best equipped. The smoothest-cheeked and cheeriest of cheeks. The handsomest and friendliest.

The noblest and brightest. All these have been true in the past and no doubt will continue to be true in the future.

From these superlatives, however, there flows one horrific inexorable. But first, whatever You may give me by way of gift or revelation or promise, will, of course, always be welcomed. Now if that gift or revelation or promise has nothing of Yourself in it, it will always be regarded by me as one brick short of a load; that's to say, it's something less than perfection. All of which is another way of saying, I look forward to the time when I'll see You in person and grasp Your Holy Hands. As the Great Augustine prayed in his Confessions *(1.1), my heart can neither truly rest nor totally relax until it rests—no, not in all Your creatures or all Your creations—only in You Yourself.*

Breathing in Jesus

O Jesus Christ, Sweetest Friend of My Friendless Soul, how can You lord over the whole universe and yet at the same time grant me license to fly anywhere in creation? And here I'm reminded of the Psalmist's dove who flew the cote and set sail for the wilderness where You reside (55:6).

Fill me with courage so that I can empty my soul.

Flood my soul with Your love so that I can drain the soil of self-love.

Just You, O Lord. No sensibilities. No methodologies. No intellectual monkey business of any kind. Just You alone and in a manner as yet unknown.

But that will be then, and this is now.

At my earthly unhappiness I frequently groan to myself, but at the same time I make a great show of my pain. It's to be expected, I suppose, what with the many evils that take place in this vale of misery.

But in quick succession I become annoyed, morose, confused. More often than not, these evils impede, then distract, unfold, then fold up. Though multifarious, the one purpose they have in common is to obstruct my access to You. I know the Blessed Spirits must be enjoying Your manly hugs, but somehow I'm prevented from joining them in that jolly exercise. All of which is another way of saying, may my snortings and snottings about the many distractions and desolations I encounter on earth move You to help.

WITHOUT JESUS, NO JOY

O Jesus, Splendor of Eternal Glory, Solace of the Wandering Soul, when I'm with You, my loquacious mouth loses its eloquence, leaving only my silence to speak to You. But when I'm not with You, I feel I must speak up.

Come, my Fleet-footed if Flat-arched Friend, come! Why has it taken You so long to make such a short trip! I'm just a verminous pauper huddled in a crumbling doorway, just a shackled prisoner shambling along on cobbles. Without You, no day, no hour will ever be happy again. Why? Because You're my joy and, besides, without You the conversation grows dull. Only You can lighten up my cell. Only You can restore my freedom. I live only to see Your friendly face turn in my direction.

So much for the little prayers of one poor Devout.

Others scour the world for You, but they look in all the wrong places. They find everyone else, but they never seem to find You.

As for me, in the same interval, I'm in just as much of a dither as they. Nothing pleases me either, but here's the difference. The only thing that's likely to please me is You, my God. You're my hope, my salvation. I should keep quiet, I suppose, but I won't. I don't care if I become raucous, obstreperous. I'll pray in public until Your grace returns; that's to say, until You return to our chatsworthy place within.

LORD

"Here I am"—that's what your prayers seem to be saying, My dear friend. Indeed, that's what the Lord said to the querulous Isaiah

(58:9), and that's what I say to you. I'm here, and here I intend to stay.

Your tears and desires, your humble soul and contrition of heart, all have turned Me toward your little prayers and hastened Me to your side.

Long have I called You, my Longanimous and Longevitous Lord, and long have I prepared myself, dumping all my earthly desires into the spittoon. Long will I continue to desire to enjoy Your presence.

As I recall, You spotted me long before I saw You. And so what recourse do I have but to bless You, O Lord, for all the mercies You've rained on me, as the Psalmist has said before me (106:45).

What more is there for Your servant to do except to huddle profoundly in front of You and remind You of his ingrained villainy and vilety?

Of all the wonderful people in Heaven and Earth, as the Psalmist has sung (40:5), there's no one like You.

Your works are extravagantly good; Your judgments, extraordinarily fair, as the Psalmist has proclaimed (19:9); Your many providences, without bounds.

Therefore, all praise and glory to You, O Wisdom of the Father, and may the cacophony of all creation praise You and bless You in chorus!

22

GOOD DEEDS OF GOD

Open my heart to Your law, O Lord God—that's what the Second Maccabist said (1:4). Teach me to walk in Your commandments— that's what the Prophet Ezekiel said (20:19). Grant that I may understand the enormity of what You want me to do—that's Paul wrote to the Ephesians (5:17)—and to appreciate the outrageousness of what I want You to do, namely, to shower me with blessings. Not only me, but the rest of Humankind as well. Do that, and perhaps my fading memory'll prompt me, at some uncertain moment in the future, to give You the thanks You deserve.

I say that now in the full knowledge that, even if I do remember, I won't have the wherewithal to thank You, not even for the least of Your gifts. How can that be? Well, for one thing, when I think of the number of Your gifts, I'm overwhelmed. That was Jacob's prayer to the God of Abraham in Genesis (32:10). And for another, when I think of the Giver of the gifts, I realize I'm just a mite before the Almighty.

Everything we have in our souls and bodies and whatever we possess, exteriorly or interiorly, naturally or supernaturally, these are Your gifts, and they reveal You as a generous, even an extravagant, giver. But why should I be surprised? Just about everything we have comes from You. One person may receive rather more and another rather less, but all the gifts are Yours. Without You not even the smallest gift can be given or gotten.

LORD

If I may add a word here, My sincere if sinful friend.

Whoever's received lots of gifts from Me can boast that he deserved them all, but no one'd believe him; Paul wrote much the same in First Corinthians (4:7). He can extol the wonderfulness of himself, at the expense of the ordinariness of others, but that'd sound tinny. He can snip and snipe at the less gifted among you, but you'd know he's just a fool.

Less is always more—that's the spiritual principle here.

For example, the modest person who humbly gives great thanks for his gifts is generally thought by Me to be greater and better than the bombastic person.

Another example: the one who closes his eyes in shame because of what he's done to Me and to others will come to look upon the simple gifts I've given him with greater appreciation.

Yes, less is always more. Put another way, more is always less.

Of course, the stuffy person who received rather fewer gifts than he thought he deserved shouldn't go all teary, or get a bad case of the pouts, or turn a sickly shade of green, envious at what he thinks are the excessive gifts of others.

What he should do is turn his attention away from himself to Me. He should praise My goodness. After all, I'm the One who so affluently, so graciously, so recklessly laid on My gifts without respect of persons. That's as Paul wrote to the Romans about who gets what, Jew or Greek (2:10–11). But that's not entirely true. Everything comes from Me, and everything bears My indelible stamp. But I know what's best for each and every person and why this one should get a little and that one a lot.

Whose gifts are these? Well, it doesn't take a syllogism, or a sorites of syllogisms, to discern that gifts, all gifts, no matter how many or how large, aren't really yours; they're Mine, and remain Mine. Try that on your logic!

As for each and every person haranguing Me about not having received his just deserts in this regard, a little time at prayer and he should quickly come to see that they're just desserts; that's to say, not wages for jobs done, but gifts meant to please and perhaps even to be used.

And what's all this fuss about who gets what? A little contemplation on your part will reveal three things.

First, each and every person receives just the right number of gifts.

Second, each and every gift has been carefully measured, cut, and sewn by Me, the Lord and Tailor of the Universe.

Third, each and every gift of Mine fits perfectly and always arrives on time!

Odd, but true. And as I've said, a little contemplation reveals all.

DEVOUT

Whence, O Lord God, I want to comment on a particularly appropriate gift of Yours; namely, the presence of gifts that is at the same time the absence of gifts; that's to say, the sort of high-visibility gifts that arouse the world's curiosity. So a person like myself, who's had a glimpse of his own spiritual poverty and vilety, shouldn't necessarily enshroud himself in rancid grave clothes; rather, he should don the airy garments of consolation and hilarity. Why? You have the temerity to ask. Because You, O Lord and Tailor of the Universe, You're the culprit! In the words of the Letter of James (2:5), You're the One who's chosen, as family and company for Yourself, the paupers and the poopers of this world. In their ragged company I'm happy to count myself.

Proof of this exotic choice, my Exoteric if sometimes Esoteric Friend, are Your very own Apostles, whom You established as princes of all the land, if I may echo the Psalmist (45:16). Nevertheless, they've passed their lives on earth as humble and simple men, compliant, without complaint, as Paul described himself to the Philippians (3:6); without any malice or guile, as Peter urged in his First Letter to the Diaspora (2:1). When, as it will to all who follow You, time came to suffer for Your name's sake, they did it gladly and with a song in their souls; at least that was Paul's summation of it in Acts (5:41).

Therefore, nothing, O Lord, ought to make someone who loves You and knows Your gifts dance with joy as doing what You want and indeed what You require. That should make him so content and so consoled that it matters not whether Your gifts make him a Minim—that's to say, a person of no particular importance—or a Maxim—that's to say, a person of inflated importance.

And it matters not to him whether in the eyes of the world he's high or low, first or last, happy or sad, nonymous or anonymous, for he's happy as a lark whenever Your will's being done. And as for all Your jolly gifts, the ones You've given and those You've yet to give, what larks!

23
PATH TO PEACE

LORD

Today, dear son and friend, I want to spend our precious chatsworthy moments together on the True Way of Peace and Liberty.

DEVOUT

Whatever You want to talk about, my Lord and Teacher of the Universe, is fine with me.

LORD

I have four points for you and all My dear friends, all of which you'll find in the Gospels.

Do the will of another rather than your own; Matthew on how to deal with a Demanding if Divine Father (26:39).

Choose to have less rather than more; Matthew on how to prepare for a missionary journey (10:9–10).

Take the last seat at the rearmost table, and put yourself hindmost when it comes to standing in line; Luke on how to behave at a wedding banquet (14:10).

Desire and pray that the will of God becomes part and parcel of your very fiber; Matthew on how to get the most out of prayer (6:10).

If ever there were such a Devout as this, he'd enter that far-off territory known only on the maps as Peace & Quiet.

DEVOUT

Well, my Lordly if Long-winded Friend, Your instruction today is unusually brief and to the point, at least as far as monastic perfection is concerned. It took You only a few moments to say it, but it'll take an age before a poor soul like me can gather the spiritual and intellectual fruit contained therein.

I think I get Your drift, though. Be faithful to these precepts, You seem to be saying, and my interior life will weather the inevitable squalls. Perhaps so. I've often felt myself bottoming out, that's to say, losing my sense of peace. But just as often, by means of simple instructions like Yours, I recover my land legs quickly enough.

But I must tell You this, O Lord and Potentate of the Universe, as Holy Job might call You (42:2), You've always had my spiritual progress at heart, and for that I'm grateful. But I can't, and won't, fulfill Your teaching or work on my salvation, as You urge, unless and until You grant me more grace. I'm sorry it always has to come back to this, but there it is.

Now as for the evil thoughts that continue to plague me, let me try out this prayer on You.

"My Lord God, don't distance Yourself from me!" thrummed the Psalmist (71:12). "My God, look down on me with help!" Why? Again the Psalmist. "There have risen up within me a band of insurrectionists" (27:12), that's to say, piratical thoughts and fears afflicting my soul. How can I pass through the fire unsinged? How can I break through the battle line unbloodied? What was that You said when You anointed Cyrus in Isaiah (45:2–3)? "I'll go before you, and I'll lay low the boastful of the earth. I'll open the doors of prisons, and I'll empty all the treasuries of their secrets, just for you to know."

Do do that, O Lord, and You'll make all these iniquitous thoughts flee from Your angry face. That's why, in every tribulation, I flee to You, confide in You, invoke You from my inmost heart, and wait patiently for Your response.

To keep my head clear, O Lord, may I address You with this prayer?

Illumine my intellect, Good Jesus, with the clarity of Your good light, and lead out of the habitat of my heart the creatures of the dark, the Harpies. Leash my wanderlust. Dash water on my supposed ability to survive the storms sweeping in from the Zee of Temptation. Fight bravely for me. Tame the riotous evil within; that's to say, my concupiscences, Sirens all, bandying and beckoning without cease. Then I'll find peace in Your virtue and praise in that holy hall, that's to say, in my conscience.

Command the winds and the storms to stop. Isn't that what You did in the middle of the Sea of Galilee? The Gospel of Mark says so (4:39). Shush the Zee, shish the North Wind, and the weather will clear.

"Beam Your light and Your truth," cried out the Psalmist (43:3) over all the land. Why? "I'm a land without features," as the Author of Genesis described everything at the beginning (1:2), that's to say, until You illumine me with Your globes. Drench my soul with Heavenly Grace. Dampen my heart with Heavenly Dew. Husband the waters of devotion so that they irrigate the face of the earth and produce bountiful harvests.

Raise up my poor mind flattened by the weight of sins, and what should You do with my desire for flashy things? You might as well hang it as an ornament in the heavens. That way, having experienced the smoothness of the Supernals, You'll find it harder to deal with the roughness of the Terrenals.

Snatch me, pluck me, from the clutches of every creaturely consolation. Why? That's because they won't let me go, even though they can't fully satisfy me; that's to say, bring quiet back to my life. Join me to You with a chain of inseparable love. Is friendship still possible? Possible, yes. With You it's fruitful, but with someone else it's frivolous.

24
CURIOSITY

LORD

My dear friend, don't go poking your nose into the virtues that may be found in the lives of your fellow Devouts. And don't sniff about the laundry for their vices. Why? Because your path is in the opposite direction. "Just follow Me." That was the Evangelist John's answer, as it was Jesus' before him (21:22).

What business is it of yours if one person is a such-and-such or another person says one thing but does another? You don't need to be responsible for your whole community. You just need to be responsible for yourself; that's how Paul put it to the Romans (14:12). And that, believe Me, is more than you can handle. Beyond that, you quickly get out of your depth.

And before you smack Me in the face with that mullet, let Me assure you I know everyone and I see everything that happens under the sun; that's what the Preacher wrote about Me (1:14). Each person I know inside out, that's to say, what he thinks, what he wants, and where he's heading; that's how My John described Me (2:25). And that includes you.

So what can I do for you? Everything, if you put it all into My hands. What can you do for yourself? Keep the peace. That's to say, forgive the agitator his agitation; he stirs the pot against you, but he can't bring it to a boil. Eventually he'll find himself in a broth of his own juices. He can't deceive Me.

Some things aren't worth worrying about. Swanning about in a sphere of influence. Being on a first-name basis with worldly notables. Dispensing tokens of affection to every outstretched hand. Why? Because these activities, harmless as they may seem, do have a tendency to distract the soul and clutter the heart.

I speak My words of wisdom and reveal My hidden thoughts to you, My beloved friend, but on one condition only. You must keep a weather eye open for My coming and leave the door of your heart unlocked; that's one of My instructions in the Last Book of My New Testament (3:20). That's to say, be on the lookout, pray while you watch, and think humble thoughts.

25
PEACE & PROGRESS

LORD

Now to peace, My son. Surely you'll recognize the following as words from the Gospel of John: "My peace I leave you, My peace I give you. It's a gift from above, not from below" (14:27).

Everyone wants peace and is willing to sweat a little for it; but not everyone cares to pay the ultimate price for the ultimate peace.

Where does My peace dwell? In the humble and gentle of heart; that's how My Matthew remembered Me (11:29). Where does your peace reside? In deep patience.

Hear My voice, follow My advice, and you'll enjoy much peace.

DEVOUT

Just tell me what my next steps should be, my Light-footed if Long-footed Friend.

LORD

Everything counts. Don't be careless. Watch every word. Guard every step. All of which means, please Me alone. That's to say, don't mess with anyone else but Me. Don't jump to conclusions about what others say or do. Stick to your monastic rule. And the result? You'll discover that your rage erupts rarely, and when it does, does little damage.

That doesn't mean you won't be thumped and thwacked from time to time—that's the way it is in the present life, but in the next? Ahhh, well!

Some "don'ts" to remember.

Don't think you've found True Peace just because you find no hub-bub in your heart!

Don't think everything's good just because you don't bump into the Devil on your daily rounds!

Don't think you've arrived at monastic perfection just because your fellow Devouts have stopped annoying you to death!

Don't think you're ready for sainthood just because you've had some fleeting moments of devotion and sweetness!

Why all these "don'ts"?

Because in all of these behaviors I can't for the life of Me discover a true admirer of virtue!

DEVOUT

And I thought I was doing so well, my Admiring if Admonitory Friend. Perhaps You'd be so kind as to tell a poor soul like me just what spiritual progress and human perfection consist in?

LORD

In offering yourself from the bottom of your heart to the Divine Will.

In not seeking out your own will, whether antsy or elephantine, in time or in eternity.

Do these, and nothing'll ruffle your calm. And continue to give thanks, in prosperous times as well as desperate ones.

Be stout of heart and long in hope. That way, when interior consolation vanishes, your heart and soul can sustain a heavier load.

Don't feel you have to justify yourself all the time; especially don't ask why you, of all people, should have to suffer all these things.

Do justify Me, though, in all your many moves and moods, and do praise Me as holy.

Then you'll walk the straight and narrow to the Land of Peace and Honey, where Hope and Doubt are no more; where, as Job put it to his Maker (33:26), you and I will be well met, finally, face to face, *in dulci jubilo*.

But that's then, and this is now. In the unlikely event that you do arrive at complete contempt of self while there's still a breath in you, know that the peace of soul accompanying it is about as good as it gets, according to the Psalmist (72:7), at least on this side of the Final Veil.

26

FREEING THE MIND

DEVOUT

As I understand You, O Lord, whoever strives for perfection should never relax his grip on the Celestials. Why? Because in his daily round he has to step smartly around and through the many and varied dumpings and dumplings of the world without so much as soiling his sandal. And he has to do it as if he hadn't a care in the world, and not at the pace of a slug, but in the sprightly manner of a person with a free and bright mind. How? By allowing no creaturely affection to cling to his soul.

To that end, I've composed this prayer.

I beseech You, Most Pious God of mine, preserve me from the cares of this life lest I trip myself up; lest I be seized by the many necessities of the body; lest I seize up from too much pleasure; lest I become depressed by the universal obstacles of the soul, broken on the wheel of trouble.

I'm not talking about the clumsy imperfections that Worldly Vanity often causes, but about those miseries that result from the Primal Malediction of Mortality. These latter seriously affect the soul; that's to say, they weigh it down and slow it down. The result is that he hasn't had the strength to enter into the freedom of the spirit as often as he desired.

O my God, Ineffable Sweetness, as far as I'm concerned, turn bitter every carnal consolation that drags me from the love of Eternals. Why? Its allure is evil. It affects my intuition. It draws me to a delectable good of the present. Don't let it conquer me, my God, don't let the flesh and blood conquer me! Don't let the World and its brief glory deceive me! Don't let the Devil and his cleverness, his bag of tricks, overwhelm me!

Grant me the fortitude of resisting, the patience for enduring, the constancy of persevering. Grant for all the consolations of the world the discreet yet manly cologne of Your spirit, and in place of carnal love, flood me with the love of Your name.

Just count them—food, drink, clothing, and the other innumerable articles that keep the body going—all these are necessary, or so they say, but they're also insufferable to the fervent spirit; so said the Great Bernard in his First Sermon for Septuagesima. Grant that I may use as little of this excess baggage of the soul as possible; that's to say, don't let me spend all my time on baggage management to the detriment of daily prayer. Truly, I'd like to ditch all these extras, but I can't. Nature has its minimal claims, and it'd be unwise to meddle with them. But to rummage about in the things that dither the soul? Holy Law prohibits that. Why? Because the flesh has this sudden capacity of overpowering the soul with its fragrance.

Because of all these, I beg You, O Lord, let Your hand direct me and protect me lest something catastrophic happen.

27

CREEPING LOVE

LORD

Well, My son and friend, the bad news is, you have to give up all if you hope to get all; that's to say, you have to lose yourself, leaving no traces or tracks behind.

Know that love of self does more harm to you than all the calamities of the World. If I were to pick one such calamity, you'd find it thriving, unbeknownst to you, among your everyday loves and affections.

If your love has been pure, simple, and well ordered, you won't be held captive by material things.

Don't look for what it's not allowed to have.

Don't acquire what can impede your progress and deprive you of your interior freedom.

It's amazing, isn't it, that you don't, from the bottom of your heart, commit yourself to Me, in whom you can desire or have everything your soul should ever need.

Wherefore, why consume yourself with false labor? Why weary yourself with worries that aren't yours? If you're always on the quest, if you simply have to have this convenience or that advantage, then you'll be in an uproar *ad nauseam*. You'll never be in quietude; in fact, you'll be up to your bum in solicitude. Why? Because nothing's perfect. That's to say, in every enterprise some defect'll flare, and in every endeavor some contrarian'll say it can't be done.

Creepers and other wildly successful plants, therefore, don't really help; unfortunately, they choke all the life out of your spiritual garden. Pretty they may be for a time, but, eventually, you'll have to root them out.

This isn't just about counting coin or amassing wealth. It's also about honors and decorations and the inflated citations that go with them. All this stuff turns to dust as the world dies; John said as much in his First Letter (2:17).

Your soul is poorly defended if it lacks spiritual fervor.

Put up a monument to Peace with the World as foundation, and it won't stand for long. Erect an obelisk within, with Me as base, and it'll never stop pointing to the sky.

You can change yourself, but you won't necessarily change yourself for the better. Try it, and see what happens. Chances are, you'll meet your same old self coming and going.

DEVOUT

Here's a prayer of my own devising.

Confirm me, O God, through the grace of the Holy Spirit, if I may echo the Psalmist (51:12).

Strengthen the interior man, if I may echo Ephesians (3:16). Empty my heart from every useless solicitude and distress. Discourage me various desires from shopping for stuff, no matter how cheap or dear.

Grant that I may see that everything is fading, if I may echo Ecclesiastes (2:11), and that I'm fading with it. Nothing under the sun remains where it is. Everything is "vanity and affliction of the spirit."

Oh, that I were wise as the person who knows this!

Grant me, O Lord, the Celestial Knowledge, if I may echo the Wisdom of Solomon (9:4), to seek and find You in all things, to be wise and love You above everything, and to understand the rest, according to the order of Your wisdom, for what it is.

Allow me to prudently decline the flatterer and to patiently bear the slanderer. Why? Great wisdom it is for a person who's set sail on a spiritual voyage not to be swayed by, as Paul put it to the Ephesians (4:14), Doctrinal Hearsay or Daresay—Sirens both, meant to distract, then to destroy!—but to continue with some serenity on the charted course.

28

KEEPING THE PEACE

LORD

You don't bear up well, do you, My dear friend, when someone trashes you in public; that's to say, when someone sets the torch to your ears? There's a reason for this; in fact, two reasons. First, you think more of yourself than you should. Second, you should think less of yourself than the slanderer thinks of you.

If you're already treading the downward-inward path, you won't pay much attention to whatever slanders come flying in your direction.

It's no small prudence to keep your peace when times are bad, that's to say, to turn yourself toward Me—that's how My John put it (16:33). That way you won't be knocked off your course by some outrageous judgment about your person or your conduct.

Don't look for your peace to come from the mouths of men. Their animadversions, whether for good or for bad, don't make you either a better or a worse person.

Just where is True Peace and True Glory? Shouldn't it be in Me?

Pleasantries, unpleasantries, it really doesn't matter. Either way, the true Devout'll enjoy great peace.

Out of unruly love and ungainly fear there arises every inquietude of heart, every distraction of sense.

29

MIDDLE OF A MUDDLE

DEVOUT

"May Your name be blessed throughout the ages." That's the way the Holy Sarah prayed it in Tobit (3:11), but she hardly knew why, so bedeviled she was by the Lord—and I don't know why I'm praying it now. You wanted this temptation and tribulation to be visited upon me. If that's so, O Lord, then flee I must, away from them and away from You but, God forgive me, also toward You. Help me to do the good and right thing!

Now that I'm in the middle of this mischief, my heart keeps pounding, and I'm breaking out all over. Father and Friend, what can I say, now that I've got the troubles except, perhaps, "Save me from this hour"—that's what You prayed to Your Father in the garden, or so the Beloved Disciple reported in his Gospel (12:27), and that's what I pray to You now.

"But that's just why I've come to this hour"—that's what You also prayed in the same place and the same verse, and so, I suppose, in the present fix I'm in, should I.

I hope You'll feel glorified when You've humbled me and then raised me up again.

"If it please You, O Lord," as the Psalmist cried, "rescue me" (40:13).

Poor beggar that I am, what can I do without You? Where can I go with You?

Grant me patience, O Lord, at this very fine turn of events.

"Help me, my Lord," as the Psalmist cooed (109:26), no matter how catastrophic my fall has been!

Still in the middle of this muddle, what shall I say, O Lord? Some words from Matthew come to mind (26:42). "Your will be done"—that sounds appropriate. That's what You said in the Great Prayer to Your Father; and that's what I should say too.

I've richly deserved to be flayed and flattened. So I have to endure it, wait patiently. But the storm'll pass. Things'll get better. Thankfully, Yours is the right hand that rocks the Cradle of the Universe.

Lift this temptation from me if You want. At least soften its impact before it crushes the life out of me.

Mercifully, many times before You've saved me, if I may take some words from the Wisdom of Solomon (11:17), although I can't help noting You waited until the last possible moment, no doubt for dramatic effect.

I've tried to save myself before, my Life-saving and Life-savoring Friend, but it's more than I could do. But You, You could save me, You could make it easier for me. And, if I might paraphrase the Psalmist (77:10), with less energy than it takes the Almighty to bat an eyelash.

30
SLOW TO TURN TO PRAYER

LORD

"Strength in the face of weakness"—that's how the Prophet Nahum described Me in his vision (1:7), and that's how you may describe Me today.

You should come to Me when things aren't going well—that's what I said in Matthew (11:28). Why? I have all this Celestial Consolation at My beck and call. So why are you so slow to turn to prayer? And why am I always your last resort?

You can plead your own case whenever you have a mind to. But often in the past, I've noticed you like to spend what I consider an indecent interval searching for relief in a variety of other venues and avenues. There's some titillation in each, no doubt, but not a lot of tintinnabulation. That's to say, here a clink, there a clink, but no one clear tone.

I'm the rescuer, the St. Bernard in the Alps, for all who hope in Me. Without Me there's no help for what ails you, no pointed advice, no lasting remedy. But, already, after the avalanche, with color returning to your cheeks, you can recover with the help of My ministrations. I'm always close by, as I say in the Psalms. What can I do? I can not only restore your basic necessities, but also add a few niceties of My own.

DEVOUT

That would be nice, O Thoughtful and Considerate Lord, but wouldn't that be out of character, to give me something I don't need?

LORD

Why would it? That's what I asked the Prophet Jeremiah (32:27). Am I a person who says He'll do something and then doesn't? That wasn't how Balaam's oracle in Numbers described Me (23:19). Is that how you see Me? Am I really a Killjoy in your eyes?

DEVOUT

At the risk of incurring Your undying displeasure, my Darling Lord and Friend, and, worse, at the risk of telling an untruth to the Truth of all truths, I must admit that some days You are indeed a Killjoy, and for the best of reasons, no doubt.

LORD

Well, I'm miffed!

DEVOUT

Other days, though, You're something of a Lovejoy and just nice to be with.

LORD

Well, that's something to be thankful for—that I'm not a total loss. But I still have to put it to you. Where's your faith, man? Stand firm and hold fast. Longanimous! Rumbustious! That's what you have to be, and consolation'll come to you in its own sweet time. Till then, wait, wait for Me! I answer the Psalmist's call (40:1). I'll come and, yes, My touch'll heal. That's what I said to the Centurion, when he asked Me to help his paralyzed servant; Matthew had the story correctly (8:7).

Out of your skin you may be, but I'm not the cause. It's the grizzly temptation that bothers you, the groundless fear that dithers you.

Why do you worry now about what's going to happen in the future? That way you'll be shedding tear after tear year after year!

"Every day has its own malice," or so the Great Matthew has pointed out (6:34).

Useless, and less than useless, it is to feel puzzled or pleased about the future. Either way you've little to gain. That's because such woolgathering rarely produces a cloak.

But isn't that just like Humankind, to play about with fanciful projections?

Your spiritual progress has been modest, I must say, if you allow yourself to be dazzled by the Enemy. Why? He doesn't care a jot whether his illusions or deceptions are right or wrong. They cause prostration, all right, but he doesn't care a tittle whether it's out of love for the present or fear of the future; I say something about that in John (14:27).

Some "don't-forget's."

Believe in Me—that's what I told My Apostles that Passover night in the Upper Room (14:1)—and have faith in My mercy.

Often when you think you've gone a step too far, you'll find Me at your heel.

Just when you think that everything's been lost, you'll find another chance for earning even more merit than before.

No, it's not a total loss when something bad happens to you.

Don't make long-term commitments to do or not to do in the light of present pleasure or displeasure.

Don't cling overlong to a mood or a mode, no matter what its source; people will think it's chronic.

Don't think you're a derelict, a beached and abandoned hulk, if from time to time I send you some tribulation or withdraw some consolation. After all, it all leads to the same destination, that's to say, to the Kingdom of Heaven.

For you and the rest of the Devouts, it's more helpful to be exercised by adversity than entertained by prosperity.

I know your hidden thoughts—that's what I told the Psalmist (44:21)—and what's wrong with that? I find it helpful in planning your salvation.

Doing without consolation for a while isn't all that bad. It prevents you from feeling too good about the spiritual tracks you're making or the ladder of perfection you're climbing.

What I've given I can take back, and what I've taken back, I can give again. Whenever I want.

When I give, it's Mine to give. When I take it back, it isn't really yours to keep.

Every gift of Mine is good, and "all gifts are good," at least according to the Letter of James (1:17).

If I send you a gift that hurts, don't get uppity, don't let your heart go pit-a-pat. I can soon lighten the load, and every burden will be changed into joy.

As for My dealings with you, I trust you find them satisfactory; that's to say, fair and just in every way, with a little mercy mixed in. So, am I right in thinking you won't mind recommending Me to others?

Every time you encounter a road block on your spiritual journey, you shouldn't go sit by the side of the road and be sad; rather, you should rejoice and give thanks. Why? I've afflicted you with woes, yes, but you're not the only one. Yes, I too know the lash, and John has let this be known to you. "As the Father has loved Me, so I love you" (15:9).

DEVOUT

Well, my Dear if Divine Friend, that's not a lot of comfort for a poor soul like myself, seeing how things eventually sorted out between You and Your Father.

LORD

And what do you mean by that?

DEVOUT

I thought You were referencing the Cross.

LORD

That's as may be, My dear friend, but that's what I said to My Disciples. I sent them off not to minor joys but to great battles; not to honors ceremonies but to contempt encounters; not to leisurely activities but to laborious exercises; not to relax without anxiety, but to endure with patience, like the seeds that fell on the good soil in My parable in Luke (8:15). As they germinated, so should you. All words worth remembering.

31

CREATOR, NOT CREATURES

DEVOUT

At this point in my life, O Lord, I should be able to make good use of the graces You've given me. But I still need more of these very same graces if I'm ever to outdistance the rest of creation. As long as a creature can lay a hand on me, I'm grounded; that's to say, I can't freely fly to the Creator. But fly I must! Certainly the Psalmist wanted to do just that when he said, "Give me the wings of a dove, and I'll fly until I find Your rest" (55:6)?

Who's achieved more peace of mind than the person who sees clearly? Who's achieved more freedom than the person who's abandoned all earthly things?

As I understand it, then, to fly over every creature, you have to pay no attention to yourself. You have to stand with an uncluttered mind and see that You, the Lord and Tailor of the Universe, have nothing in common with the rest of creation.

If you haven't freed yourself of all creatures, then you're still tethered to the ground; that's to say, you're off the ground a bit, but you can't rise any higher to the divine.

Perhaps that's why there are so few contemplatives; that's to say, that's why so few know how to sequester themselves from the creation daily perishing around them.

To do this great grace is required, a grace that raises the soul off the ground and keeps it airborne. And unless you are airborne in spirit and freed from all creaturely ties and rising to God, whatever you know, whatever you have, is only a drag.

Whoever thinks he's found something important outside of the One Sole Immense, the One Eternal Good, is destined to fly small, fly low.

The moral?

God is all, and what's left is nothing and ought to be counted as such; at least that's what the Great Augustine wrote in his *Confessions* (3.8).

There's a world of difference between Devouts illumined by Divine Wisdom and Clerics well versed in humane knowledge. Much more noble is the doctrine dripping from the Divine Tap than the science drawn from a well.

Many people think contemplation a pleasant, fashionable way to pass the time; they long for it, even lust for it. But when they learn it's hard work, they quickly lose interest. There's a mammoth misunderstanding here. They want to enjoy its consolations, yes, but they don't want to endure its mortifications. Go figure!

If we Devouts are caught sharing this opinion, then we've clouded our own minds into thinking, as the public has every right to think, that we're spiritual men.

We labor so hard and so long, and what do we get for it but more anxiety about the transitory, everyday things? As for our interior interests, we rarely gather our wits and our senses to try to figure out where we really stand.

Some real pains!

After a modest period of recollection we have to rush outside for a breather!

When it comes to evaluating our works, we can't hold our focus for more than a minute!

Where our affections are at any particular moment in time, we have no idea.

Impurities invade our souls, and we'd like to deplore them one by one, but there's not enough time in the universe for that!

"Every creature has lost its way or fouled its nest"—that's been obvious since that notorious Garden Party in Genesis (6:12). Is it any wonder, then, that the Great Deluge is never far off?

Our interior affections have sustained so much damage that we can no longer rely on them for True Direction. Only a pure heart, which comes from a good life, as Paul wrote in First Letter to Timothy (1:5), can discern the shortest distance between two spiritual points.

The populace is interested in everything celebrities do, but they don't pay much attention to their motives, that's to say, whether their actions are virtuous or not.

Courage, wealth, good looks, nice personality—that's what the populace looks for first. Can the celebrities carry a tune, write a decent paragraph, do something adventurous—that's what seems to be newsworthy.

Mum's the word, though, about whether these glittering creatures have about them any whiff of poverty of spirit, patience, mildness, or any other desirable internal qualities.

Nature looks at what Humankind does; Grace looks into how Humankind does it.

Nature hopes in the Enemy, but its hopes are often hoodwinked; Grace hopes in God, and its hopes are often fulfilled.

32

SAYING NO TO SELF

LORD

Say no to self and mean it, or you'll never find yourself a free man— that's what I told My Disciples, that's how Matthew recorded it (16:24), and that's what I'm telling you, My dear friend. Until that sweet time comes, count yourself a prisoner, under house arrest, in your own body as in a bedlam.

Well, you feel as if you own your own self, are your own best friend, lust for tacky stuff to decorate your own domain, peep through the arras at others more fortunate than yourself.

You feel you're something of a dervish whirling in a circle until you turn to butter, or a Sybarite seeking soft sheets for yourself instead of the rock-hard life of Jesus Christ. Paul wrote much the same thing to the Philippians (2:21).

Maybe you feel you're one of those tinkers who spend their time thinking up and putting together gadgets. They'll work for a time, but then they'll break down. Which is another way of saying, I think, no project is likely to be successful unless it has its source somewhere in Me.

Here are some words of advice that you could never logick your way to.

Give up everything, and you'll find everything. Leave greed behind, and you'll find rest. With this sort of attitude and this sort of resolve, you'll understand all things.

DEVOUT

As You describe it, my Understated if sometimes Overwrought Friend, Ezra the Priest was right when he spoke to the guilt-ridden, rain-soaked people of Judah and Benjamin (10:13). This isn't the work of one day.

LORD

No, it isn't.

DEVOUT

Nor is it a child's game.

LORD

No, it isn't.

DEVOUT

You've put a whole dictionary into just one dictum, and it has all a Devout needs to know to become the perfect Religious.

LORD

My dear Devout, just being within earshot of the way of perfection shouldn't turn you away or make you depressed. Rather, it should provoke you to fly higher, and if that makes your nose bleed, to sigh more for such a life while still on earth.

Would that you'd arrived at a point where you no longer love yourself above all else! Would that you stood at the ready for My command, and the command of the Father I've put over you. That would please Me much, and your whole life on earth would pass in joy and peace.

But up to this point, if I may be permitted a painful observation, My dear Devout, you have a lot of excess baggage to leave behind. You could resign it totally to Me. Then you'd get what you want. "Gold refined in the fire by Me—that's what I want your actions to buy from Me—I want you rich." That's to say, as it is in the Last Book of the New Testament (3:18), rich in Celestial Wisdom, poor in all other wisdoms.

I've said it before, and I say it again. While on this earth, you should buy duller, cheaper items in preference to flashier, pricier articles.

Whatever happened to Wisdom, *Sapientia, Sophia?* Such a mighty presence she used to be, and quite a beauty too! Now she's thought to be a hag and a terrible nag. Even as I speak, she's being carted off to the Hall of Forgotten Virtues, a victim of benign neglect.

Poor babe, perhaps she saw it coming. She was shy; shunned parties; was thought innocent, some would say naive, and had this tendency toward the tendentious. That made her an amusing conversationalist, though sometimes she'd say the most annoying things; not that they weren't true—they were all too true. Qualities all that seem so quaint to so many in our own day! When people speak of her now, they do so warmly, but their cold lives belie their tepid belief.

Wisdom, if she must, then, is content to be the Precious Pearl of My parable in Matthew (13:46), that's to say, perhaps hidden from the eyes of the many, but always on view to the chosen few.

33

SWINGING & SWAYING

LORD

The Mutables, My dear Devout—no doubt you've made their acquaintance. They wreak havoc with your affections. What's true today is false tomorrow—that sort of thing. Will you or nill you, that's the rhythm of life, so long as you shall live. You're happy one moment; the next thing you know, you're sad. At peace, then in an uproar. Fervent, then tepid. Studious, then stupid. Serious, then supercilious.

But the wise person who's well instructed in the ways of the spirit isn't swayed by the huffs and puffs of the Mutables. He pays little attention to the flips and flops of affections within. Nor does he care from which corner of the chart the wind of instability blows. All he does is bend his mind to the task at hand; that's to say, to make progress toward the vowed and desired destination.

How can one remain firm of purpose through the topsy-turvy of a lifetime? Simply by placing one eye on the intention and the other eye on the Lord.

The purer the eye of intention, the longer the glass through which it peers. But even the long glass, pure as its intention is, will dawdle at the middle distance when something delightful presents itself. A dipping caravel, for example, laden with cloth and silk, sugar and diamonds, heading for Antwerp.

Self-seeking leaves strawberry marks on the soul, and rare's the person without them.

Self-seeking always damages the sight of the soul, and rare's the person who has the vision he was born with.

As John the Evangelist told it (12:9), the Jews of old went up to Bethany to Martha and Mary's. "It was to visit with Jesus, of course, but they also spent some time with Lazarus."

Which couldn't be right. I'm the ultimate sight, and indeed the ultimate site. Always aim the lens in the right direction and focus it at the farthest point. That's where you'll find Me. If not, try cleansing the lens.

34
WITH GOD, WITHOUT GOD

DEVOUT

What, ho, my God, my All, if I may hail You with the words of the Great Father Francis of Assisi! What more can I want? How much happier can I be? But can there be room for more? I'd like to know.

Give me Your word, O Word of words, O Book of books, that there's nothing more I could want! John said as much in his First Letter (2:15). You can tell me, a true admirer of Your Word for what seems at times like an eternity. All right, don't tell me. Just don't go wasting Your word or Your time on wordlings and worldlings whose only thought is to stack high and deep the things of this world.

"My God and my All!"

To the thinking person these words say it all.

To the admirer, these words may say it all, but there's more. They should also be said often, with great reverence and with great warmth.

When I feel You next to me, everything seems to go so swimmingly. But when I think You're out and about, I plummet like a rock.

You bring to the heart tranquillity and a certain festival joyfulness.

Pleasure with You near, how sweet it is! Pleasure with You nowhere to be found, how brief it is!

Pleasure for us Devouts can be had, O Lord, only if You have something to do with it. Either that, or Your grace has to be an ingredient somewhere in the mix, perhaps a soupçon of sapience.

When one of us has a moment of happiness with You, O Lord, it has an unexpected effect. The rest of creation seems to have this pleasant patina on it.

Who is there in the world to whom You haven't already been a cause of delight? Alas, there are quite a few. They're the worldly wise and the fleshly wise, but when it comes to Your wisdom, they're noways wise. Paul advised the Romans on this very point (8:6). But wherever they are, Vanity runs riot, and Death hangs in the air.

And where are Your followers, O Lord? If anywhere, they're off the beaten path making their way through bog and fen; that's to say, up to their hips in Contempt of the World and Mortification of the Flesh.

But why are these last, at least by some, generally recognized as the truly wise persons in this world? Because they've made the pilgrimage from Vanity to Verity, Flesh to Spirit.

God has found them, and under the guise of good they find God in creation and praise Him so for all the good in creation.

How different, how wildly different, are the pleasures of the Creator from the pleasures of the creature! They're as different as Timelessness from time, Uncreated Light from created light.

My prose begins to turn to prayer.

O Perpetual Light, transcending all sources of created light! Let the ragged lightning bolt from the sky search the nooks and crannies of my soul. Purify, glorify, clarify, vivify—with all Your powers—my spirit that it may cling to You with joyful hugs.

Oh, when will this blessed and desirable moment come, when we'll see each other face to face?! That's the sort of moment Paul wrote about to the Colossians, where everyone—Greek and Jew, slave and slaver, circumcised and uncircumcised, civilized and not so civilized—all are one in Christ (3:11).

Why hasn't it happened already?

How much longer do I have to wait?

Up to this point in my sad life, there lives, in a shack out back, the Old Man Paul's Letters speak of; that's to say, the unregenerate man who's climbing all over the Cross, but has yet to learn which side is up; he says he's dying to himself and to the World but, if he is, it's the longest death scene since Prometheus on the rock! Paul wrote something similar to the Romans (6:6).

Up to this point the itch outlasts the scratch; concupiscence attacks the defenses within—Paul to the Galatians (5:17); the quiet kingdom of my heart is aflame with war and the fumes of war.

If I may use the words of the Psalmist . . .

But You, O Lord, who "dominate the power of the sea and mitigate the roll of the wave" (89:9), rise up to help me (44:26). "Scatter the peoples who want to war" (68:30). Pulverize them with the engine of Your virtue. Dazzle them with Your wonders, I beg You, and Your powerful right hand will be glorified, as Jesus son of Sirach would say (36:6). Why do I want You to do all this? Because there's no other hope or refuge for a bloke like me, except in You, my Lord God.

35
NO PLACE TO HIDE

LORD

My dear Devout, as you already know, there's no security in this life. As long as you live, you'll have to bear spiritual arms. Why? Every day you traffick among enemies, and every day you're impugned from the right as well as from the left; that's as Paul described the Christian condition in his Second Letter to the Corinthians (6:7). Indeed, they're coming at you from all sides. If, therefore, you don't protect yourself with the Psalmist's shield of patience (91:4), you won't be long without a wound.

Moreover, if you don't place your heart firmly in Me, with the pure intention of suffering everything for My sake, you won't be able to sustain that ardor of yours, nor will you be able to reach the palm of victory at the end.

What to do now? Verily, you have to act virilely, that's to say, heat up your resistance against all who oppose you. For the Torrid there'll be manna at the end, or so the Book of Revelation promises (2:17); but for the Torpid there'll be only misery in the aftermath.

Rest and repose you'll have, but do you want it in this life or the next? Choose one. But which one?

Which is better to choose, great rest or great patience? Choose the latter.

Seek True Peace, not on Earth, but in Heaven; not in Humankind or in other creatures, but in God alone.

For the love of God you ought to freely undergo everything; that's to say, labors and dolors, temptations and vexations, anxieties and necessities, infirmities and injuries, apprehensions and reprehensions, humiliations and confusions. All these are stepping-stones to virtue. They test the raw recruit for Christ; they're the materials of the Heavenly Crown.

Reward time. For a good if short life, I'll return Eternal Life. For finite confusion on this earth, I'll give Infinite Confirmation.

Do you think you'll always have spiritual consolations? My Saints didn't have them all the time. Most of the time what they had were depressions, temptations, and desolations. But they withstood them patiently, knowing that, as Paul had told the Romans (8:18), "The passions of this time aren't to be compared to the attainments of future glory."

Do you want to have right away what many have scarcely obtained after many tears and great labors?

"Wait for the Lord like everyone else," advised My Psalmist (27:14), "then act like a man!" And take comfort. Don't be diffident. Don't give it up. Let your body and soul constantly radiate the patience of God. I'll be with you every step of the way, as My Psalmist has promised (91:15), and in the end I'll reward you handsomely.

36

FALSE JUDGMENTS

LORD

Don't fear the judgment of Humankind, My dear Devout, especially when your conscience judges you innocent and returns a verdict of not guilty. Rather, cast your heart firmly in the Lord.

But when the tongue of another stings, know two things. First, that something good and blessed may actually have happened. Second, that your trust in God as opposed to yourself cushioned the blow.

Many people can blither and blather, but they're no more convincing at the end of an hour than at the beginning.

Of course, satisfying everybody is never really possible. As the Great Paul reported in First Corinthians, he strove to do it in the Lord (10:33), and the Lord made him all things to all men (9:22). Nevertheless, he thought it pretty small beer when he received good reports from his peers (4:3).

Paul did about as much as any one person could do for the edification and salvation of others. But try though he did, he knew that he couldn't prevent himself from offending others. The best remedy was to commit himself totally to God, who knew all his strengths and weaknesses.

With Patience and Humility as his only allies, then, he was able to defend himself against whatever mouthings came from the thinking crowd and whatever hurlings came from the drinking crowd. And there was another reason why he responded; his silence could be interpreted, at least in the minds of the weak, as admission of guilt.

If I may use the words of My Isaiah (51:12), who are you that you should fear Mere Mortal Man? He's here today but gone tomorrow, if I may use the words of My First Maccabist (2:63). Fear God, yes, but don't lose your water over manmade terrors. What real harm can insults or injuries do you? The tout or the lout who specializes in this sort of behavior actually does more harm to himself than to you. And that's in this life; in the next, there's nowhere to hide, nowhere to run. The judgment of God awaits him, no matter who he is; Paul assured the Romans of that (2:3).

The remedy? Put God in first place. And don't waste time and energy tossing quarrelsome words about. Good advice from Paul in his Second to Timothy (2:14).

But what happens in the present moment if you do succumb to concussion and suffer contusion you don't deserve? First off, don't get indignant, and don't threaten your eternal crown by outbursts of impatience. Rather, when terror strikes, turn to Me in Heaven. After all, I'm the One who'll rescue you from all confusion. And I'm the One who'll reward you according to your just deserts. My Paul assured the Romans of that (2:6), and so I assure you.

37

SURRENDER & FREEDOM

LORD

Some mysterious advice.

Lose yourself, and what'll you find? Me.

Stop dead in your tracks! Don't make another move! Another choice isn't necessary. No need to consult your own self-interest. Do these, and you'll regain all the self-worth you thought you'd lost forever!

Fall on your face when you're following Me, but don't flounce right up. Down is better than up, and a new shipment of grace will arrive on your doorstep tomorrow.

DEVOUT

How often do You want me to give up, surrender myself?

LORD

As often as you move without My permission.

DEVOUT

Is there anything of mine You're particularly interested in, or do You just want all my stuff?

LORD

Small things, big things, it makes no difference to Me.

DEVOUT

Well, it makes a difference to me. I don't need them, but I want them.

LORD

Well, I don't want them, and I certainly don't need them—and what's more, you don't either.

DEVOUT

Well, there's another fish in the face!

LORD

What I'm trying to say to you is, your chiefest possession is self-love, and on the Heavenly Market it has no value. Hence, in every situation I want you to be found stripped of your self-love. Otherwise, how can you be Mine, and I yours? Disrobe and leave your soft garments on the floor. The quicker you do this, the better the hold you'll have on the situation. And the fewer your conditions and the sincerer your attitude, the more you'll please Me and the more you'll gain for yourself.

Some make the Unconditional Surrender in public, but in their hearts they've retained certain private conditions; that's to say, they don't put their trust wholly in God. You can usually tell who they are because they take every precaution not to be caught with an empty buttery.

Others offer themselves up whole and entire right from the start. After some time, however, bullied and sullied by temptation, they return to their old ways. Baby steps, not manly strides, that's about the only spiritual progress they make after that.

They live a life that has little to do with freedom of heart or grace of friendship. Which is just another way of saying, they haven't really surrendered themselves fully and sacrificed themselves daily to Me. Without continued acts like these, a friendship has no roots, let alone any fruits.

It's one of My very favorite sayings, and I know I've bored you to tears with it many times. Indulge Me just once more. Lose yourself, surrender yourself, and you'll enjoy great internal peace.

Give up all your stuff. Don't try to snatch it back. Don't start a campaign to get it back.

Stand tall and strong for Me, and you'll get My attention. You'll be free in heart and, as My Psalmist has said (139:11), darkness will no longer frighten you. Try this, pray for this, sigh for this. Despoil yourself of everything you possess. Naked you are; that's to say, there you stand, in all your baptismal beauty, with no possessions and no prepossessions. And naked you must be if you want to follow the naked Jesus.

Die to yourself, and you'll live eternally for Me. Then will slip away all the airy elephants, all the evil roughhouse, all the needless needlings. Then also will unbridled fear quiet down and unruly love come home to roost.

38

RELIANCE ON RULE, RECOURSE TO GOD

LORD

To that end, My dear Devout, you ought to tend diligently. That's to say, in every place and in every act, whether occupation or diversion, you should feel more comfortable with yourself and in command of yourself. Everything should be under your control, and not the other way around. You should be the lord and tailor of your own actions, not the slave or mercenary. You should be above it all and a true

Hebrew to boot, that's to say, enjoying the lottery and the liberty of being a son of God; Paul wrote as much to the Romans (8:21).

These last stand above the parochial state of affairs and look toward the eternal perspectives. With their left eye, they spot the Transitories, and with their right, the Stationaries. They aren't drawn to acquire the Temporals, but do manage to use them rather well. Their supposition, if I may so phrase it, is that the fabric of the Universe was created by the Lord God and cut and sewn by the Great Tailor Himself, having this meticulosity about everything in its place, not a frill out of place.

Whatever the onslaught, you must stand firm, let the smoke and din of battle settle, and see what actually happened, not what you would have liked to happen. That's to say, do everything you can to make an accurate assessment of everything you saw and heard.

In this, you'd have common cause with the Great Moses. When bedeviled with problems and perils he couldn't handle, he fled to the Tabernacle, as the Exodist reported it (33:8), where he consulted with the Lord. What did he learn? Never ever to shut his eyes and ears to the Divine Response! And Moses never did. No wonder he left the Tabernacle refreshed, much wiser on many accounts concerning the present and future.

And so should you. That's to say, you should flee to the secret garden of your heart, there to implore Divine Help more intensely. That's what I advised in My Matthew's Gospel (6:6).

On this point I'd ask you to recall Joshua and the sons of Israel. They were outsmarted by the Gibeonites (9:14), who could have killed them but, worse, made them hewers of wood and drawers of water. That wouldn't have happened if the Israelites had consulted the Lord first; He'd have straight-talked them onto the safe and narrow. Instead, they listened to the Gibeonites' chatter, were entertained by what they said, and in the end fell prey to their sweet talk and fancy prayer.

39
A NOT-SO-MERRY CHASE

LORD

Always bring your case to Me, My dear Devout. I'll dispose of it well when the Final Court sits. Don't worry. I'll straighten things out. Just the thought of that should give you the strength to go on making spiritual progress now.

DEVOUT

At last, my Lordly if Lawyerly Friend, I've got will enough to commit all my affairs to Your representation. Up to now, trying to do good on my own, it's been such a trudge. Perhaps it's that I feel so drawn to what's going to happen in this world! If only I'd felt the same strong urge to take You up on Your continued offers of friendly help toward the next world.

LORD

I know all this, My dear Devout, because I've seen it happen so often. Humankind gets so antsy about acquiring just one more bauble, one more bangle. Odd thing, though. When they actually have it in their hands, there's always something wrong with it. It has this desperate flaw. That's to say, their affections play with it, then get tired of it. And it's off again on a not-so-merry chase from one unsatisfied desire to another.

Therefore, when it comes to desirables, two easy conclusions. Obviously, one should leave the maxiatures alone. Not too obviously, the same goes for the miniatures.

The truly spiritual activity of Humankind is saying no to self. The result? Abnegated Man. He's denuded himself of all material things, but still he's managed to be a breezy sort and quite secure in his own self-esteem.

The Ancient Enemy, on the other hand, is a nervous, queasy sort, a skulker, always on the prowl; that's as Peter's First Letter described him (5:8). Everyone he meets on the road he considers a perfect target. He never lets up, even in the field. Day and night he beats the bushes to arouse the unsuspecting and drive them toward invisible nets and covered traps.

What's the defense? "Watch and pray," I said in Matthew, "that you enter not into temptation" (26:41).

40

TO BOAST OR NOT TO BOAST

DEVOUT

"What's man that I should be mindful of him?" It's the Anxious Psalmist again (8:4). "What's the son of man that You should visit him?"

What has Humankind done that You should respond with Your grace? Reward us for not doing a thing, and we'll see no reason to change. We're a hopeless lot. So why should we shed a tear if You get up and leave forever? But we will.

If You don't give me what I ask for, who else will?

Certainly I can think about this in verity and come up with a few mouthings.

O Lord, I am nothing. O Lord, I can do nothing. O Lord, I find no good in my self. O Lord, there's nothing I don't need. O Lord, I'm headed nowhere. Odd but true. And unless You give me a helping hand and prop up my sagging spirit, I'll just end up a feeble, faltering wreck.

"You, however," You, O Lord, "are always Yourself, and You remain as such for eternity," said the Psalmist (102:27). That's to say, You're good, You're just, according to the standards of both spiritual and earthly wisdom. But I, who am proner to regress than to progress, find it hard to stay long in one state of soul. As the Prophet Daniel saw in one of his visions (4:16), so I see myself passing from one stage to another in my life, and I'm never in one phase long enough to establish a firm hold.

One thing I've noticed. My spiritual condition quickly improves when You stretch Your hand to help.

Another thing I've noticed. Sometimes You come to the help of us human beings even without our having to ask.

But here I ask. Stop moving! Stand still! I'm turning my head every which way, and I still can't catch sight of You. Only in You alone'll my heart find conversion and quiescence. And may my face brighten up like Hannah's after prayer! A tender moment in First Samuel (1:18).

Whence, it follows, if I know well enough to dump every consolation known to Humankind in my continuous pursuit of devotion and the Devotion of devotions, why do I have to ask, as Jeremiah did right at the beginning of his Lamentations (1:2), "Is there no one who can console me?"

That being said, I have high hopes for Your grace and will exult when it comes.

As often as good stuff happens to me, I give my thanks to You, whence everything comes. I, however, am vanity and "nothingness before You," if I may echo the Psalmist (39:5), a quack, a *quondam,* a quisling. I'd like to boast, but I don't have anything to boast about. Whence can I find something to boast about? Why do I seek to be thought well of? Aren't my desires just droppings? And isn't all this world Vanity gone mad?

Glory at its emptiest is disease at its sickest, Vanity at its noisiest. That's because it draws a Devout's attention away from the One True Glory and denudes him of Heavenly Grace.

Here's an example of what can happen. A Devout is quite pleased with himself for what he's been able to accomplish outside the monastery walls; that's to say, he's made so many friends among the rich and the famous. Now I know that makes You nervous, my Joyful if sometimes Jealous Friend, and I don't want You to think I don't know why. Why? Because he spends his time in the unhappy pursuit of false celebrity instead of the happy pursuit of True Virtue.

However, there's True Glory and Holy Exaltation to boast in You and not in himself, to rejoice in Your name, not in his own virtue, and certainly not to take delight in any creature, except insofar as it has something to do with You.

May Your name be praised, not mine. May Your work be magnified, not mine. May Your Holy Name be blessed, and may no praise from human mouths be attributed to me. You're my glory, You're the exultation of my heart. In You I shall glory, and I shall exult all day long; Psalmist again (89:16). As Paul wrote in Second Corinthians, "All I have are my infirmities —precious possessions all" (12:5).

The Jews hoped to find glory from among their tribes. But the sort of glory I require "comes from God alone"; that's as You said on a Sabbath in Jerusalem, and as John wrote it down (5:44). Every alp, every medal, every decoration, when compared to Your eternal glory, is mean, not to say meaningless.

My Truth, my Mercy, my God—Blessed Trinity!

To You alone be praise, honor, virtue, and glory for ever and ever.

41
FEELING GOOD ABOUT FEELING BAD

LORD

What do you do when you see others being honored or elevated? You could feel bad about their feeling good. Or you could consider these as occasions for your feeling good about feeling bad. Why? The contempt of men on earth, if only you knew it, shouldn't cause you to shed one single tear. What should you do? Direct your heart toward Me in Heaven.

DEVOUT

In the face of Your blinding glory, O Lord, we have to be blinkered. Perhaps that's why, without our peripheral vision, we're so easily hoodwinked by Vanity.

If I assess myself correctly, never has an injury been done to me by another creature, and hence I've no right, at least not yet, to make a ruckus against You, my Righteous if Riotous Lord.

Why? Because I've sinned against You frequently and gravely. Deservedly, therefore, should every creature pick up his pike against me.

So it's only reasonable to conclude that confusion and contempt are my just due. Yours, however, is praise, honor, and glory. And in the light of these considerations, unless I prepare myself—by being looked down upon by every giraffe, outsped by every gazelle, over-looked by every gryphon—I can be neither pacified and stabilized interiorly, spiritually illuminated, nor fully one with You.

42

LOVE AS FRIENDSHIP

LORD

My dearest Devout, if you place your peace in some person—that's to say, if you feel comfortable with him and enjoy dining with him— you'll be unstable and entangled. But if you have recourse always to Ever-living, Everlasting Truth, your friend won't shed a tear if you live or die.

In Me the love of a friend should stand. It's because of Me that he should be loved, that's to say, everyone who's seemed good to you and who's very dear in this life.

Without Me the love of friendship won't have the strength to last. Nor is the love of friendship true and clear unless I'm an integral part of it; that's as My Augustine described it in his *Confessions* (4.4).

Which is another way of saying, you ought to be dead to two-person friendships, especially when the other person's another creature. But when the other person is Myself, then something odd happens.

The closer you approach God, the farther you recede from every friendly solace. Also the higher you ascend to God, the deeper you descend into yourself and the viler you appear to yourself.

Whoever attributes good to himself only makes it more difficult for himself to receive the grace of God. Why? Because, as the spiritual wisdom echoing in Proverbs (3:34), Psalms (55:22), and First Peter (5:5) has it, the grace of the Holy Spirit always seeks the humble heart.

To annihilate yourself, to empty yourself of all created love—that's what you ought to do. And what I ought to do is fill that very same space with a very great grace.

When you warm to the wonderfulness of the created world, the Creator's respect for you begins to cool. Because of the Creator, if for no other reason, learn how to conquer yourself in all things. Do that, and you'll have the strength to reach out to Divine Knowledge.

However slight it may be, unruly love and irregular respect retard, even detour, your spiritual progress.

43

THE UNIVERSITY WITHIN

LORD

My dear Devout, don't be swayed by the well-oiled, smoothly reasoned words of human wisdom. As the Great Paul wrote in First Corinthians, "Virtual words won't get you into the Kingdom of God; only virtuous acts will do that" (4:20).

Pay attention to what I say. It'll set fire to your heart and illumine your mind. It'll loosen your conscience and infuse—who knows?—a little consolation.

My point? Never say a word that'll make you seem better educated than another. Instead, strive to mortify your verbal vices. Why? Because spiritual progress, though sometimes painful, does you more good than any amount of philosophical knowledge, which often enough can be quite pleasant, or so I've been told.

When someone reads from a random pile of books, he often increases his learning; but just as often he strays from the One True Principle. At once he must return to the One True Book. Why? I'm the One who's given adults what little knowledge they find in their petty encyclopedias; and I'm the One who's given the children their pretty abecedaries. The Psalmist has said much the same (94:10; 119:130).

Whoever hears My word will quickly become wise and make much progress in virtue.

Woe to those who are out whiling away their time in flea markets and curiosity shoppes when they could be at home strenuously serving the Lord!

The time'll come when the Teacher of teachers, the Christ of christs, the Lord of Angels, will appear; My Paul promised that to the Colossians (3:4). Yes, I'll, come to audit all the lectures, examine all the students. That's to say, "Jerusalem'll be searched by lamp light," as the Prophet Zephaniah has said (1:12) and "all the errors will spring out of the darkness," as Paul in First Corinthians has said (4:5). That should quiet the querulous once and for all!

Case in point: two humble Devouts. The University takes ten years to educate the first. As for the second, I can raise his mind to where he can grapple equally well with the rationalizations and ratiocinations expected of any university graduate—and I can do it in a trice!

My pedagogy? Well, I'm the Logos, and so I don't need a lot of logorrhea to make My points. Philosophers and Theologians like to entertain other opinions; I don't. Academic pride, intellectual arrogance, public disputation whose only aim is to have the upper hand, not that the Truth may appear—all these are nice, but they're certainly not My style.

My thesis is simple and simply put: Despise this life. Shrink from the present. Seek the next life. Look forward to that happy time. Flee honors. Endure scandals. Hope in Me. Desire nothing but Me. Love Me ardently above all things.

About the last, loving Me ardently. If you do this, you'll learn what the University has promised but failed to deliver; that's to say, the secrecies and prophecies of the Divine.

That's to say, you make more spiritual progress when you leave the public disputation before it's over than when you linger to make yet another *distinctio rationis ratiocinatae minor*.

Sometimes I lecture in halls; sometimes I tutor in rooms. Occasionally I make a personal impression by a miracle or a verbal expression by a metaphor. Once in a while I even take the drape off a mystery.

A book has one voice, but its many and varied readers don't necessarily come away from it with the same message. In the University Within, however, Mine is the only voice, and One is the only message. I'm Lecturer, Examiner, Invigilator. I interpret all thoughts, prompt all actions.

All of which is another way of saying, and perhaps another way of rendering a passage in Paul's First Letter to the Corinthians (12:11), I mark each examination with *alpha, beta,* or *gamma*, enhanced or diminished by pluses or minuses. Wow to the *Alphas!* Woe to the *Gammas!*

44

LOSS & GAIN

LORD

Two things, My dear friend. Be grateful for all the things you don't need to know about life on this earth. Consider yourself, though you're still alive and kicking, dead to the World. As far as you're concerned, as Galatians would put it (6:14), you're already hanging on the cross.

Yes, you have to pass through many noisy patches as though you were deaf, and yes, you should open your ears to the things that bring you spiritual peace.

Sometimes it's better not to meet the gaze of a troubled soul. He wants to talk, yes, but does he want to listen? If you do stop to talk and the phlegm begins to fly, you're not the less pleasing to God. That's to say, if you're worsted in a hostile exchange and could have come to blows but didn't, then at least your worsted's still intact, and so's your virtue.

DEVOUT

O Lord, how long it's taken us to travel such a short distance! Look how a temporal loss sets the eyes to weeping! Even for a modest profit, we have to labor and lumber. As for a spiritual loss, it's scarcely noticed, let alone repented or retrieved.

LORD

Often what manages to get the public eye ends up with little or no spiritual profit. But just as often what the public eye fails to notice is of the greatest possible spiritual importance.

Why is it that people are dazzled with this-worldly thingamajigs? Well, unless they come to their right minds soon, they'll amuse themselves to death.

45

CONSISTENCY IN HUMAN BEHAVIOR

DEVOUT

I'm in a pickle, O Lord! "I've fallen, and I can't get up." That's how the Psalmist put it (60:11), and that's how I'm putting it now. "I've called for human help, and no one's come. You're my last resort!"

How often on earth have I put my trust in a fellow human being, even in a Devout, and yet been disappointed! But then again how often have I found a helping hand where I had no reason to expect one? The conclusion? Vain is the hope for consistency in human behavior. But You, O God, You're always consistent; if the Psalmist had it right (37:39), then the Just are always saved.

Only You, my Lord and my God, can find the good in everything that happens to us. Left to ourselves, we're infirm and unstable, fallible and fallable.

Devouts like me keep a good monastic muzzle on ourselves in everything we say or do. But will that caution and circumspection really prevent us from being axed and battleaxed?

All I know, O Lord, is that whoever confides in You and "speaks from a simple heart"—a characteristic much favored in the Wisdom of Solomon (1:1)—doesn't fall so easily. Oh, he'll slip—he's bound to—but You'll come to his rescue or, at the very least, You'll offer him some help. That's because You don't desert whoever's put his hope in You for the Long Haul.

A rare find is the faithful friend who perseveres through all the ups and downs of friendship. You're the most faithful of friends, O Lord, and without You there's no such thing as Friendship.

LORD

Once there was a holy soul, St. Agatha, a wealthy girl who'd vowed her virginity to Christ in the third century. As the official record of her martyrdom showed, she was brutally tortured and died in prison, but not before dropping this pearl of spiritual wisdom: "My mind is grounded and founded in Christ." If only that were your sentiment also, then your every fear wouldn't sting so, nor every unkind word stab.

DEVOUT

Who can read the future? Who can contradict disasters yet to occur? Even if we do have a whiff of what's to come, the future can still hurt and maim. But if we don't prepare for what may happen, then we'll all suffer the gravest consequences.

Wherefore, why haven't I, a Devout who has firsthand knowledge of his own wretchedness, prepared better? Why have I relied so heavily on others who know no more than I?

LORD

Often you Devouts are thought of as, or declared to be, Angels. In reality, you're only men, and all too fragile men at that.

DEVOUT

Why, O Lord, do I believe in anyone else but You? You're Truth; but Truth doesn't deceive; therefore, You don't deceive. Something of a syllogism here. But it's really a reference to something You said to Your Apostle Thomas; John was Your recordist (14:6).

The Great Paul to the Romans had no illusion about this (3:4). "Every man's a liar." Wobbly, waffly, especially when it comes to speech. What someone says may sound right when we hear it, but we shouldn't necessarily believe it right away.

How prudently You warned us, my Admirable if Admonitory Friend! Matthew gave us the clues. Humankind's worst enemy is itself (10:17). "The enemies of Humankind are the members of its own household" (10:36).

Nor is there necessarily any truth in the Devout who finds a prophet, a messiah, behind every shadow. "Look, here He is! Oops! Where the devil did He go? He's over there now!" Matthew on You in Your last discourse (24:23). I learned this lesson to my loss. Would that I'd be goose in the future, and not just a gull for every bit of juicy gossip!

Watch it, watch it, watch it! That's what someone says to me as he entrusts a secret. Keep to yourself what I'm about to tell you. And so I do, but while I keep my lips sealed and believe I'm keeping a secret, he doesn't hold his tongue. He wags it all over the house, betraying himself and me, and then, before I can berate him, he's off to another monastery. From cautionary tales like this and the incautious people who tell them, protect me, O Lord. Don't let me fall into their hands, and don't let me repeat such a gaff ever again.

Grant that I may speak in a straightforward manner, not with a forked tongue.

What I'm unwilling to put up with others, I should avoid at all costs myself.

A tangle of "not's."

Not to say bad things about good people.

Not to believe bad things about these very same people.

Not to spread a shaggy story about someone else.

Not to reveal my inmost secrets to anyone else but You, O Lord, now and always the Inspector General of Hearts.

Not to be swept away by every barrage of verbiage, but simply to desire all *esoterica* and *exoterica* to be regulated according to the Divine Pleasure!

How can Devouts and Celestial Grace enjoy safe conduct? They must all flee human contact. They must avoid the winsome things of this world. But they should always be on the lookout for the things that'll bring them closer to the next world.

Many a humble soul has died the death when someone's outed their virtuous life and held it up for public praise!

Grace grows best under a bridge where it's dank and dark. On the bridge itself, it'd be tromped by every itinerant temptation, tramped by every mercenary troop.

46
WHEN EVERY WORD STABS

LORD

My beloved friend, stand firm, and hope in Me, as I tell you this. Words are just words. They fly through the air, airy aerialists that they are. But if they're harsh words, they land on your head with a thud. No, no lumps, but yes, a lot of pain.

If you deserved the lumps for something you did, think how willingly you'd reform in order that the pain'd stop. But if you're not conscious of having done a wrong, then think how you can turn the pain to your spiritual advantage.

Even if you couldn't survive an all-out war of words, you could put up with a few verbal volleys for a while without making a big deal out of it. But tell Me, My dear friend, how can these little darts pierce you to the heart unless you're a carnal man who pays more attention to what the carny man says about him. That's because you're afraid of being despised; you don't want to be reprehended for your excesses, and so you seek refuge under an arbor of excuses.

Spend more time on introspection, and you'll find—surprise!—that even now, after some years away from the World, the World is still very much alive in you; in fact, you're still doing what Humankind thinks quite fashionable in the World.

Why do you refuse to come down from your marble pedestal and be confronted with your faults? It just stands to reason that you're not a truly humble Devout, nor from the look of you a Devout truly dead to the World, nor does the World appear crucified to you—I can tell by your eyes. These are the characteristics that Paul stressed to the Galatians (6:14).

But hear My word, and you won't care a fig for the wagglings of ten thousand tongues. That was Paul's own tongue-lashing to the Corinthians in his First Letter (14:19).

Look here now, My dear friend, gather the most malicious words in the dictionary, then imagine they all apply to you. How would you react? You could scream! You could howl! Or you could think, What harm can they do? Especially if I shrug them off. After all, they weigh as little as a tittle and haven't enough pluck to pluck a hair from your head. And no one has a more accurate hair count than I, as Luke rightly reported it (21:18).

A Devout whose heart isn't in the monastery and doesn't have God in his sights is an easy target for a vituperous word. On the other hand, the Devout who's shared confidences with Me and has no appetite to be his own man will be able to stand down all verbal abuse.

I'm the Judge, Knower of All Secrets. I know all the ins and outs of every human act. I know the wrongdoer as well as the wrong done. The wrong itself comes by way of Me, and I permit it to happen. Why? As Luke would put it (2:35), that "the thoughts from many hearts might be revealed." I'll sentence the guilty and the innocent in public; I've tried them already in My chambers.

The testimony of Humankind often falls short of the truth. My judgment, on the other hand, is always true. It'll stand and won't be reversed on appeal. The record's not available to the general public; only a few have access. The transcript's been read for errors, omissions, emendations, and so on. None found; none needed. When the foolish among us hear this, they get that milky, faraway look in their eyes as if to say that Truth, whatever else she may be, just isn't fair.

Therefore, whenever you need a quick decision, come to Me. In no instance rely on your own good judgment. As the Book of Proverbs put it (12:21), the just person won't be confused or confounded because "whatever happens to him will come from God."

Even though some unjust charge is brought against you, you shouldn't pay much attention to it. Best thing to do is shrug it off.

If a charge against you is resolved when some believable witnesses come forward, you shouldn't throw a victory party for a hundred of your closest friends.

"I read the hearts and loins of Humankind," rightly said My John in the Book of Revelation (2:23), and I don't pass judgment the way that Humankind does; John put down these words when I was teaching in the Temple (7:24).

Often someone found guilty in an earthly court is praised for his conduct by the Celestial Court.

DEVOUT

O Lord God, Just Judge, strong and patient, You know the fragility and depravity of Humankind. Hence, be my strength and my total trust. Conscience isn't enough for me. You know what I don't know. And so I ought to humbly accept Your penance for my every transgression.

Act forgivingly toward me every time I commit a sin of omission, and yet again grant me more grace of sufferance.

Your copious mercy is better for my obtaining indulgence than Your justice against my defending my conscience.

"I'm not conscious of anything bad I've done," as Paul wrote in First Corinthians (4:4); nevertheless I can't justify my behavior in this. The reason? Remove mercy from the equation, as the Psalmist once said (143:2), and no living creature will ever be justified in Your sight.

47

HAPPY DAYS, UNHAPPY DAYS

LORD

Two "don'ts," My dear friend. Don't let the labors you've assumed on My account break your spirit. Don't let the troubles I've sent you get you terribly down. My promise'll strengthen and console you at every turn. I'm flush enough to reward you beyond all means and mea-sures. And remember this. You won't have to labor long for this, nor will you have to be dragged down by your dolors.

Keep watch for a little while, and then you'll see a swift end to all evils. The hour will come when all labor and tumult will cease. The passage of time will be short and pass quickly.

In the meantime, do what you're doing; no need to stop. Labor faithfully in My vineyard. Yes, I'm the Vintner in the parable in Matthew (20:4), and yes, I'll reward you with the Vintage of vintages. Write, read, sing, sigh, shush, pray, behave virilely against a contrary. Eternal Life is worth fighting for, large battles and small. Peace will surely come, but when? That's known only to the Lord. But when it does come, then there'll be no day, no night; only perpetual light, infinite clarity, firm peace, and safe rest.

Then you won't be able to ask, as Paul asked the Romans (7:24), "Who'll free me from this death ride in my carcass?" Nor will you be able to whoop "Woe!" as the Psalmist liked to preface important say-ings (120:5), "my journey has been delayed once again!"

As Isaiah partially foresaw (25:7–8), Death'll take a header on thick ice, and Salvation'll coruscate on thin ice. Anxiety'll evanesce, and there'll appear in her place Jollity, Beatitude, and all the other grand companions in the Heavenly Society.

You should see the perpetual crowns of the Saints in Heaven! Once the Contemptibles in this world, they got to join in the glory of the next world.

As for you, My dear friend, you should immediately humble your-self. Stay in that lowly but not unlovely position until you come to the inevitable conclusion: You're subject to everyone and everything else. This you must do before you ever again assume a position of authority over another.

Another thing. Don't waste your time wanting all the days of your life to be happy ones. If you want to make hay with God, then thank

Him profoundly for all the days of toil and trouble He's sent you. After all's said and done between you and Me, to be accounted as nothing among men—that should be your greatest loot!

If only you'd get the full flavor of these remarks and take them profoundly to heart! Then you wouldn't dare utter a single syllable against them. When Eternal Life's the goal, shouldn't all back-breaking tasks be borne with a grin?

To gain or lose Heaven—that's not your normal task. Therefore, lift your face to Heaven, and what'll you see? All My Saints! While they were on earth, it was just one battle after another; that's the way the Letter to the Hebrews put it (10:32). Now they rejoice, and they're refreshed; they're free from care and ready to rest. And they'll remain with Me without end in My Father's kingdom; that's the promise I made in the Upper Room, and Matthew was the recordist that night (26:29).

48

HARD TIMES & HEAVENLY TIMES

DEVOUT

That sprawling mansion in the Supernal City—it's quite a handsome structure really! Where every day is clear, and everyone can see forever! Where night isn't dark, and the beacon of Truth burns with steady flame. Everybody's joyful and without a care in the world. And never ever again will anybody worry about having the Contraries to tea.

Oh, how I wish that day had dawned already and all the peoples of the earth had arrived at that Happy End! For the Saints that splendid day has already begun with a clarity that never ends. As for us poor pilgrims, as the Letter to the Hebrews might refer to us (11:13), this reality still seems a long way off, a sort of reflection of a reflection, as Paul might have put it in his First Letter to the Corinthians (13:12).

The citizens of Heaven know how joyful it is there. But we "exiles of the children of Eve," as the Marian prayer has it, and denizens of the Earth, know how mournful it can be here. Days are fast and foul, full of sore spots and tight spots; Jacob's words about himself to the Pharaoh in Genesis (47:9). Sin strolls the streets of Humankind. That's to say, the good are snared by passions, strung out by fears, distended by cares, distracted by curiosities, surrounded by errors, bruised by labors, flustered by temptations, enervated by delicacies, tortured by want.

A winnow of "when's."

When will evil end?

When will I be free from the servitude of my vices?

When will I remember You alone, O Lord?

When will I put all my enjoyment in You?

When will I be without shackle and manacle, without sin and imperfection?

When will there be a solid peace, peace imperturbable, peace within and without, peace from every part?

When will I stand to see You again, Good Jesus?

When will I contemplate the glory of Your kingdom?

When will You be all things in all things for me? A question Paul could have asked the Colossians (3:11).

When will I be with You in Your kingdom, that's to say, in the kingdom You've prepared for Your beloved from all eternity, the one You spoke of in Matthew (25:34)?

I'm a derelict, a pauper, and an exile on a hostile ground, where fortunes are won daily and lost nightly.

My every breath is for You, my Loyal Lord and Friend. Hence, make my exile happier by lessening my pain. After all, the World's not slow to come; it wants to lighten the load, but succeeds only in making it heavier.

I desire to enjoy Your friendship. I stretch out my hand, but it can't reach Your grasp. I do opt to stay on the celestial path, but earthly affairs often command my attention. And my passions, which I thought were long ago dead—they cling to me for dear life.

Mentally, I want to be on top of everything; however, my flesh is so unwilling, I'm really at the bottom of the well.

Unhappy creature that I am, I fight with myself, and, as Job put it so well about himself (7:20), I've made my self into an ass, an idiot; that's to say, my spirit soars, but my flesh takes a nosedive.

Whenever I try to delve into celestial considerations, I drain my brain. Whenever I try to pray, the Carnals gather round me and fill me with pretty pictures!

My God, don't distance Yourself from me! That was always the Psalmist's fear (71:12). Don't make me say what You forced the Psalmist to say (26:9): "Don't be angry with me and turn Your face in the other direction."

Waggle Your lightning bolts, my Bravo if Bravado Friend, and send these distractions packing. Release Your Celestial Arrows, and all the Enemy's phantasms will quickly fade. Plaints from the Psalmist (144:6).

Gather my far-flung senses back to Yourself, my Friend. Make me forget all these worldly things, and condemn all those ghastly if ghostly manifestations of the Vices. Succor me, Eternal Truth, that Vanity may never be my motivation. Approach, Celestial Suavity, and spritz the schmutz from the face of my soul.

Be merciful to me, my Merciful Friend, whenever I have a distraction in prayer. It seems I just can't help it. So many times, whether I stand or sit, I'm just not there. Where am I? I'm with my thoughts, and they've sailed away. Where to? Is it so surprising that my thoughts are where my loves are, where I find some natural delight and pleasure?

Whence you, my Verity, have openly said, as Matthew has said before you (6:21): "*Herz und Geld*, Heart and Gold—fraternal twins! Trashy treasures both!"

Loving Heaven as I do, I frequently ponder heavenly things.

Loving the World as I've done, I rejoice at its felicities and mourn for its adversities.

Loving the Flesh more than I should, I can't prevent my imagination from parading naughty images past my eyes.

Loving the Spirit as I've been slow to learn, I like to think of spiritual things and bandy them about in spiritual conversations.

All these pictures are, for better or worse, part of my permanent collection.

He's blessed who's taken Your hint and given all creatures permission to retire; that's to say, to bow themselves backward out of the room.

Happy also is he who holds the whip hand over his own nature and in a spiritual fury nails his fleshly concupiscences to the cross. Harsh sentiments from Paul to the Galatians (5:24).

That's the sort of person who can pray without distraction and with a clear conscience. He's suspended all animation from within and without. And, though never entirely conscious of this, he's thought worthy to mingle with the Angelic Choirs.

49

FIGHTING FOR ETERNAL LIFE

LORD

When, My dear friend, can you stare at the sun without a parasol, that's to say, contemplate My clarity without blinking an eye? The Letter of James prompted Me to ask that question (1:17). Only when you sense the desire of Eternal Beatitude rising in your soul. Only when you think your soul's about to make the Grand Exit. To hasten that time, open your heart, spread wide your desire, and accept this holy inspiration.

Return the fullest thanks to Supernal Goodness; she's dealt so decently with you, visited you so thoughtfully, grabbed hold of you so powerfully, before your own fat self fell to the earth.

Just don't think you had anything to do with any of this, My dear friend. You didn't think it up, and you didn't sweat it out! But it had everything to do with Supernal Grace and Divine Kindness.

As you stockpile your virtues and increase your holdings in humility, you'll be preparing to battle for Me, and eventually to buttle for Me, as is the duty of a fervent servant soul.

Flame glows, as you have no doubt noticed, but without smoke it doesn't ascend. So as the desires for Celestials on your part flame up, they don't smoke; that's to say, they're not free from the temptation of carnal affection. You do the right thing for the honor of God—that's to say, pray desiringly to Him—but all's not right with you. Why? More soot than wisp.

Isn't that often the case with your own desire? You've clouded your own mind into thinking that your desire was perfectly suitable. But it wasn't! It wasn't white smoke rising; it was just black soot falling.

How to put time to good effect. Don't go looking for delectables for yourself. Do find what's acceptable and honorific to Me. If you can make this midlife correction, then you'll prefer My regulations to every *desideratum* of yours, whether in the past or the future, and follow it cheerfully.

I know your desire, and many's the time I've heard you lusting for it in the night.

You'd like to be cavorting around the playing fields of the Lord with the children of God; Paul would have it that way, that's what he wrote to the Romans (8:21). That'll be then, but here is now. The thought of the Eternal Home and Celestial Homeland delights you. Alas, that hour's yet to come. Yours is another clock, ticking another time. The time for war, the time for labor, the time for temptation. Replenish your depleted soul with the *Summum Bonum*—that should be your wish. But alas, the time's not ripe. I'm the One. Look for Me, says the Lord, until the Kingdom of God comes; Luke's quoted Me on this already (22:18).

Up to this point, My dear friend, you had to be put to test and exercised in many different situations. For these, intermediate consolations've been issued to you, but the Final Lump Sum isn't due just yet. Therefore, "Stay cheery and keep in fighting trim." That's what Moses said to Joshua before his death, as recorded by the Deuteronomist (31:7), and what the Lord said to Joshua after Moses died (1:6). Especially when it comes to fighting against, as well as to just enduring, the contraries of nature.

It's important for you to put on the New Man, as Paul encouraged the Ephesians to do (4:24), and to play this new part as a Christian.

Often you have to do what you don't want to do; and it's important to leave behind what you truly hold dear. That'll forward others' interests, but it won't necessarily promote yours. What some say'll be heard, but there's no guarantee that what you'll say will be worth hearing. Some'll beg on the streets, and their pockets'll be filled; you'll hold your hand out on the corner, and no one'll look your way.

Some will develop a large following, but you'll remain a comparative unknown. Bits and bobs'll be done by others, but your immense contributions'll go unnoticed. Because of experiences like these, your nature'll always be thrown into a hissing fit. But if you can manage to hang on to your tongue, you'll take a giant stride along the path of spiritual progress.

In these and many similars, the faithful servant of the Lord usually has to be proved; that's to say, to bring himself low and to snap his attachment to all things.

Die you must to the things of this world, as you already know. But there's scarcely a somesuch in which you need to die more than this; namely, to endure, to suffer what makes your will scream, what goes against your grain, what makes you wince at the mere scrape of it.

That's especially so when disconveniences are the order of the day. Why? They just don't make sense to you. Even so, because you don't dare resist the Higher Power, you insinuate yourself into an already existing line of authority.

Now that must seem hard to you, My dear friend—to walk around awaiting the nod from another Devout who's no worthier than yourself. It's like looking into a mirror and trying not to see yourself.

But think of the fruit of these labors, My dear Devout, the swiftly approaching End and the extravagantly large Reward. Do that, and you'll lose your grounds for complaint, but you'll surely have the strongest possible ground for patience.

From just a small investment in Free Will Limited here on earth, you'll be able to trade up to Free Will Forever in Heaven.

There's where you'll find everything you want, everything you can possibly desire. You'll have the faculty of doing nothing but good, without fear of losing a thing. Yours'll be always one with Mine—no secrecies, no privacies.

There, nobody'll cross you; nobody'll complain about you. Nobody'll trip you up. No one'll go around you.

All your *desiderata* will be present to you at one and the same time, and each and every one will entertain your whole spirit, filling you with refreshment and continuing to top you off.

In Heaven I'll match Celestial Comelies—that's to say, glories—with each of the Earthly Uncomelies—that's to say, contumelies—you've had to endure; the woolly white *pallium* of distinction, as the Prophet Isaiah might have put it (61:3), in place of the rough bronze monk's cloth of sorrow; a seat in the Kingdom of the Ages in place of your stool of ignorance.

In Heaven, making special guest appearances will be two fruits of Obedience. Labor of Penitence will rejoice, and Humble Subjection will be crowned with glorious fanfare.

That'll be then, but this is now. Incline yourself humbly under the hands of Humankind. Don't let yourself get hot and bothered about what someone may've said about you or another may've ordered you to do. But take great care that whether a Prelate, a Priest, or a Devout demands something of you, you do it whole and entire for the good of the situation and to fulfill all expectations.

Odd thing, though! One person asks for a tit; another, for a tat; both become celebrities and are praised to the skies. But when you do the very same thing, no joy or glory attaches to you. Why? It's that your only joy, if I may say it, My dear Devout, will be found in contempt of self. Which mayn't be so bad if it means in the Long Run that you'll become My pride and joy.

One desire, and one alone, is all you'll need, this side of death or that side of life: that God will always be glorified in you. That was Paul's wish for the Philippians (1:20).

50

A DEVOUT ABANDONED

DEVOUT

Lord God, Holy Father, may You be blessed now and forever. As You wish, so it's done. May Your servant rejoice in You, not in himself and not in any other; You alone are my True Joy and Honor, O Lord; You alone are my Hope and my Crown.

What do I have except what I receive from You? Paul asked that in his First Letter to the Corinthians (4:7). What do I receive, except what I haven't earned or deserved? All is Yours, not only what You gave me, but also what You did for me. As the Psalmist put it (88:15), "I'm a pauper, and have been in the throes since I was a youth."

I'd like to say my soul has never been moved to tears, but I can't. I'd like to say my soul has never ever been thrown into confusion, but I can't. Oceans of passions never leave me in calm.

I desire the joy of peace, and I demand the peace Your children enjoy; the lambs in Your pasture You feed in the light of consolation. If You grant me peace, if You flood me with joy, Your servant's soul will be full of melody and prayerful noise. But if You absent Yourself from me without notice, as You have this very bad habit of doing, I'll run afoul on Commandment Street; as the Psalmist named it (119:35).

With You just a memory, I'll beat my breast and bend my knees. That's because I'm not the person I was yesterday or even the day before yesterday. That was when Your lantern was swinging above my head; Job had the same experience (29:3). And that was when Your huddled wings protected me like an umbrella from falling temptations; the Psalmist had the same experience (17:8).

LORD

Let me tell you, My Dear Devout, how I pray to my father.

O Father, Just and Always to Be Praised, the hour comes for Your servant to be proved. O Father who must be loved, it's the right time—this very hour—that Your servant suffer something in Your behalf. Father Perpetually Venerated, my time has come—You knew it already from all eternity—that Your servant should lower his public profile for a while and live only the interior life with You.

For the briefest time he'll be treated as dirt, humbled and homeless, trod under the feet of Humankind, writhed by his passions, wreathed by his sargassos. All that so that he may rise again with You in the dawn of new light and be clarified in the Celestials.

Holy Father, so You ordained, and so You wished. This is a fact, and I perceive it as so.

DEVOUT

So this is how You treat Your special friends, my True if sometimes Truant Friend, by sending them trials and tribulations. How often and wherever is Your business, but You do it because You love them. You permit them to happen, and You don't advise Your friends or give them due warning. Without Your permission—or is it cause?—nothing happens on this earth. The Psalmist on the subject, as it's found in the Latin Bible (118:71): "Good thing, Your humbling me, knocking me down a peg; it tells me how Your justifications work." As a result I fling off all elations and relations of the heart.

Yes, it's a good thing every now and then, getting hit in the mush with a mullet, that's to say, being faced down with disgrace; the Psalmist has said something similar (119:71). Two lessons. First, that as long as I require consolation to survive, I choose Yours, not the World's. Second, that Your inscrutable judgments give me the shivers; the Psalmist had the same experience (69:7); that's because You seem to bedevil the pious about as much as the impious, even though You seem to employ equity and justice as useful guidelines.

But I must say, thanks are due because You didn't spare me from the troubles, because You took it out on me with whips, laying on stripes, inflicting wounds, troubling me greatly both inside and out.

There was no one under the sun to console me, that's to say, except You, my Lord and God, the Celestial Wounder and Healer, as the Deuteronomist describes You (32:39). You it is who, according to the Book of Tobit (13:2), leads an excursion to the Lower World and brings them back again.

The knotted cord whipped across my shoulders, the rigid rod laid across my limbs—these'll teach me what I'm so reluctant to learn.

Here I am, Father Beloved! I'm in Your hands, as indeed was the Psalmist (31:15). And I incline myself under the rod of Your correction. Whip my bent back and my bowed neck until the blood runs, until I straighten my cricks and cranks to Your will. Make me a pious and humble Disciple, as You've made so many before, that I may respond to Your every nod, Your slightest nudge.

I commend myself to You, baggage and all, for correction. Why? Search and seizure are better in this life than in the next.

You know each and every thing, as Your Apostle discovered and John recorded (16:30); and nothing in the human conscience is hidden from You. Before they happened, You knew they would. And You don't need anyone to preach to You or bring You up to date about what's happening now.

You know what'll help me make spiritual progress and just how much tribulation is needed to scrape the rust from my hull, that's to say, the decay caused by my vices.

Make Your pleasure one of my *desiderata*.

Don't despise my sinful life, which is a lot to ask, I know, since no one knows me better than You.

These are my terrible "to's," O Lord.

To know what has to be known.

To love what has to be loved.

To praise what tickles You the most.

To appreciate what You think precious.

To vituperate what soils the eyes.

To put less reliance on visible and audible evidence when it comes to forming a judgment; that's what the Lord in Isaiah did (11:3).

To inquire always, first and foremost, into the pleasure of the Divine Will.

Often human senses fail when it comes to making a sound judgment. There fail too lovers of the present age when they allow what they see to cloud their judgment.

Thinking something doesn't make it so. For example, is a person to be thought better just because his peers have decided he is so? I don't think so. That's how one liar deceives another liar, by praising him to the skies! And so on with the vain, the blind, the infirm. All of which is another way of saying, cheap praise is never a bargain for those who buy it.

In the end "the only thing that matters is how a person looks to the eyes of the Lord; that's it, nothing more." That's the humble way Holy Father Francis from Assisi put it.

51

HUMBLER RATHER THAN HIGHER

LORD

My dear friend, you just don't have the staying power when it comes to upping your desire for the virtuous life. I might say the same thing when it comes to moving up a grade in contemplation.

While you're attempting both, you have to, because of the Original Corruption, descend to the Lower Depths, carrying, however unwillingly and tediously, the burden of life among the Corruptibles. Therefore, while you're still in the flesh, you have to weep about the burden of the flesh. So weep this! You don't have the strength to continue your spiritual pursuits.

But if you want to persevere, hie yourself to the nearest humble acts and find recreation in doing good deeds. Do continue to expect My Adventual and Supernal Visitation. It's going to happen! As for your feeling of exile and alienation, patiently endure until I visit you again and free you from all these anxieties. That's when I'll make you forget your labors and enjoy your quiet. I'll extend before you a vista, that's to say, a meadow of fragrant Scriptures in which to graze.

You'll run, with expanded heart and lung, the straight and narrow way of My Commandments, as My Psalmist has sung (119:32). And you'll say, if the Letter to the Romans is any guide (8:18), "The passions of the present aren't comparable with those of the future; that's to say, no glory now, but all glory then."

52

CONFESSIONS, NOT CONSOLATIONS

DEVOUT

O Lord, I'm not worthy of Your consolation, nor of any spiritual visitation from You. Just treat me justly when You leave me empty and desolate. At this point in my life, even if I could weep tears like the waves of the sea, I still wouldn't be worthy of Your consolation. Whence, I'm worthy of nothing more than flagellation and incarceration. That's because I've sinned mortally and frequently and been derelict in all sorts of responsibilities. Therefore, as True Reason has parceled it out, I'm not worthy enough even of the least of Your consolations.

But You, O Clement and Merciful God, You don't want Your good works to die the death, do You? You'd pour the riches of Your Goodness into *amphorae* of mercies, then deign to console Your servant, who's got only a few merits in his pocket, beyond his capacity to count; that's Your Paul to the Romans again (9:23). All of which is another way of saying, human stories often rely on a causality that produces a happy ending; spiritual stories, on the other hand, have a causality all their own; that's to say, they produce only the most extravagantly happy endings.

What have I done, O Lord, that You'd confer Celestial Consolation on me? Not a great deal, sad to say. I've always been prone to vices, and supine to doing anything about them. It's true. I'd like to deny it, but I can't. If I were to say otherwise, You'd stand against me, and no one'd rise to defend me.

What have I earned for all my sins but Hell and Eternal Fire?

In all truth I confess that I deserve only contempt; that's to say, to be made a laughingstock in a world that shuns public laughter. Nor is it decent of me to want to be remembered as one of Your Devouts.

Although it'll bruise my ears, nevertheless I'm going to say it. Just to set the record straight. Yes, Sin and I have been keeping company. The only reason I make a public statement of it now is to make it somewhat easier for me when I try to gain an easier, better access to Your mercy.

What can I say, I'm a criminal who doesn't know one part of his anatomy from another. I don't need a mouthpiece—I can say this word myself. *Peccavi.* I've sinned, O Lord, over and over again. Have mercy on me. Please forgive me. Let me follow poor Job's path "a little while that I might lick my wounds, before I have to make my way to that tenebrous land where the willows weep and are covered with the darkness of death" (10:20–22).

Why do You require so much of me? I'm only a criminal, and a wretched sinner at that. Beat me, batter me, humble me for my derelictions.

Hope of Forgiveness in conjunction with True Contrition and Humiliation of Heart produces two things. One's conscience, having been driven mad, is finally reconciled. And one's welfare is protected from future wrath. These done, who'll run to meet each other with a holy embrace, but both God and the Penitent Soul.

Humble Contrition for Sins—does this smell like an acceptable, old-fashioned sacrifice to You, O Lord? Doesn't the sickening, sweet stench arising from the temple sacrifice do more for Your hairy nostrils than a good censing from a smoking thurible?

Again, Humble Contrition for Sins—doesn't this seem like an agreeable unguent? The Psalmist seemed to think so (51:17). The kind of slow-flowing, cool-feeling nard that Magdalene poured over Your feet? Luke made such a tender scene of that in his Gospel (7:46). Why do I think that? Because, if I may cite the Psalmist again, again in the same place, You've never looked down Your nose at a contrite and humbled heart.

Heaven's the place of refuge from the Enemy's wrathful face. Heaven's also the place where the cracked crockery's repaired and the soiled linen washed and bleached.

53

GODLY GRACE & WORLDLY WISDOM

LORD

My dear Devout, My grace is such a precious commodity. Therefore, don't allow it to be watered down or thinned out with extraneous things or terennal consolations.

One of the things you have to do is ditch all impediments to grace; that's to say, if you hope to keep receiving My grace on a regular basis.

Look for a secret garden of your own. Spend some time there. Alone, preferably. Leave your friends at the path, leave your books at the gate, and I'll be there waiting in this fine Chatsworthy place. We can pray together, you and I, and I'll give you a few snippets on how to keep your spirit penitential and your conscience pure.

As for the rest of the world, don't give it a thought. Do God first; do all the rest later, if there's any time left over. That's to say, you won't be able to wait on Me and at the same time tickle your own Transitories. As for your friends and acquaintances, tell them you're going on holiday. But if you're going on holiday with Me, then leave behind all your usual baggage. So prayed Blessed Apostle Peter in his First Letter, that those faithful to Christ should describe themselves as "strangers and wayfarers" (2:11).

When you're about to die, will you have enough faith in your wallet to let go of those final affections of the world? Will your sallow and indeed shallow flesh ever let your soul escape to the Freedom Beyond? Sentiments similar to those in First Corinthians (2:14).

If you truly wish to be spiritual, you have to renounce everything near and far and take care of no one more than yourself.

If you've perfectly conquered yourself, then you'll be able to subjugate the rest of the world more easily.

The perfect victory? To triumph over oneself.

If you keep yourself in check—that's to say, if your sensuality obeys your reason, and your reason obeys Me in all things—then you can truly claim victory over yourself and have yourself proclaimed lord of the world.

If you're determined to scale this crest, then you should follow the advice of John the Baptist, as it's recorded in Matthew (3:10); that's to say, you have to begin by picking up the ax and putting it swiftly, virilely, to the roots, uprooting and destroying all the wildly successful plants that are destroying you.

Self-love is the radical vice, the root that needs to be eradicated at all costs.

Evil once conquered and captured must be led in triumph through the streets! After that, there'll be a period of peace and tranquillity.

Only a few take seriously this business of dying to self, and even they've had only partial success. Some, caught up in the wonderfulness of themselves, remain entangled in their own desires and can't rise above themselves in spirit. Others, on the other hand, who freely desire to walk with Me in the Garden have to leave all their clingings—that's to say, their diddly depravities and fickle affections, their creature comforts and private stashes—at the gate.

54

NATURE & GRACE

LORD

My dear friend, pay close attention to the movements of Nature and Grace, because they can be very subtle, sometimes quite contrary. It takes a spiritual and enlightened Devout to discern them. Hence, let Me discern them for you.

DEVOUT

Is this another fish in the face, my Fine Fisher of Friends?

LORD

Am I going to smack you with a smelt?

DEVOUT

My question exactly!

LORD

Why would I do that?

DEVOUT

Beacause you've done it before!

LORD

Don't be silly! My point—and I do have a point—is a philosophical one.

Every Devout has his heart set on good, as indeed does all Humankind—Aristotle, My pagan philosopher friend, put that down right at the beginning of his *Nichomachean Ethics* (1.1). And every

Devout pretends there's something good in what he says and does. And so it is that many Devouts fall by having clouded their own minds into thinking they were doing something good when, actually, they were doing something quite bad. Horace, My pagan poet friend, expresses much the same sentiment in his *Poetic Art* (25).

Natura, as Dame Nature is familiarly known, is hot, and as if to prove her point, she's dragged any number of Devouts under the bushes; she's a tramp, a deceiver who always gets her way.

Gratia, as Lady Grace, is commonly known, cool, walking in the Garden at twilight, pruning all the deadly nightshade; she's not pretentious or fallacious and has the pure intention of doing everything for God, in whom all Finality rests. First Thessalonians recommends much the same thing (5:22).

Natura won't entertain the possibility of death; nor does she allow herself to be oppressed, overwhelmed or underwhelmed, or tamed by a master.

Gratia, though, truly strives to mortify herself, asks for direction, desires to be taught, and has no intention of dancing naked in the fountain; that's to say, she resists sensuality. She thrives under discipline and abhors the thought of disciplining someone else. But she lives, stands, and exists under God, and because of God she's always prepared to defer to every other human creature. Here I'd refer you to First Peter (2:13).

Natura labors only for her own advantage and looks only to what financial gain she can squeeze out of a situation.

Gratia has it the other way around. She expresses no interest in promoting or advancing her own career; she does only what'll be good for others. First Corinthians (10:33).

Natura freely accepts honors and decorations she doesn't deserve.

Gratia attributes all honors and decorations to God, on whose bountiful breast they should be proudly displayed. Psalms (29:2).

Natura likes to be in control; when she's not, she fears confusion and contempt, disgust and disgrace.

Gratia likes protocol and rejoices when she's asked to suffer some contumely for the name of Jesus. Acts of the Apostles (5:4).

Natura likes to lounge about in silk and have her body bathed in milk.

Gratia cleans up quite nicely, thank you very much, but she doesn't spend a lot of time in front of the mirror; there's too much to do, too many people to help, for her to loll around.

Natura surrounds herself with curios and *objets d'art* and abhors the cheap and the dull, as if she knew the difference.

Gratia doesn't clutter her residence with cutesy artifacts; no bibelots or furbelows for her; she delights in humble fabrics with simple designs and swans about in secondhand splendor.

Natura has to keep pace with the latest fashions, is a bad winner and a poor loser, and bristles at the slightest barb, real or imagined.

Gratia takes the long view, with Eternity at the end of the scope. She hardly notices when things come into, let alone when they go out of, fashion; nor do her lips go pouty when she's slapped in the face with an insult. That's because she keeps her treasure and joy where it's truly secure, that's to say, in the Vaults of Heaven. Matthew (6:20).

Natura has to have one of everything. Slower to give than to receive—that's her motto.

Gratia, however, prefers none of anything, develops the common touch, avoids particular friendships, and has modest needs and desires; that's because she judges it "more blessed to give than to receive." Acts of the Apostles (20:35).

Natura has a fondness for creature comforts, flashy displays, witty dinners.

Gratia is attracted to God and the virtuous life, doesn't invest in unguents or ointments, turns her back on the World, detests carnal desires, restricts her travels, and blushes when she has to appear in public.

Natura's not beneath getting her jollies by sipping the sort of drinkies that make her skin crawl.

Gratia's not above seeking a little consolation for herself, but she finds it in God alone; her delights aren't in the visible world of the *Summum Malum,* but in the invisible world of the *Summum Bonum.*

Natura's a heartless businesswoman. No *pro bono* work for her. As for remuneration, she expects better than equal pay. In lieu of that, she'll trade up to preference or praise from those who set the standards. For her benefactions, paltry and tawdry as they are, she wants instant public recognition.

Gratia, on the other hand, seeks nothing ephemeral, certainly not a reward; she prefers God, the greatest reward of all. She does with only a few necessities in this life, a comb and a brush and just enough diet to get her through to the next life.

Natura arranges a ball for a thousand of her closest friends—as if she had that many!—not so much for them to dance and to sing as for her to boast about the stateliness of her home and the lengthiness of her lineage. She flashes her teeth at the powerful and rubs up against the rich. And she's assembled a virtual retinue of viragos like herself.

Not so *Gratia*. She feels affection even for those who've shown no signs of friendliness. Nor does she surround herself with yea-sayers and gainsayers. She takes no extraordinary pride in her distinguished family or historical home, and rarely lets slip that Virile Virtue is the *major domo* managing her estates. She favors Lazarus to Dives, feeling more warmly for the indigent than for the potentate. She rejoices with Truth and politely refuses Untruth. She has this habit, annoying to some, of exhorting the good to yearn for greater charisms; as for herself, she yearns only to be assimilated through virtues to the Son of God. Matthew (5:44) and First Corinthians (12:31).

At the hint of famine or drought, *Natura* begins to binge.

In the face of want, *Gratia* keeps on an even keel, eating and drinking like a bird.

Natura quickly turns the conversation back to herself, always pestering and pummeling until she gets her own way.

Gratia begins with herself, but very quickly leads the conversation back to God, whence everything came in the first place. She ascribes nothing good to herself, nor does she give off even the faintest aroma of arrogance. She's neither contentious or sententious. And she submits her senses and intellects for the Divine Examen by Eternal Wisdom.

Natura wants to know all the secrets and to hear the latest news; she appears in public with daring dress and brazen mouth. She acts audacious and talks salacious, yet desires to be thought gracious.

Gratia, though, doesn't care a fig about the latest in fig leaves. That's because this whole thing had its start with the Primal Corruption; that was when there lay over the earth nothing new and nothing lasting. So she trains her senses to avoid Vain Complacency and Empty Ostentation, humbly hides in herself what's considered laudatory and wonderful in others, and seeks in every situation and every branch of knowledge to find something for the praise and honor of God. She doesn't wish to advertise the importance of herself or the magnitude of her gifts, merely to choose that God be blessed when He gives His gifts; after all, He's the One who's showered everyone else with gifts, and just for the love of it all.

Gratia is supernatural light. She's a certain special gift of God, properly a little sign of God's favor to the Elect, and a pledge of Eternal Salvation. She's meant to lift up Humankind from Terrenals to the Celestial Lovables, that's to say, to make a carnal Devout into a spiritual Devout. Ephesians (2:8).

In conclusion, I may say, the sooner Nature's impediments are removed, the freer Grace's improvements'll flow. And when that happens, the interior Devout'll be reformed according to the image of

God by a new series of daily visitations. That, according to Colossians
(3:10).

55

CORRUPTION & EFFICACY

DEVOUT

O Lord my God, who created me to look like You, grant me this grace
You keep talking about, the one that's greatly necessary for salvation.
Perhaps it'll help me get hold of my lowest nature—it's dragging me
down to sins and into Perdition itself.

I feel in my flesh the law of sin contradicting the law of my mind,
as Paul so haply put it to the Romans (7:23), and lashing me with
silken bonds to sensuality. I'm helpless! Help me! I can't resist my
passions unless Your Most Holy Grace, branded hotly onto my heart,
assists me.

Your grace is necessary, and a great grace it has to be if it's to do
the job. My nature has to be overthrown. It's been plaguing me since
adolescence. That was God's appraisal of human nature in the aftermath of the flood, at least as it was recorded in Genesis (8:21).

Yes, it was through Adam, our Primal Father, that our nature was
pocked and pummeled by Sin until it finally fell. And from that
moment on, as Paul reminded the Romans (5:12), the punishment
left that terrible strawberry blotch on the human soul.

Since that time Dame Nature herself, who was fathered by You in
Your goodness and rightness, has been in a compromising position.
Poor babe, now that she's slipped from her pedestal, she's had to shop
such putrid wares as Vice and Weakness and Corruption. A mere
remnant of her former self, though, she still has power enough in
her little finger to grab your foot and drag you under the bushes
where all mortal and venial sins are committed.

Modest, like an ember in the ash, is the force for good that remains in her, that's to say, Natural Reason. Up to this point in human history, it's managed to survive as if in a dear but dark night. It still has the ability to distinguish good and bad and to discern the distance between truth and falsehood. All this Natural Reason can do, but, oh, the powers she's lost! To logick the universe, illumine the Truth, restore Sanity to its own terribly troubled affections.

Hence it is, my God, that, as the Letter to the Romans has said (7:22), "I'm truly delighted with the rules of engagement You've laid down for the interior self."

But then again, I knew Your commandment would be good, just, and holy, arguing as it does that every evil and every sin has to be fled. But, oh, the reality! Again the Letter to the Romans, the next verse (7:23).

But "when I follow the law of sin, I'm enslaved by my flesh." Which is, I think, another way of saying, I err more in favor of Sensuality than Reason. Romans again (7:25).

Thence it is then that, again from the same chapter in Romans, but an earlier verse (v. 18), "I want to do good for You, but I often find I just can't pull it off."

Hence I often propose a flurry of actions that far exceed the grace in my purse. Thence, my infirmity returns with a vengeance, and I have to advance to the rear.

Hence, it happens that I know the path of perfection and see clearly where it is on the map. Thence, donkeyed as I am by the deadly weight of self-corruptions, I just can't climb any faster or indeed any higher.

Oh, how much I need You, O Lord, You and Your grace! To begin well, not to flag in the middle, to finish strong! Without it I can't do anything; that's if I remember correctly John on God as the Vintner and You as the Vine (15:5). With Your grace comforting me and in You I can do everything; that's as Paul encouraged the Philippians (4:13).

O Truly Celestial Grace! Without You there'd be no proper merits, nor would any of the gifts of nature have any value!.

Without grace, O Lord, there'd be no validity to, no vitality in, art, wealth, beauty, courage, talent, eloquence.

These gifts of nature are common to both the good and the bad. However, the appropriate gifts for Your Elect are Grace and Love; emblems of You and Eternal Life worn on the sleeves of Your Elect.

This grace has an eminence of its own. Without it there's no such thing as the gift of prophecy, the operation of miracles, the revelation of Theology, the reasoning of Philosophy.

Without Charity and Grace, neither Faith nor Hope nor any of the other virtues are acceptable to You.

O beautiful grace! How You make the poor in spirit rich with virtues! How You make the rich into persons of humble heart!

Come, each morning, descend on me, let me break my fast with Your consolation. If You don't, my soul'll falter, my intellect buckle.

I beseech You, O Lord, that I may find grace in Your eyes, as Abraham begged favor of the three lordly gentlemen suddenly in front of his tent, as Genesis recorded it (18:3).

I know from the Great Paul in his Second Letter to the Corinthians (12:9) that "Your grace is always enough to do the job." I say that now, and I'll say it again, even though I don't get all the other things my lousy nature desires.

If I'm going to be taxed and vexed by many trials and troubles, I've nothing to fear from evil. That's to say, so long as Your grace is with me. The Psalmist himself could live and die on that promise (23:4).

That's my courage, my counsel, and my help. It's stronger than all my enemies combined; wiser than all the wisdoms universal.

Grace teaches truth, monitors the monastery, illumines the soul, lightens pressure, banishes sadness, reduces fear, nourishes devotion, produces tears. What am I without her, but dead wood, the dry rot of a family tree not good enough even for the Final Fire?

If I may, the Collect of the Sixteenth Sunday after Pentecost: "May Your grace, O Lord, always precede me and succeed me, and keep my mind constant only on good works, through Jesus Christ, Your Son. Amen."

56
WAY OF THE CROSS

LORD

Some random thoughts.

My dear friend, as strong as your pull's away from Me, that's the strength of My pull toward you.

Desiring nothing outside the walls will give you peace inside the walls. Make the external surrender, and you'll be invited to join Me.

In addition to what you already know, I want to teach you how to say no to yourself once and for all.

Some "don'ts." Don't interrupt, don't contradict, and, above all, don't whine!

"Follow Me!" That I said to Matthew, and that's what he recorded in his Gospel (9:9); indeed, that's what he did.

"I'm the way, the truth, and the life." I said that also, and My good John noted down what I said (14:6).

Without the way, there's no going. Without the truth, there's no knowing. Without the life, there's no living, that's to say, no life at all.

I'm the Way you ought to follow, the Truth you ought to believe, the Life you ought to hope for.

I'm Way Inviolable, Truth Infallible, Life Interminable.

I'm the straightest road, the supremest truth, the truest life, the blessed life, the uncreated life, actually.

If you stay on in My life, you'll learn about Truth, and Verity'll set you free; that's what I said to the Jews who believed in Me; and that's as John recorded it (8:32). At last you'll get the handle on Eternal Life.

Tough talk for the not-so-tough!

"If you want to enter Eternal Life, keep the commandments." Matthew (19:17).

If you want to learn the truth, believe in Me.

"If you want to be perfect, sell everything in sight." Matthew again (19:21).

"If you want to be a Disciple of Mine, just say no to yourself." Matthew, an earlier chapter (16:24).

If you want to possess the holiness of the next life, then say no to the worldliness of the present life.

If you want to rejoice in the next world, then "humble yourself in this world." Matthew, a later chapter (23:12).

If you want to reign with Me, then carry the cross with Me. Only those who get on with the carrying will find the beatudinous way, the True Light.

DEVOUT

O Lord Jesus, Your life was such a small stretch in human history, and even that was despised by Humankind. Despite what the history of the world has said and done, grant that I may imitate You in all respects.

"The servant isn't greater than the master, nor the student, the teacher." That's how Your Matthew put it (10:24).

We Devouts will be exercised in this life because there's where we'll find our Salvation and True Sanctity.

Outside of these applications of the spiritual life, whatever I read or hear about You won't give me the same pleasure as knowing You personally.

LORD

My dear friend, you've heard and read all there is to know about the spiritual life, but you won't be blessed until you put the words into action. That's what I said when I washed the feet of My Apostles, John among them (13:17).

"How do I know who loves Me, and whom I should love in return, and to whom I should pay a visit? That's rather simple, really. He's one who has My commandments in his heart and keeps them." I say that to you, but it's also what I said to My Apostles after the last Passover feast, again, John among them (14:21).

And, in conclusion, I'll make room for you on My throne in the Kingdom of My Father; the Book of Revelation has promised that (3: 21).

DEVOUT

Lord Jesus, as You've said and promised, so it'll be. And so hopefully it'll be for me too.

I've received the Cross from Your very hand. I'll carry it as You handed it over to me, carry it to the death.

Truly the life of a good monk is the Cross, and the Cross is the passage to Heaven.

The Way of the Cross is an uphill trudge, and once begun, you can't just stop and turn around and go downhill.

Ah, my brothers, let's make the trudge together—Jesus'll be with us. It's because of Him we took up this cross, and it's because of Him we'll persevere in the Way of the Cross. He'll lead the way, and we'll follow. If He falls, we'll help. And the other way around.

Look, there He is. Our King enters before us. He'll fight for us. Let's follow him virilely, and no one'll fear the terrors. Let's be prepared to die bravely in the war. "Let's not bring disgrace on our glory," as the First Maccabist would say (9:10), by fleeing from the Cross.

57

DEPRESSION & SLIPPAGE

LORD

My dear Devout, a little patience and humility in adversity will please Me more than a lot of consolation and devotion in prosperity.

Why do you become depressed when a small insult is sent your way? If it'd been a bigger one, a real calumny, say, you still shouldn't have let it bother you. Let it pass. It's not the first time or the last time, just the present time, and they'll keep coming, no matter how long you live.

Verily, you'll do virilely most days, that's to say, until something prickly gets in your way.

You're very good at giving advice on vice to others, how to battle the Enemy, that sort of thing. But when tribulation suddenly comes a-knocking, you quickly lose your water.

Pay some attention to how fragile you are, especially in the small things of life. They're for your salvation, all these dreadful little things that happen to you.

Put the bad stuff out of your heart, as best as you know how. And if it does get to you, don't let it depress you or entangle you for long. As for consolation, if you aren't getting any, then at the least bear up patiently.

Also if you accidentally overhear an insulting remark and feel your gorge rise, reprimand yourself and don't let a wisecrack escape your mouth, lest the tots and tykes be scandalized.

If a commotion arises, quickly muffle your drums, and from that, the internal pain will be suitably and soothingly hummed with grace.

Up to this point I've lived, prepared to help you, and I'm prepared to help you more. But first you have to have faith in Me, then invoke Me directly, and address Me nicely.

Keep your head on straight! Cinch up your cincture! There're worse battles ahead. But don't fuss and fume if you have to skirmish with tribulation, or worse, come under heavy fire from temptation. Why? Well, I should have thought it obvious by now. You're *homo sapiens*, not *Sapientia* herself! You're fleshy, not feathery; man, not Angel.

Just staying in the same old place as far as virtue's concerned isn't really a virtue in the spiritual life. The First Angel as well as the First Man found that out. And now they're out of Heaven, out of Paradise.

I'm the One who raises up those who are down and out about their own welfare. But those who know their own infirmity, these I'll carry to My divinity.

DEVOUT

A prayer about the Final Good.

O Lord, blessed be Your word, sweeter than honey, thicker than the honeycomb, if I may quote the Psalmist (119:103). What could I do in these great sore spots and tight spots unless You comforted me with Your Holy Words? Until I finally arrive at the Gate of Salvation, what should I watch out for, what should I have to endure? Grant me the Final Good. Make my passing from this world to the next a smooth one. Remember me, God of mine, and set me on the straight and narrow to Your Kingdom. Amen.

58
WAY OF THE SAINTS

LORD

My dear friend, beware of public disputations on matters that are beyond your humble intellect. And you'd be well advised not to pry into what's behind the judgments of God. Same reason; that's to say, they're Divine Judgments, not human ones. For example, why one man has lost out, and another has lucked into a verdict in his favor. Or why one person has had the book thrown at him, and yet another has gotten off with a slap on the wrist. Instances of justice such as these exceed the capacity of each and every human faculty. All of which is another way of saying, no rationalization or disputation can delve the niceties of Divine Judgment.

Next time, therefore, the Enemy—or worse, the Schoolman from the University—suggests a nice topic like the Saints for public disputation, you respond with the prophetic words of the Psalmist (119:37): "You're just, O Lord, and Your judgment's right." And again, "The judgments of the Lord are true, and need no further human justification than that" (19:9).

Well, I must say, My judgments are meant to scare you to death, not to be debated to death by you. That's how My Paul put it to the Romans (11:33). Why? Need I say it once again? They're incomprehensible to the human intellect.

Also there's no real call to make philosophical inquiry into the merits of the Saints. That's to say, "*My* patron saint is holier than *yours!*" "*Your* patron saint is lower in Heaven than *mine.*" That sort of thing.

Such animadversions quickly lead to animosities that eventually lead nowhere. Whence comes pride, whence vanity, whence jealousy, whence dissension, whence riot!

Can't you just hear it? One person proclaims that his patron Saint as the all-time all-star best; another shouts out that that Saint was a fake, a myth, that he never really existed, and bleats out his own nomination for the Saint of All Saints. Then they come to blows.

Such delvings rarely bear fruit, and in an applied sense they displease, even embarrass, the Saints themselves.

And another thing. I want to set the record straight. I'm not the God of dissension—I'm the God of peace, the sort of peace that consists in True Humility, not in pompous self-postulation. That's how Paul described Me in his First Letter to the Corinthians (14:33).

Just what's the attraction of the Saints? Some are drawn to them with the zeal of love; others, with more ample affection than they realize. But that's the human way of looking at hagiology, not the divine.

Don't forget, I'm the One who invented Saints in the first place. I gave them grace; I set them up in glory; I knew the merits of each; I prepared their way with sweet pavers. That's how My Psalmist saw it (21:3).

I foresaw that I'd love them before creation; Paul put that in his Letter to the Romans (8:29). I chose them personally after creation— they certainly didn't preselect Me; John got My words right in his Gospel (15:16, 19).

I called them with grace as My trumpet, as Paul could have said to the Galatians (1:15). I attracted them through mercy; I held their hands through how many temptations. I showered them with magnificent consolations; I gave them perseverance; I crowned them with patience.

I know the very first Saint and the very latest Saint. I encompass them all in one humongous hug. I'm prepared to be praised in all My saints, blessed above all things, and honored in each and every Saint, whom I've magnified so gloriously and predestined before they've had the chance to earn a merit on their own.

One thing I'd like to convey to you My dear if sometimes dim Devouts. To condemn one of the least of My Saints, and I've got a lot of them, isn't the same thing as honoring a great Saint, of which I've all too few. The reference here is to Matthew (18:10). And I love them all, from the silly to the sincere.

Another thing. Derogate just one Saint, and you derogate Me, and all the rest of the Saints to boot!

The many and varied Saints are all one, linked with the silken cord of Charity. They have the same thoughts, the same wishes, and they love each other as they love themselves.

Up to this point, however, the Saints love Me more than themselves or their merits. Drawn out of their own personal love, they sail on, totally in love with Me, in whom they fruitfully rest.

There's nothing that can turn them away from Me or depress them about Me. You know why? The Devouts who're full of Eternal Truth burn with Charity's eternal flame.

Along this line the sensualist and the secularist at the University don't have a great deal to say. Rather, they think it supremely important to distinguish the many and varied levels of Sainthood. But how could they do that when they don't know anything about the subject of love, except perhaps what their own petty toys and joys may teach them? Such Schoolmen from the University just don't know their thesis from their arsis. That's to say, you'd think they'd be happy discerning black or white, but they aren't. They'd rather distinguish a thousand shades of gray!

In many of you there's a certain ignorance. That's to say, not all that expert in the spiritual life yourselves, you rarely know how to love someone with a perfect spiritual love. You find attractive this one or that one; the first instance is natural affection; the second, human friendship. Then you make the ghastly assumption that the way love's expressed here on Earth is the way it's going to be in Heaven. Sad to say, there's an incomparable distance between those *Obscurati* who see as through a glass darkly and those *Illuminati* who look as through a pane clearly.

Beware, therefore, My dear friend, of being drawn into public disputations about topics like these. Why? They're just too much for your small head. Instead, try to figure out how you can be discovered the least in the Kingdom of God. And if anyone wants to know who's holier than who or who's greater than who in the Kingdom of Heaven, then he should ask Me. What'll I tell him? That such a piece of knowledge has market value, no street value. Recognizing this as fact, you should humble yourself in My presence, and when you rise, you'll be praising My name all the more.

This is how you'll learn something about the magnitude of your sins and the parvitude of your virtues. You may even learn just how far you yourself are from the perfection of the Saints. Then and only

then can you move up a few places in the line to God. That's in sharp
contrast to the bloke who insists on arguing heatedly, perhaps even
elegantly, that some Saints are highbrow and others lowbrow.

It's not all that bad, delving the secrets of the Saints with the frail
instruments of Philosophy and Theology. But it's quite a bit better
invoking these very same Saints with devout prayers and pious tears,
imploring their glorious intercessions with humble mind.

The Saints are contented beyond contentment. If only you knew
how to be this content, you'd stopple your logorrhea.

The Saints don't boast about their merits; they don't ascribe any
goodness to themselves; they give it all back to Me. And with good
reason. I gave it all to them first, from My fund of Infinite Charity.

The Saints are so flooded with love of divinity and joy that it's hard
to find a glory, a felicity, they don't have.

All Saints, the higher they are in glory, the humbler they are in
themselves, and the nearer and closer they are to Me.

And so you have this single and indeed singular scripture, in the
Last Book of the Scriptures (4:10), to the effect that the Saints laid
down their crowns before God, fell on their faces before the Lamb,
"and adored the Living God for ever and ever."

Many of you, like the Disciples in Matthew's Gospel (18:1), spend
too much time asking who's the greatest in the Kingdom of God.
Rather, you should devote all the time to computing how to reserve
even the farthest seat at the farthest table in that Holy Hall.

It's a great thing to be a small Saint in Heaven, where all the
Saints are great by definition. That's because all have received the
call to be, and indeed have become, the children of God. The reference is to John's First Letter (3:1).

"The least in Heaven will be as a thousand men on earth"; the cal-
culation was the Prophet Isaiah's (60:22). "And the sinner who's lived
to a ripe old age will still have to die"; Isaiah again (65:20).

When a couple of the Apostles asked which of them would be the
greater in the Kingdom of Heaven, they got a response they didn't

expect; as it was recorded by the Great Matthew (18:3–4): "You've got to change your life. You've got to become like tots and tykes; otherwise you won't be able to enter the Kingdom of Heaven. The adult who's able to recover his childhood innocence will become one of the great Saints in Heaven."

Woe to those who think it beneath their dignity trying to recapture their spiritual childhood! Yes, the door to the Heavenly Kingdom is low, and no, getting down on all fours won't help them through.

Woe also to the rich, having their consolations in their money bags! I tucked this among My Beatitudes, and Luke put it in his Gospel (6:24). Fat cats that they are, they'll be the first ones sobbing and fobbing outside the tiny portal as the paupers parade into the Kingdom of God.

Paupers all, rejoice! Yours in the Kingdom of God! Luke again (6:20).

All you have to do is walk in the truth! John's Third Letter (v. 4).

59
HOPE & TRUST

DEVOUT

O Lord, how would You characterize my trust in this life? Let me put it another way. What's the greatest solace I can have under the big sky? Isn't it You, my Lord God, whose mercy is without end? Where else would I do so well but sitting alongside You on Your throne? When can anything be bad if You're around me?

I prefer to be a pauper because of You. I'd choose rather to vagabond around the world with You than to travel Heaven without You.

Where You are, there Heaven is.

Where You aren't, there Death and Hell are.

You're my desire, and so I feel I have to sigh after You, cry out and implore You.

When all's said and done, there's no one I can fully confide in; no one who'll give me the help I'll need when I'm pinched by the unforgivingness of life. No one, that is to say, except You alone, my Lord God.

You're my hope, my trust, the consoler of my soul, and the best friend I could ever have.

"Everyone looks for a way to get ahead" according to Philippians (2:21). You, offering me salvation and spiritual progress, give me an edge.

Even if You expose me to various temptations and adversities, You manage to turn the whole thing to my advantage.

You have, my dearest Lord and Friend, this well-known habit of tempting the daylights out of Your friends!

LORD

Just know, My dear friend, that in every probationary period you won't be loved or praised the less than when I'm topping you off with My Celestial Consolations.

DEVOUT

In You, therefore, my Lord God, I place my whole hope and refuge. In You also I place all my sore spots and tight spots. In You everything looks firm and stable; outside You, everything's fluid and chaotic!

In this regard, personal friends sometimes help. Experts in their fields always think they can help. Wisdom literature has gone to great lengths writing help down. Philosophical and theological treatises have compressed help into a few syllogisms. A gem with magic properties is no help at all. A secret garden with high walls can be a sad refuge. But all these are useless if You, O Lord, don't aid and abet, comfort and console, instruct and guard.

Everything seems to lead to peace and felicity, but with You absent, my Dear and Noble Friend, all this seems a hill of beans; that's to say, felicity and truth seem to wilt.

Therefore, the only conclusion I can draw is that You are the end of all goods, the height of my life, the depth of my eloquence. And to hope in You above all—the strongest solace of Your servant Devouts.

A maze of "may's"!

May my eyes be on You, O Lord God, if I may follow the Psalmist (123:1)!

May I, as Paul in Second Corinthians (1:3), confide in You as Father of Mercies!

May You bless and sanctify my soul with Heavenly Benediction!

May my soul become Your home away from home, Your country seat, your Chatsworth!

May nothing be found in the temple of Your dignity that'd offend Your eyes!

May You keep one eye on the magnitude of Your goodness and the multitude of Your mercies, and the other eye on me! That's what the Psalmist implored, and he was no fool (69:17).

May You hear the prayer of Your pauper servant, crying from afar as if in the region of the shadow of death!

May You protect and preserve the soul of Your small servant among the many perils of the corruptible life!

And may You set me, with Lady Grace as companion, on the road to peace; that's to say, to the Land of Perpetual Clarity! Amen.

BOOK FOUR

✠ ✠ ✠

The Sacrament of the Altar

✠ ✠ ✠

How to Prepare for It
&
What It Tastes Like

EXHORTATION

JESUS

Here are some of My sayings on the subject of Holy Communion, as recorded by My Evangelists.

"Come to Me, all you who labor and lumber, and I'll take up your load," wrote Matthew (11:28).

"The bread I give you is My flesh—there's enough to nourish the world," wrote John (6:57)

"Take it and eat it—this is My Body. Do it again, whenever you think of me; it's in remembrance of My part in the Original Deal." Matthew recorded that too (26:26), and so did Paul in First Corinthians (11:24–25).

"Whoever communicates Me in this way—that's to say, who commemorates Me by eating My Flesh and drinking My Blood—he'll take up residence with Me, and I with him!" John again (5:64).

"These words I've spoken to you—breathe them and live." John too (6:63).

1

INVITATION

DEVOUT

Yes, yes, O Christ, Eternal Truth. Yes, I've read these sayings, and what's more, I've copied them. And I can't help but notice they're not all from the same place; they weren't set down at the same time; they didn't appear all in one passage or indeed scattered about on any one page. But that's the copyist in me! They're Your words, no doubt about that, and, as such, I welcome them with open heart and open soul.

And now they're my words also—favorite sayings, all—because You uttered them for my salvation. They flew from Your mouth, like seeds from a sower's hand, coming to rest on the topmost soil of my soul. So full of piety and promise, they arouse me, but, alas, my sins drowse me off again. You still want me to approach the Great Mystery, but the very thought of it, when I do think of it, makes my conscience cringe, my bones creak.

I still want to break bread with You but, as the Evangelist John might have asked (13:8), do You still want me to approach the Holy Table?

JESUS

Of course I do, My dear Devout.

DEVOUT

But my feet are stuck to the ground.

JESUS

One act of faith at a time, My dear Devout, will get you to the Holy Table in plenty of time.

DEVOUT

I still want to obtain Eternal Life and Glory, but are You telling me to accept the Alimony of Immortality?

JESUS

"Come," I said once, and Matthew recorded it; and I say it again, "not just you and you, but you also!" (11:28).

DEVOUT

Honied and homely words, these, when they fall into the ear of a sinner! That You, my Lord God, should invite the likes of me—that's to say, the pocketless and the pauperous—to the Communion of Your Most Holy Body.

But who am I, O Lord, that I should presume to approach You? Look, the Heaven of heavens can't contain You—if I may echo the

Author of the First Book of Kings (8:27)—and yet You say to me, a leaky sieve, what You said to the others in Your lifetime on earth. "Come, all those of you who break your backs and bust your butts, and I'll pour you a draft." Isn't that how the Great Matthew put it (11:28)?

JESUS

I know what you must be thinking, My dear friend. It's such a Comedown for Me, and so it is. But for you? Can it be anything else but a Comeliness if I choose to send such a friendly invitation?

DEVOUT

A Comeliness, yes, and of course respond I must, but how shall I dare, I who can't find a spot of good in me to save my soul? How am I to introduce myself when we meet face to face, I whose malign conduct I've continually thrown into Your benign face?

Surrounded by such heavenly heavyweights—Angels and Archangels, holy people from the Old and New Testaments—You still have the nerve to say, "Come to Me, one and all"?

That's outrageous! No one else'd make such an invitation. Who'd believe it? Nobody'd give such a command. Who'd pay any attention?

JESUS

Let's not get stalled on comings and goings, My dear friend. I have here an exegetical involving three gentlemen from the Hebrew Scriptures.

First, from Genesis (6:9). Noah, a just man if there ever was one, fabricated an ark that could save just a few—that's how Peter's First Letter put it (3:20). It took him a hundred years . . .

DEVOUT

A hundred years? I know where You're going with this one. It'd take no more than an hour to prepare myself to receive, with all reverence, the Fabricator of the World.

JESUS

Good. The second's from Exodus (25:10–11). Moses, My great servant and special friend, made the Ark of the Covenant out of wood, durable and fragrant. Then he plated and lined it with purest gold in order that he might lay the Tablets of the Law in it . . .

DEVOUT

Your point's well taken, my Friend and Founder of all Law, Giver of All Life. I, lawless creature that I am, have the gall to receive You without having to break a sweat?

JESUS

Two out of two, My dear Devout. The third's from the Author of First Kings chapter 6. Solomon, wisest of the kings of Israel, took seven years to build a magnificent Temple in which My name'd be praised. When he came to dedicating it, he declared a feast, a celebration, lasting eight days; at least as the Second Maccabist recalled it (2:12). He attended to the offerings first, 22,000 oxen and 120,000 sheep, according to the Author of First Kings (8:63), slaughtered and burned, all for peace. With that godly and yet ungodly smell in the air, with brassy trumpetry and airy jollity, he solemnly situated the Ark of the Covenant in the place prepared for it . . .

DEVOUT

Seven years for the Temple? Eight days for the feast? Well, I'm miffed! I can hardly pull myself together to spend half an hour in prayerful devotion? Truth to tell, I don't think I can manage even that!

JESUS

How hard these three old men strove, and how puny your young efforts have been! What little time you take to prepare yourself for Communion! Certainly not enough time to gather your wits! Not enough time even to drown your kittens; that's to say, purge your distractions!

DEVOUT

I can do better, O Lord, and indeed I must. In Your salutary presence no indecent thought, no unhealthy distraction, shall ever rear its ugly head. Why? Because I'm about to welcome into my heart and hearth, however humble it may be, not an Angel, but the Lord of Angels.

JESUS

What a difference a distance makes! There's a world of distance between the Ark of the Covenant and its holy contents; between My unstainable Body and its unspeakable Virtue; between a sacrifice required by the Old Law and the Sacrifice of sacrifices required by the New Law; that's to say, the one prefigures the other, and the New Bread that's host to my Body complements the Old Sacrifice.

DEVOUT

Wherefore, therefore, am I so slow to catch fire when it comes to Your venerable presence? Why don't I prepare myself with greater care for the taking of the holy things; that's to say, the Bread and the Wine? Especially when those holy ancients—Patriarchs and Prophets, Kings and Princes—all offered us such good examples when it came to divine worship?

JESUS

David, a most devout person for a king, danced in the presence of the Ark of God until he dropped—as Second Samuel had it (6:14)—all the time remembering the kindnesses from above bestowed on his predecessors in the royal line. He carved all kinds of instruments that made melody, as the Prophet Amos recalled (6:5); he turned psalmistry into psalmody. He taught people how to sing with joy, and he frequently accompanied them on the harp. Filled with the grace of the Holy Spirit, the people joined him in hymning God in the highest; and he encouraged them to continue this sort of praise to God for the rest of their lives.

DEVOUT

Such great devotion was in vogue then, as was remembrance of divine praise at the Ark of the Covenant. But that was then, and this is now. Shouldn't I, and indeed the rest of the Christian population, have more reverence, more devotion, in the presence of the Mystery and in the reception of the Sacrament?

JESUS

Every year, My dear friend, any number of Christians go to great pains to visit as many shrines as they can, there to pay respects to the relics of the Saints and to hear of the wonders worked through the Saints' intercession. Of course, the pilgrims reverence with their lips the holy bones resting on silk and cased in gold, but they also gawk at the sumptuousness of the churches housing the shrines.

DEVOUT

Stop! I know what's wrong with this word picture!

Right in front of me, on this very altar, without my having to lift a finger, let alone a foot, You're alive and well. That's to say, God, Holy of Holies, Creator of Humankind, and Lord of Angels. But if I may ask, dearest Lord and Friend, what do You have against pilgrimage?

JESUS

Plenty, My dear friend! This flurry of activity seems holy at first, but in reality it's a curiosity that plagues all Humankind. That's to say, there's a certain freshness that comes with hithering and thithering, with seeing new things in exotic places. But when people tally up the expense of pilgrimaging, they've paid too much for too little.

That's to say, the fruit of a pilgrimage is conversion, reform of life. But that seems to have taken a back seat in their minds, if not their souls; they've preferred happy times in holy places to the True Contrition they could find at home, at Chatsworth, the shrine where their souls reside.

DEVOUT

But here and now, in the Sacrament of the Altar, You're totally present, Jesus, Man and Christ. Right here, within my grasp, Eternal Salvation awaits, to be harvested just as often I undertake Communion with dignity and devotion.

JESUS

Pilgrims, beware! The paths to this shrine are rocky, and slippery are the pavers marked Levity, Curiosity, and Sensuality; for true cobbles, rely only on Firm Faith, Devout Hope, and Sincere Charity.

DEVOUT

O God, Invisible Creator of the world, how wondrously You treat us! How sweetly and graciously You carry on with Your chosen—these are the people You've invited to join you in Your Sacrament!

Yes, I know Your low opinion of Us Devouts, but I just have to say that the Sacrament has a special appeal to our hearts. We're truly faithful friends of Yours, and we've planned our whole lives around reformation of soul. As a result, we frequently receive this Most Worthy Sacrament, and from it we derive the great grace of devotion and the love of virtue.

O admirable yet hidden grace of the Sacrament, only the faithful of Christ have known it well! The faithless and the sinful, however, have no experience to match it.

JESUS

So much for what you know, My dear Devout. Now let Me tell you some things you may not know. When you receive this Sacrament, Spiritual Grace is conferred, and Virtue dimmed is restored to its original beauty. Once covered with soot and sin, the pallid soul will soon blush into a full palette of colors.

Sometimes this grace is so great and devotion so pent that they burst, coursing through not just the mind, but the body, replacing weakness with strength.

DEVOUT

Nevertheless, my Lord and Friend, if I may the Teacher teach. Our own tepidity and negligence cause a great deal of pain, even misery. We should be drawn to receive You, O Christ, with greater affection, but we aren't. How is this possible since You're the Total Hope, Total

Merit, of those who'll be saved? You're our Sanctification and Redemption, aren't You? The Consolation of us poor wayfarers, and the Eternal Fruition of the Saints?

JESUS

And so it is that I grieve—and grieve again—that so many turn so little to this Salutary Mystery, which praises Heaven and supports the world!

DEVOUT

Alas, how blind, how hard, the human heart is! We should develop more devotion to the Ineffable Gift we receive every Sunday. As for the rest of the days of the week, if our devotion to Communion takes a dip, then we should do something about it.

JESUS

An exegetical, My dear friend.

Suppose it's come to this, that the Most Holy Sacrament is being celebrated only at the farthest altar in the universe, and the words of consecration are being said by the last Priest alive. What then?

Why, Humankind would fall all over itself trying to rush to that place to see that Priest of God celebrate the Divine Mysteries one last time.

Now, fortunately, just the opposite is true. Many Priests have been ordained, and I'm being offered in many places around the world. The moral? As Holy Communion spreads, Divine Glory increases.

DEVOUT

Thanks to You, Good Jesus, Eternal Pastor, for thinking us poor paupers and poopers worthy of refreshment by Your precious Body and Blood.

Thanks also for Your personal invitation to come to a better understanding of the mysteries surrounding Communion; that's to say, when You said, "Come to me, all you who're lumbered and encumbered; I'll find places for you to slumber."

2

PREPARATION

DEVOUT

Your great goodness and mercy have made me well again, O Lord; nonetheless, I'm sick as a dog. That's why I come to You, my Savior, with empty mouth and dry tongue, to the Font of Life, a destitute in the Court of Heaven, a slave to the Lord, a creature to the Creator, a desolate to the Consolate. The remedy? The Sacrament.

I have trouble with that; and so did Your Evangelist Luke (1:43). I should be going to You; instead, You're coming to me. Well, I'm miffed again! You can't come to my house. I'm a sinner, and You should know what that means. I mayn't be discovered in the same room as You.

Yes, I confess my vilety. I acknowledge Your goodness. I praise Your piety. I thank You for Your charity—it seems to know no bounds.

Of course, I realize that You're just doing this for Yourself. My meager merits have nothing to do with it. That's to say, it's just Your way of bringing to my attention Your goodness, Your charity, Your humility. It pleases You to do so. But at the same time it teases me, my Divine Friend, this comely Comedown of Yours.

Would that the floor weren't littered with my iniquities!

O Sweetest, Gentlest Jesus, how much reverence and gratitude with praise unending I owe You when I receive Your Holy Body! No man alive can be found who can fully unfold the dignity of this act!

But what shall I think of this Communion? It gives me access to the Lord, whom I'm unable to reverence devoutly enough and yet whom I devoutly wish to receive?

What better, more salutary course of action can I take in Your presence, except perhaps humbling my poor self and exalting Your infinite goodness?

I praise You, my God, and I exalt You forever. I despise myself and subject myself to You. Why? My vileness has yet to bottom out.

Look at You, the Holy of Holies! And what am I? A Shittite among Shittites.

Yes, I can see You across the crowded floor. I'm looking right at You, in fact. But are You gesturing me to come forward? There must be some mistake. I'm not worthy to return Your glance, let alone to meet Your gaze!

Yes, it's awkward, but it gets worse! You're coming toward me. You actually want to be with me. You invite me to join You for a meal. You want to show me just how good the Divine Diet can be. Especially, Bread of Angels. That's how the Psalmist described it (78:25). Which, of course, is none other than You Yourself, the Living Loaf, who descended from Heaven to give nourishment to the world; my reference here is John (6:33, 51).

Some questions for You, my Eclectic if Encyclopedic Friend.

Where does Love come from?

What gives Largesse its glow?

How many grateful acts of praise are due You for these two virtues?

But before You answer, here are some exclamations.

How helpful and practical Your counsel is!

How pleasant and comfortable that dinner was when You Yourself were the food!

How admirable Your operation, O Lord!

How powerful Your Virtue!

How ineffable Your Truth!

Now, some conclusions.

You just gave the command, and the world was created. You gave the command again, and the Sacrament was created. Apparently, everything went according to plan.

Worthy of wonder, worthy of faith, worthy of warping the human intellect! You, my Lord God, True God and True Man, You're contained whole and entire in some modest species. The Bread is eaten and the Wine is drunk, but Your Body and Blood remain forever.

O Lord and Tailor of the Universe, so far as I know, You don't keep a list of wants and needs. Yet You have long wanted to dwell in us through Your Sacrament. Help keep my body and soul sinless. Why? So that with a spotless yet sportive conscience I can celebrate the Mysteries—that's to say, receive the Sacrament—more frequently. For my perpetual salvation, then, help me receive the Sacrament that You sanctioned and instituted as a special honor and perennial memorial to remind us of Yourself.

Rejoice, my Soul, and give thanks to God for the Sacrament, that noble gift and singular solace left behind for me in this valley of tears! Every time I receive the Body of Christ, it rekindles this Mystery. Every time I become a co-conspirator in all Your redemptive work, O Christ, as well as a co-participant in all Your merits.

JESUS

No matter how extravagantly I've squandered My charity, My dear Devout, it never seems to lessen. No matter how recklessly I've paid out the fruits of My propitiation, they never seem to be exhausted.

Every time you approach the Sacrament, you ought to spend some time recollecting your soul and meditating on the great Mystery of Salvation.

Whether you celebrate the Sacrament or just hear the Mass, come afresh. That's to say, think of it as the very day that Christ descended into the womb of the Virgin and was made Man. Or the very day that Christ hung on the cross, suffering and dying for the salvation of Humanity. That's how to turn an experience grown dull into a truly enormous, novel, joyful event.

3

FREQUENCY

DEVOUT

Behold, I come to You, O Lord, that Your Gift will do me well. Also I want to rejoice at the party "You've so thoughtfully prepared for the poor, O God"; that felicitous phrasing is the Psalmist's (68:10).

Behold, in You is everything that I can and ought to desire. You're my Salvation and Redemption, my Hope and Fortitude, my Grace and Glory. Therefore today, "Make joyful the soul of Your servant, for he's turned to You, Lord Jesus," if I may paraphrase the Psalmist; "for today's the day I lift up my soul" (86:4).

JESUS

It's all about desire, My dear friend. I desire you to receive Me devoutly and reverently. I desire you to lead Me into your home and, as I favored Zacchaeus with a blessing—Luke is the recordist here (19:1–10)—so I'll favor you. And by a similar stretch over the centuries, I desire to number you among the sons of Abraham. May your soul desire My Body in your Host. My heart desires to be united with you.

DEVOUT

Hand Yourself over to me, O Lord, and that'll be enough to satisfy my desires. For without Your Holy Presence consolation grows stale, falls flat, loses its flavor. Without You I have the staggers. Without Your sacramental visits, I won't have the strength to carry on.

JESUS

As a remedy for what ails you, My dear Devout, I encourage you to approach the Holy Table frequently. If you don't, I'll stop the Celestial Alimony, and you'll lose what little sense of direction you have.

When preaching to the people and healing their maladies, I in My mercy have sometimes had to stop Myself cold, and say, "Those of you who're fasting, I can't send you away on empty stomachs for fear you'll never make it home." That's how Matthew put it (15:32).

DEVOUT

And so may You treat me, my Dearest Friend and Companion. But is that really the reason why You left Yourself behind in the Sacrament—as a consolation of the faithful?

Well I must say, then, You're a fine refection for the soul. And what was that You just said? Whoever makes a worthy dinner of You will be a partaker and heir of Eternal Glory? Is that to say there's a rebate? The cost of the dinner will be refunded at a later date?

JESUS

That's as may be, My dear friend, but first, don't you have something to tell me?

DEVOUT

How did You know that? I work hard and long, and yes, I occasionally sin. That's to say, I begin the race with all deliberate speed, but before very long I have to flop. But, through frequent prayers and confessions and the sacred reception of Your Host I get my wind again and rejoin the race. If I don't do this or something like this soon, I'll just never have the strength to stay the course.

JESUS

From adolescence on—the Author of Genesis knew this (8:21)—the senses of Humankind are prone to evil, and unless Divine Medicaments help, Humankind will go to the dogs; that's to say, proceed from the lesser sins to the greater. That's how Holy Communion pulls you back from evil and pushes you toward good.

DEVOUT

So often I've been lazy and lukewarm when I went to Communion or to Mass, but what if I didn't go? What'd happen if I didn't receive the Cure, and didn't seek out the Great Apothecary?

JESUS

Some days it may be well, when you're ill or indisposed, not to hear or celebrate Mass. Nonetheless, you should feel the obligation, at the appropriate times, to receive the Divine Mysteries.

Why? it seems to me I hear you ask.

This is the principal consolation of the faithful soul. As long as your soul is entrapped—should I say, enshrined?—in your mortal body, it travels through life apart from Me; that's as Paul put it in Second Corinthians (5:6). Therefore, your soul should be mindful of God Himself from time to time and receive its beloved Friend with a devout mind.

DEVOUT

I have to say it again, my Dearest Friend. What a wonderful Comedown for the Godhead! What a wonderful Comeuppance for Humankind! That's because You, Lord God, Creator, Bellows Maker of All That Breathes, deigned to come to my hovel of a soul; once there, to fatten up the leanness of my soul with the plumpitude of Your Sacrament; that's to say, with the plenitude of Your Divinity and Humanity.

JESUS

Blessed is the soul that's finally prepared itself to receive Me, the Lord God, with devotion! In return, I'll fill that soul with spiritual joy!

Happy is the mind that receives the Great Lord, welcomes as guest, receives a congenial companion, accepts a faithful friend, embraces a noble bachelor in front of a party of friends, a Friend of friends!

DEVOUT

May Heaven with all its pendants and Earth with all its ornaments pause in their tinkling orbits for a moment of homage to You, my Sweetest Friend!

Whatever praise seeps or grace drips from the largesse of Your Comedown, it's only spillage from Your Ever-flowing Fount. As the Psalmist has sung, "There's no accounting for Your Wisdom" (147:5).

4
ANXIETY

DEVOUT

My Lord God, do take an interest in Your servant, and do bless me with
Your sweetness, as the Psalmist would say (20:4). With that I may feel
worthy and devout enough to approach Your magnificent Sacrament.

Arouse my loitering heart, excite my listless mind. "Visit me with
Your medicines" (Psalm 106:4). I need a tonic, a purgative, something, anything, to cleanse my palate before I savor Your spirit in the
Sacrament; that's to say, encounter the sudden sweetness that flares
up as if from a secret fountain.

Pop my eyes—the Psalmist yet again (13:3)—that I may see the
Great Mystery, and prop me up to believe it with undoubted faith.

JESUS

Let me put it to you, My dear Devout, the way the Schoolmen do.
Mine is always Act; yours, only Potency. I'm always the Causation;
you, only the Instrumentation. Now who can imagine, let alone
grasp, concepts like these? The University thinks it can, but I doubt
the Schoolmen are any the better off for their silvery syllogisms.

And why am I not surprised? Their thinking leads to more than
Philosophy and Theology, more than Reason and Revelation, more
than Angelic Intuition can do. It's a merry chase, but can the
Cherubim and the Seraphim pass the test? Why, they'd founder and
they'd flounder and eventually they'd have to be sent down. How,
therefore, can you, a wretched student with earth and ash for a
brain—that's how Jesus son of Sirach would have put it (17:32)—
ever hope to apprehend, let alone comprehend, the High Holy Secret
of the Sacrament?

DEVOUT

Don't be so quick to despair, my Hectic if Hopeful Friend. I try to be
simple of heart and firm of faith; this is something of an echo from
First Chronicles (29:17). But if it weren't for Your invitation I could

never hope to approach You with reverence. And here You are in the Sacrament. God and Man, no less. One and the same time.

What next?

I've got You under my tongue; that's to say, I've received the Host and You in the Host. But are You suggesting that at this very same time You've got me under Your tongue? That's to say, You've received me whole and entire?

Well, I must say!

To do it once is staggering. But to do it again and again—I pray Your clemency and I pray Your grace. Not only to receive You again, but also to sour all other consolations that may compete with it.

JESUS

I think you begin to see.

DEVOUT

This Most High Worthy Sacrament means many things to me. The salvation of my soul and body. The medicine for what ails my spirit. The pool in which my vices are healed. The reins by which my passions are whoaed. The brawn with which my temptations are brawled. The broom that sweeps my nightmares away.

The Sacrament makes several things happen. More grace is infused. Virtue begun becomes Virtue increased. Faith is thewed. Hope is sinewed. Love is torched and spread like wildfire.

JESUS

That's precisely what happens.

You've given me more gifts than I know what to do with, my Beneficent and Munificent Friend. And You've done the same to all the others who've received You in the Sacrament. It's no wonder, then, that we think up more names for You, our God. Protector of Human Infirmities. Purveyor of Internal Consolations.

As proof of Your goodness, as if we needed yet another one, is Your grafting of consolation onto tribulation. The resulting staff can then be used to ward off various harms.

When my interior acropolis crumbled and I despaired in the rubble, You gave me hope. Using new grace You restored the scaffolding and relit the sconces.

Looking forward, before they receive Communion, some Devouts feel anxious; that's to say, their souls feel like stones, they've lost all their affections. Then comes the Communion. Looking back, after dining on the Heavenly Food and Drink, they find themselves changed for the better.

JESUS

Do what you can, My dear friend, to find out what the trouble is. If you go about it in an honest way, you'll make two discoveries: how much infirmity has wormed its way into your soul and how much goodness and grace you can worm out of Me.

On their own, the Anxious are often frigid, dense, not all that devout. With Me as Companion and Friend, they're becoming fervent, responsive, and devotion returns.

DEVOUT

What Devout happening upon a fountain of sweetness in the wood wouldn't hurry back to report on his good fortune! As proof, he'd wave the aromatic branch he'd dipped into the pool.

What Devout hogging the fireplace doesn't feel his bottom growing warm!

You're the Fount, the splish, and the splash! You're the Flame, the cackle, and the crackle. The Great Augustine himself didn't put it better in his *Confessions* (10.29).

You're the Pipe of wine that flows freely; that's to say, the Heavenly Cask containing the graces and consolations. At least for others if not for me. But if I'm not allowed to drink from the butt, I'll die of thirst. Perhaps the tap's in the off position. There'd still be some drippage, some droppage. I could survive on that. Anything to slake my thirst, make my fever subside.

I'm not a total Cherub or Seraph yet, flitting about like a celestial firefly, but I do experience a flicker of Divine Fire that comes from the humble reception of the Life-Making Sacrament.

Whatever I need but don't have, Good Jesus, Holy Savior, do supply me from the Divine Bin, and do it so it doesn't hurt. After all You're the One who deigned to halloo the crowd. "Come to Me, all you carters and haulers, tremblers and trundlers, I can lighten your loads." Matthew again (11:28).

I labor by the sweat of my brow, as Genesis put it (3:19); I'm tortured with the pain in my heart, I'm burdened by sins, I'm disquieted by temptations, I'm implicated and compromised by my many evil passions. "There just doesn't seem to be anybody to help"—and the Psalmist wasn't the first, and certainly won't be the last, to make this cry (20:12).

Is there no one who can free me up, make me feel safe again. Alas, no one else but You, Lord God, my Savior, to whom I commit myself and all my cartage and haulage, that You may guard me and guide me through to Eternal Life.

Receive me in the praise and glory of Your name, You who prepared Your Body and Blood as food and drink.

I feel a prayer coming on . . .

Grant, O Lord God, my Salvation, that the affection of my devotion may increase with the frequency of Your Mystery.

5

DIGNITY

JESUS

Even if you had the purity of the Angels and Archangels or the sanctity of John the Baptist, you still wouldn't be worthy enough to receive this Sacrament, let alone handle it with your fingers. Worthiness has got nothing to do with it; that's to say, worthiness as Humankind defines it. There're just not enough human merits to go around when it comes to consecrating and handling the Sacrament of Christ.

Consuming the Bread of Angels the way one eats a loaf—it's a Grand Mystery and a Great Dignity for the Priests. That's to say, this priestly power could've been given to Angels, but it wasn't. It was given only to Priests ordained in the rite of the Church. Only they have the power of celebrating the Mass and consecrating the Body of Christ.

The Priest is a minister of God, using the Word of God the way God set it up. God's the Principal Initiator and the Invisible Operator of all things.

Furthermore, you ought to put more faith in Omnipotent God, as He appears in this most excellent Sacrament, than in your own sensible yet silly world. To make this major readjustment, you must tiptoe through the tulips, that's to say, walk with fear and reverence.

Pay attention to Me now as I refer to First Timothy (4:16, 14). The ministry that's been given to you comes from the imposition of the hands of the Bishop.

That done and you're made a Priest, ready to consecrate and to celebrate. All you have to do now is to offer sacrifice to God at the appropriate times and places and see that your behavior is above reproach. First Timothy again (3:2).

But with all the dignities of the Priesthood newly heaped upon you, one might expect that you could slough your other burdens, lighten your load, that sort of thing. Yes, one could think that, but just the opposite is true. Now you're bound with a tighter chain of discipline, and you're held to a higher level of holiness.

The Priest's conduct should show off all the virtues to their best advantage; that's what the Letter of Titus urged (2:7). That's to say, in his daily round the Priest should show that the good and virtuous life can indeed be lived on this earth. As for his conversation, he should shy away from the things people like to gossip about. Rather, he should save his own talk for the Angels in Heaven—an echo of Philippians (3:20)—and the other men on this earth who're seeking perfection.

The Priest clothed in sacred vestments carries on what I began. In My stead, yet as a humble suppliant, representing not only himself, but all the rest of the populace, he speaks in your behalf to God the Father; sounds like Hebrews (5:3).

On the front and back of his vestment, to make him mindful of the Passion of Christ, he wears the sign of the cross. The one on the front of the chasuble reminds him to look for the footprints of Christ and to follow them fervently; I'm making a passing reference here to First Peter (2:21). The one on the back of the chasuble, to bear up under whatever the mob'll toss at him.

The cross in front reminds him to mourn for clemency for his own sins. The one in the back, to lament through compassion the sins of others and know that he himself is an intermediary between God and sinner.

May the Priest not lose his interest in prayer and offering the Holy Sacrifice. Rather, he should hammer these home until he deserves, somehow, to receive Grace and Mercy.

When the Priest celebrates Mass, he honors God, cheers up the Angels, strengthens the fabric of the Church, helps the living, and gives rest to the dead. And he makes himself partaker of all good things between God and Humankind.

6

MYSTERY

DEVOUT

When I weigh Your dignity against my vilety, O Lord, I put Your *Mysterium Tremendum* against my *delirium tremens* and I turn into a terrible jelly.

You urge me to action, but my choices are limited. If I don't approach You, I flee from life. But if I do approach You and introduce myself into the company wearing the wrong garment or under a false pretext, I'll incur yet another offense. What, therefore, can I do? You're my Facilitator and Conciliator whenever I'm in a bind.

For most human activities, I do clean up quite nicely, if I may say so, but for the reception of Your Sacrament, or even for the celebration of Your Sacrifice, I have to do rather better than that. Teach me the right way. Propose some exercise that'd fit me for Holy Communion. Something practical, useful, sensible.

7

EXAMINATION

JESUS

The Priest of God should approach the celebration of this Sacrament, the touching and consuming of this Sacrament, with humility and reverence, with full faith and pious intention to the honor of God.

As for your conscience, give it a thorough going-over. Clean it up and clarify it with True Contrition and Humble Confession. I know there's no such thing as the perfect Confession; just do the best you can, however imperfect it may seem at the time. The result is to rid yourself of mortal sin; that's to say, anything that would bar your access to the Holy Table.

You can never be truly happy because you're a sinful creature from the start, and you should be particularly sad about your daily excesses. Whenever time allows, you confess to God in secret how your passions run wild, your concupiscences hoot and holler.

Well, you asked for it, and here it is. A veritable litany of venial sins derived from a so-so spiritual life.

So enslaved by your external senses, and yet so often enthralled in your airy fantasies.

So deeply involved in the outer life, and yet so uninvolved about the inner life.

So lithe to weep tears of laughter, and yet so loath to shed tears of sorrow.

So quick to languor and torpor, and yet so slow to rigor and fervor.

So conversant with the lively and the lovely, and yet so confounded by the sickly and the lowly.

So desirous when it comes to having, and yet so parsimonious when it comes to giving, and yet so tenacious when it comes to what you already have.

So inconsiderate when talking, and yet so restless when listening.

So disorderly when it comes to manners, and yet so reckless when it comes to actions.

So overwhelming when it comes to the food on the table, and yet so underwhelming when it comes to the Word of God.

So quick to quiet, and yet so slow to labor.

So alert for courtly stories, and yet so drowsy when it comes to nightly vigils.

So swift off the mark, and yet so rambling when it comes to the tape.

So negligent in reciting the Holy Office, so tepid in celebrating the Mass, so arid in communicating the Host.

So easily distracted, and yet so rarely recollected.

So quick to pleasure oneself, and yet so quick to displeasure others.

So prone to quick decision and yet so supine when it comes to calm discussion.

So exhilarated in prosperity, and yet so debilitated in adversity.

So able to draw up a long agenda, and yet so unable to make a short list.

So much for the No-No's as derived from the lives of the So-So's!

Confess these and your other defects. Express great pain and displeasure at your continuing self-infirmity. Make a firm purpose to amend your life. Promise to do better.

Then, with full resignation and yet wholeness of will, offer yourself, in honor of My name, as a perpetual holocaust on the altar of your heart. Faithfully commit your body and soul to Me.

Then and only then will you worthily deserve to approach the Holy Table to offer sacrifice to God and receive the Sacrament of My Body to salubrious effect.

No oblation's worthier and no satisfaction for getting rid of sins is greater than to offer oneself to God, pure and whole, when the bread and wine are offered up as My Body and Blood, both in Mass and Communion.

If you look into yourself and are truly sorry for your sins, then you can come to Me as often as is necessary for forgiveness and grace.

"I live, says the Lord; so why would I want the sinner to die? I just want him to reform his ways and live"; that's the Prophet Ezekiel to the captives in Babylon (33:11).

"His sins I'll stop recording, and his punishments I'll see excused"; that's the Prophet Isaiah putting words into the Lord's mouth (43:25).

8

SACRIFICE

JESUS

For your sins—that's why I wanted to do it, and that's why I did it. And what did they do? They ripped off My clothes and hammered My hands onto the cross. It was a sacrifice the old-fashioned way. Perhaps that's why God the Father seemed so pleased.

In the same way, you, My beloved Devout, ought to be willing to offer yourself to Me—I ask you the way My Father asked Me—in pure and holy oblation, everyday in the Mass, with all strength and affection, until the day you drop.

Surrender. Unconditional surrender. That's all I require of you. Not your possessions—I could take those anytime and scatter them over the landscape; you'll find this in Philippians (4:17). Just you— that's all I want. Of course, I could take you as a prisoner of war and do with you what I want. But what I really want is for you to give yourself to Me as a gift.

Of course, the same is true for you. If you had all the baggage in the world, but didn't have Me, would you be any the better off? You'd have a full cart, maybe, but also an empty heart. And the other way around is also true. It's not your silly stuff I want—it's your silly self!

Offer yourself to Me. Make that the only package, and it'll be an oblation that will be welcomed.

Look at Me! I offered My whole self to the Father for you; I also put My whole Body and Blood into food and drink that I might be totally yours and that you might be totally Mine.

If, however, you hold something of yourself back or are slow to give your all, it'll be a pretty poor offering made not by any friend of Mine, but by a pretty poor acquaintance.

To prevent that and to acquire illumination and liberation of spirit, you ought to make a spontaneous oblation of your very self into the hand of God. When? Before each and every thing you do.

Such an attractive proposition, I thought, but I must ask, Why are there so few *Illuminati* and *Liberati* today? That's because so many don't know how to denude themselves of imperfections.

My firm opinion is this, and it appears in the Gospel of Luke (14:33): "Unless a person renounces everything that he has and everything he is, he can't be My Disciple." Therefore, if you want to be my Disciple, offer your whole self to Me; that includes your scruffy affections.

9

PRAYER

DEVOUT

I'll gladly do as You suggest, my Lordly Friend, and I'll pray to boot. Do tell me if the following is an appropriate way to begin.

O Lord, I begin this prayer by acknowledging that everything's Yours—Heaven, Earth, and everything in between. That's a sentiment from First Chronicles (29:11).

I sincerely desire to offer myself as a spontaneous oblation to You, and for You to offer Yourself to me as a Fast Friend forever!

Mine is a simple heart, O Lord, but I offer it to You today in perpetual servitude of friendship, worship, and sacrifice of perpetual praise.

Take me together with Your holy oblation of Your precious Body, which I offer to You today in the feathery presence of Your Angels, invisibly assisting. This I do not only for the salvation of myself, but for all Your people.

Here's another prayer, one suitable, I hope, for offering my sins at the altar.

O Lord, I offer to You all my sins and near sins, which I've committed in Your presence and the presence of Your feathery choir— that's to say, the ones I first committed right down to the ones I've just committed—on this placable altar of Yours.

May this offering burn with even flame, and Your charity turn it to ash.

May You scrub out every sinful stain from my conscience; that's what the Letter to the Hebrews would urge (9:14). May You restore all that grace of Yours that I lost by sinning. May You make a clean sweep of Chatsworth—that's to say, my inner digs—and may You welcome me with the merciful kiss of peace.

Here's an act of contrition of sorts.

With regard to my sins, what else can I do but confess them humbly and pray unceasingly for Your forgiveness?

I pray You, my Deft if sometimes Deaf Lord. Turn the Divine Ear Trumpet in my direction, and let me pour my worldly whispers therein.

All my sins displease me—I don't want to perpetrate, let alone perpetuate, them ever again. But I grieve over them and will continue to

*do so as long as I live, prepared always to do penance and offer satis-
faction however I can.*

*Forgive me my sins, O God; forgive me for the sake of Your Holy
Name—that's as the Psalmist would say (25:11). Save my soul,
which You've redeemed with Your precious Blood—words reminis-
cent of First Peter (1:18–19). Behold, I commit myself to Your
mercy. I surrender myself to Your hands.*

*Do with me what Your goodness dictates, not what my malice
demands. A holy echo from the First Maccabist (13:46).*

Here's a prayer offering up my good deeds.

*I offer up all my good deeds, although they're precious few in
number, and all are chipped or cracked from constant use. Do mend
the chips and cracks, and do put them to Your Holy Purpose. Do
glaze them with grace, and make them acceptable to Your Holy
Table. Even better the design, if You want. But don't for a moment
think of not leading me, huge homely human that I am, to Lauds'
End.*

Here's another prayer for offering your necessities and the necessities of others.

*I offer You all the pious desires that arise from all the Devouts. I
offer also all the necessities of parents, friends, brothers and sisters,
and all those who're dear to me or who've been my benefactors,
motivated only because of Your love.*

*And there are the ones who've desired to have petitionary prayers
and propitiatory Masses said by me for them and others, for those
now living as well as for those long dead. That they all may sense
the approaching hoofbeats of Your Grace, Consolation, Protection,
and Liberation. And that, having been snatched from all evils, they
may dutifully and joyfully render solemn thanks to You.*

Here's a prayer for sinners.

*I offer You prayers and masses, especially for those who at some
moment in the past have slashed me or depressed me or done me
some other grave damage. And I do make the same offering in behalf*

of those whom at some time or other I've saddened, confused,
insulted, scandalized by words or deeds, knowingly or unknowingly.
Forgive us all equally our sins and mutual offenses.

O Lord, pinch from our hearts every suspicion, indignation, dis-
sension, deception, and whatever else can bruise Charity or fracture
Fraternal Love.

Have mercy, have mercy, O Lord, on those who are loudly
demanding Your mercy. Give grace to the spiritually indigent. And
make us such people as may enjoy Your grace and make progress to
Life Eternal. Amen.

10
EXCUSE

JESUS

It's good you frequent Holy Communion, that's to say, to revisit the
Font of Grace and Divine Mercy and the Font of all Goodness and
Purity. The reason? You have to be cured of your passions and vices.
You have to be more vigorous, more vigilant, against the windmills of
the soul and the whirligigs of the Devil. A cunning enemy, he tries to
deflect the faithful, as much as he can, from Holy Communion, that
great cornucopia of spiritual fruits and remedies.

When some prepare themselves for Holy Communion, they
undergo the tortures of the Damned. One thing Satan does—and the
Great Job himself encountered this (1:7)—is to disguise himself and
mix with a crowd of believers; suddenly he'll reveal himself, popping
noisy and noisome tricks out of his devilish bag. Another thing he
does is to candy people with Timidity and Perplexity until they can
move no longer.

Satan's overall strategy toward us is to squish our affection, then
squash our faith. The results? First, we find it increasingly harder to
fit Holy Communion into our already overcrowded schedule. Then

we start missing Communion without actually missing it. Finally, we relinquish the practice of Communion altogether.

Apparently there's no real antidote for the Devil's crafty fantasies, just as there are no counters to a really bad case of the Torpors or the Horrids. But one thing is certain. A *phantasma* springs from the Devil; it must be sent packing back to its source before it turns into a *stigma*.

That Miserable and Derisible Creature must be denounced. Despite the hackles he raises and the emotions he arouses, Holy Communion must never be omitted.

Another important thing, scrupulosity and anxiety about making Confession can get in the way of cultivating devotion. What to do in a situation like this?

Follow the wisdom of the ages and take the wind of it. Scrupulosity hinders the grace of God and destroys the devotion of the mind. Even when beset with serious peccadillos, don't pass up Holy Communion.

Go to Confession, and do it more often than has been your custom. Don't take offense so easily at the actions of others. And in the very likely event that you're offending just about everybody in sight, pray forgiveness humbly, and God will forgive you freely.

What do you get out of putting Confession off for a long time or deferring Holy Communion for as long as you can?

Purge your souls of the fetid spurge as soon as possible. Swiftly suck out the venom. Hasten to accept the antidote, no matter how vile it tastes. Do these, and you'll feel better, quicker, than if you just put the whole thing off indefinitely.

There are a host of reasons and excuses that will try to convince you not to receive the Host. Indeed, there's no end to them, and their merriness, if you let it, will carry you away from the One True Host for ever.

Don't receive the Host today, for whatever reason good or bad, and you'll do the same thing tomorrow. That's to say, there's no end to finding good reasons for not receiving the Host. Eventually, you'll stop going to Holy Communion altogether. Finally, you'll no longer remember what the Sacrament was like. Is that what you truly want?

Just as soon as you can, drag your carcass off your cot. Why? There's no great virtue in living the anxious life, trafficking with confusion, sequestering yourself from the divine things just because of some daily obstacles. Moreover, it causes a great deal of spiritual harm when you fight Communion off for a long time, for that generally induces the sort of lethargy from which one rarely reclaims his original fervor.

What a pain it is! There are some tepid and dissolute souls, I know, who're only too willing to find ways of postponing Confession, and there's always an excuse for putting Holy Communion off. Why? They fear that they'll have to put their rascally rabbits—that's to say, their rapidly increasing bad habits—under severer discipline.

Alas, you who so easily postpone Holy Communion seriously compromise your charity and devotion! How happy you'd be if you regularly patrolled your own consciences; then you'd be prepared to communicate on any given day, whenever it was scheduled, without having to give the impression that you were Holier-Than-Thou's.

In the meantime, humility about one's self or charity toward another may be a legitimate reason for not approaching the Sacrament, and there may be others. If you have to resort to such an excuse, you're still to be praised for your reverence. But if Old Torpor has overcome you, you ought to rouse yourself out of it. At the faintest sniff of reform in this regard, the Lord will bound to your aid. As we've come to learn, recovery's become one of the Hound of Heaven's specialties.

When you have a truly good excuse for not communicating, you still retain the goodwill and pious intention of communicating. And so you don't go lacking the fruit of the Sacrament. Indeed, you can, every day and every hour, receive Christ in Spiritual Communion without any prohibition and with all spiritual nutrition.

Nevertheless, on certain days and at times set aside, you ought to receive, sacramentally, the Body of the Redeemer Himself, with reverence frothing over with affection. That way you'll be tendering praise and honor to God rather than just seeking your own consolation.

Every time you communicate in this mystical way and are refreshed in this invisible way, you continue to rekindle the mystery and passion of the Incarnation of Christ and rise in His love.

But whoever loses track of time and thereby is surprised by a feast day or a day of obligation coming fast upon him will often find himself unprepared for Holy Communion.

Blessed are you who offer yourselves to God in holocaust—you are the ones who celebrate and communicate.

When it comes to celebrating Mass, don't be a tortoise and don't be a hare. No need to set a record in either direction. Just accommodate the devotion of those with whom you live.

Te Deum laudamus, not tedium for the ages—that's what you should cause in others. Rather, you should serve the common good as it's laid down in the Institution of your Founders. And when it comes to a choice, look to the needs and wants of others before looking to your own devotion and affection.

11

SIMPLICITY

DEVOUT

What a splendid dining companion You are, Lord Jesus! How sweet it is to make merry with You at the Heavenly Banquet. Odd thing, though, or perhaps not so odd: there's only one entrée on the menu. You Yourself are the dish, and a most delectable one at that, at least as my heart ranks tastes.

When it came to devotion, I used to be able to turn it on and turn it off, it came in such abundance. Sensing Your presence was such a sweet thing. Being such fast friends and all, I used to tear up and, like the pious Magdalene in Luke (7:37–38), drizzle Your feet with the drops. But where's my devotion gone? Where have my tears fled?

Certainly in Your purview, O Lord, and that of Your Holy Angels, my whole heart ought to burn and to cry for joy. Why? I have You truly present in the Sacrament, although, I must say, You've hidden Yourself under some rather common species.

JESUS

Yes, I know, My dear friend, but I have a very good reason for doing so. It's for your own protection, so to speak. That's to say, if you were to stare at Me in the light of Divine Clarity, I don't think your eyes could stand the glare. In a like manner the whole world would have to be blindered when the glorious strokes of My Majesty flash across the skies, sometimes even singeing the earth.

DEVOUT

Are You giving me to understand, my Deft if sometimes Daft Friend, that I'm an imbecile?

JESUS

In a manner of speaking.

DEVOUT

That's it, then! That's why You've dumbed Your dazzle down to a single Sacrament. I think I understand it now.

JESUS

Yes, you do hold Me up and adore Me, whom the Angels adore in Heaven. I admire you for doing so. But at least up to this point in your existence, you've been kept very much in the dark; remember Paul says very much the same in his Second Letter to the Corinthians (5:7). Faith has been the only sconce. The Angels, on the other hand, have chandeliers; indeed they are the chandeliers; that's to say, they see Me in person, face to face, without veil, temperamental or sacramental.

DEVOUT

I'm quite content with the little illumination You've allowed me. Faith sheds more than enough light to believe by and to walk in. That's not to say I don't look forward to the dawn of the Day of Eternal Clarity when the shadows of the night will leave all our figures revealed fully and forever. I hope it's all right for a monk to read the Song of Solomon (2:17).

JESUS

"When the Time of times comes," as Paul wrote in First Corinthians (13:10), the Sacraments will have done their job. That's because the Blessed in Heavenly Glory will no longer have any need for a medicament, let alone a sacrament. They'll rejoice without end in the presence of God, face to face, their glory mirroring His; Paul has said something similar in Second Corinthians (3:18).

Back to the sconces. As I've just said, they've been transformed into chandeliers. Our perspective on earth was abysmal; now it's abyssal, and the Deity Himself is visibly at home in Heaven. And the Blessed taste the word of God made flesh, as it was in the beginning and remains for ever.

DEVOUT

Whenever I'm mindful of these wonderful things, a deep gloom descends. Even spiritual consolation can't cut through the fog. And there appears to be a good reason for it. As long as I couldn't see You, my Godly Friend, openly and in Your full glory without blinking, I counted as nothing everything I saw or heard around the world.

You, Dear Jesus, are my witness, if I may borrow a word from Romans (1:9). Nothing can console me, no creature quiet me. Only You, my Lord God, whom I desire to contemplate to the end of time and beyond. But of course, at the present time, this isn't possible, at least while I have to endure this mortal coil. So, as You say, I have to aim for greater patience and submit my every desire to You.

The Saints who're jamming the Kingdom of Heaven now, O Lord, once lived a life of expectation on Earth, waiting for the advent of

Your glory, as the Letter of Titus described it (2:13). Faith and Patience played a large part in their survival; the Letter to the Hebrews would certainly second that (6:12). They believed it then; I believe it now. What they hoped for then, I hope for now. That's to say, where they've arrived already, I trust I'll one day come through to Your grace.

In the meantime, I'll walk in faith, as the Great Paul has said in Second Corinthians (5:7), comforted to know that I'm following the footsteps of the Saints. I'll also have with me, as my *vade mecum,* the Holy Books as a consolation—a sentiment expressed by the First Maccabist (12:9)—as well as a mirror to life; and above all these things, Your Most Holy Body as a singular remedy and refuge.

My body's a prison, and the view from my cell is grim. I survive, but barely. I do without things in this wretched state, but two things I just can't live without. Food and Light. And You, Dear Lord, You bring them to me in the middle of the night.

Food? Your Sacred Body, which revives my sagging mind and body.

Light? Your Divine Word. As the Psalmist has sung in similar circumstances, it's a lamp for my shackled feet (119:105).

Without the Food and without the Light, I wither. Without the Bread and without the Bible, I wander. Without the Sacrament of Life and the Book of Life, I perish.

From my cell I see—or think I see—an altar. A Holy Table from which rises Holy Church in all her splendor. On one side is the Holy Bread; that's to say, the precious Body of Christ. On the other, the Holy Bible; that's to say, the Divine Law that contains Holy Doctrine, teaches right faith, leads even the imprisoned soul through the veil of veils to the Holy of Holies, as the Letter to the Hebrews has led us to expect (6:19).

I thank You, Lord Jesus, "Light of Eternal Life"—that's the title the Wisdom of Solomon assigned to *Sophia* (7:26)—for the Holy Doctrine, which You've administered through the ages to the Prophets, the Apostles, the Disciples, all who've come after.

Thanks to You also, Creator and Redeemer of Humankind, for displaying Your charity to the whole world. That's to say, You prepared a great banquet, the centerpiece of which wasn't the requisite lamb, but rather Your Most Holy Body and Blood. All the faithful are jumping for joy at the Holy Meal, dipping the Bread of Life time and time again into the Chalice of Salvation, brimming with all the paradisal vintages. The Holy Angels dine with us; we, quite humdrum with knife and fork; they, quite fascinating without limbs or implements.

JESUS

So much for the banquet, but that's yet to come for you, My dear Devout. In the meantime let's look at the Priesthood.

Oh, how great and honorable is the office of Priests! They consecrate with sacred words the Lord of Majesty, and bless with their lips, hold in their hands, consume with their mouths, and minister to others!

Oh, how clean their hands ought to be, how pure their mouths, how holy their bodies, how immaculate their hearts! After all, the Author of Purity has passed through this way so many times already!

From the mouth of a Priest nothing but the Holy Word, nothing but the honest and useful word, ought to come forth, especially since that very mouth has so often itself received the Sacrament of Life.

A Priest's eyes should be simple and modest, for they're accustomed to look into the Eyes of Christ. His hands should be pure and raised in prayer—that was First Timothy's prescription (2:8)—for they're accustomed to handle the Creator of Heaven and Earth.

There's this saying about Priests in Leviticus (19:2), "Be holy because I'm holy; I, Your Lord and God."

A priestly prayer.

Omnipotent God, may Your grace help us to undertake the sacerdotal office, and may we serve You worthily and devotedly in all purity and in good conscience; First Timothy again (1:5). And if we can't carry on in such innocence of life as we ought, then grant that

we may weep worthily over the bad deeds we've done, and in the
spirit of humility and with the resolve to do good, serve You more
fervently in the future.

12

IMPERFECTION

JESUS

As you, My dear Devout, I'm a lover of purity and the Giver of All
Sanctity. A pure heart is the sort of thing I seek. And in a place like that
I like to take My rest; a Chatsworth, as it were; that was Luke's senti-
ment in Acts (7:49). Prepare for Me a dining room with some suitable
furniture—that's how the Evangelist Mark recorded it (14:15), and
I'll make Passover with My Disciples and invite you to come.

I'll be glad to come to you and remain for the celebration of the
feast, but first you'll have to scour the leaven from the room—Paul
reminded the Corinthians to do just that in his First Letter (5:7)—
and sweep out the inner room of your heart. Get rid of everything
secular. Banish the sounds of the noisy vices outside. Then sit as a
solitary sparrow on a roof tile, as the Psalmist once put it (102:7),
and stew about your regrets in—as the Prophet Isaiah described it so
well (38:15)—the vinaigrettes of your soul.

Every loving Devout has already done this, prepared a Chatsworth;
that's to say, the best, most beautiful spot for his own beloved Friend.
Why? To show what great affections would greet the arrival of his
Best Friend.

Mark you, no preparation is ever perfect. Try though you do, there
are still foreign particles about, and even if you were to spend a year
doing it, there'd still be dust in the air.

Taking into consideration My piety and grace, you'd be permitted
to approach My table. You'd have to do it, though, as an indigent to a

rich man, with nothing in your pockets and no way to repay the kindness other than to eat humble pie and give humble thanks.

Just do what you can do and do it diligently, not out of habit or necessity, but with fear and reverence. With affection receive the Body of your Beloved Lord and God, who thought you were a worthy enough chap to receive a visit.

I'm the One who called you, the One who ordered it to happen, who cleaned you up so nicely. Come and receive Me.

If perchance I should shed some grace of devotion on you, give thanks to Me, your God. Not because you're worthy of it, but because I look down with mercy on your pathetic state. If you don't have grace, but feel increasingly arid, insist on prayer, groan, and beat your breast, saying *"Mea culpa, mea culpa, mea maxima culpa";* the Evangelist Matthew said something similar (7:7). And don't stop until you receive a morsel of medicinal grace. Without Me you're poor— not the other way around. You don't come to bless Me and make Me feel good—it's the other way around. You come to be sanctified by Me and to be joined to Me in friendship, and to be encouraged once again to do better; First Timothy yet again (4:14). Don't overlook this grace. Rather, prepare your heart with all diligence. Then bid your Beloved Friend to enter.

It's important to note here that you should not only prepare yourself for devotion before Communion, but also save yourself solicitously after Communion. The recollection after shouldn't be less than the preparation before, for the post-Communion glow is the best preparation for attaining major grace.

Whoever flees from Communion back to the World for fear of missing some worldly consolations loses what spiritual consolations have already been detailed to him. Beware of lengthy conversations. Remain by yourself in the church or chapel, and enjoy your special time with God, for you have Him whom the whole world cannot wrest from you. I'm the One to whom you ought to give your com-

plete self. That so that you may live not in yourself, but in Me—do
that, and you can kiss care good-bye.

13

UNION

DEVOUT

Who'll let me know how to find You alone, if I may echo the thoughts
of the Song of Solomon (8:1)? I'll open my whole heart to You and
enjoy Your company as my soul desires, and no one'll despise me for
it. Nor will anyone move me and give me a second look. But we'll
have a good conversation, just You and me, and speak as one good
friend to another, and then to a good meal!

This I pray. This I desire, that I be totally at Your disposal, and that
I withdraw my heart from its many worldly commitments. What's
more, through Holy Communion and frequent celebration of the
Mass, I'll develop a taste for the Celestials and Eternals.

Ah! Lord God, when will I be totally united and absorbed with You
and totally oblivious of myself? You in me, and I in You, as the
Evangelist John once put it (17:21). Fast friends forever!

You truly are my Beloved Friend, chosen out of thousands and
thousands, but how did I ever find You? That was the central question of Solomon's Song (5:10). You're the friend in whose friendship
it pleases my soul to spend the rest of the days of my life with.

You bring peace to my life, which isn't all that odd; You're the
Great Peace and the True Rest, outside of whom there's nothing but
grudge and grief. You truly are my hidden God, tucked away, secret;
that's how the Prophet Isaiah saw it (45:15). And Your words of wisdom are not with the Impious, and Your small talk is with the
Humble and Simple. "O Lord, how sweet is Your spirit," as the Book
of Wisdom has it (12:1).

You're the One who, to demonstrate Your sweetness toward Your children, thought them worth feeding with sweetest bread descending from Heaven; that's how the Deuteronomist described the feeding of Moses and his friends for so many years (4:7). "Truly there's no other nation so grand as the one whose gods approach as closely as You, our God, have approached us." You're present with all Your faithful, and You give them their daily bread, raising their hearts to Heaven, to eat, to enjoy.

What other tribe has been so honored as the Christians? What other creature under the heavens has been so loved, so chosen, as the soul of a Devout in whom God has made an entrance that He may nourish him with his own glorious substance.

O Ineffable Grace! O Admirable Dignation! O Immense Love bestowed on Humankind alone!

But what return do I make to the Lord for that grace, for such extravagant charity? A question frequently asked by the Psalmist (116:12).

There's no better return than to present my heart on a platter to the Lord, with the hope that He'd accept it as I intended. Then all my intestines will jounce for joy when my soul's been perfectly united to God.

Then He'll say to me, "If you want to stay with me, I'll stay with you."

And I'll respond to him. "Do please sit with me, and I'll willingly sit with You. This is my desire, whole and entire, that my heart be united with Yours."

14

DESIRE

DEVOUT

"O how great is the multitude of Your candies, sweets that the fearful know not of," wrote the Psalmist (31:19). When I call to mind some Devouts approaching Your Sacrament with great devotion and affection, O Lord, I turn a hundred shades of pink that I should even think of approaching Your altar, the table of Holy Communion so tepidly, so frigidly. The result is that I remain arid and without affection of heart, that I'm not totally ascended to Your presence, my God, not so vehemently attracted and affected as many others have been.

These last couldn't restrain themselves from crying when confronted with the desire for Communion and sensible love of the heart. But they longed, equally with the mouth of heart and body, for You, God, the Living Fountain, the Source of the Well. They weren't able to temper, let alone to satisfy, their appetite except when they received Your Host with all spiritual eagerness.

How truly flaming is the faith of the Devouts! And how truly amazing that that's not a bad proof of the existence of Your Sacred Presence! For the Apostles truly knew their Lord in the breaking of the bread, as noted by the Evangelist Luke (24:35); their hearts burned strongly in them as they walked with Jesus by the lakeside. Such great affection, such vehement love and ardor are often a long way from my reach and devotion.

I know I'm a pathetic case, Good Jesus, my Divine Friend, sweet and mild. Grant that I, a poor pauper who's always had his hand out, may feel a little of the cordial affection of Your love as it's found in Holy Communion. May my faith convalesce more quickly, and my hope progress in Your goodness. Your charity once holocausted and Your manna once tasted, may they never fail me.

Since Your mercy is powerful, O Lord, grant me the desired grace, and in the spirit of ardor, when the Day of Your Pleasure comes, greet

me like Your long lost friend. Although I don't flare up with the great
desire of those special Devouts of Yours, nonetheless I do keep a
steady flame with the help of Your grace, that's to say, a desire for
that Great Desire, praying and desiring that I might become a partici-
pant in all such friendships of Yours and to be numbered among that
Holy Company.

15

DEVOTION

JESUS

Waste no time! Hop to it! Look for the grace of devotion. Alas, the
search for it may take some time. Be patient and faithful. Accept the
fact that there may be a waiting period.

When it does return, welcome it warmly, and don't let it out of
your grasp. Follow it wherever it leads. What else can you do? Except
perhaps to commit to God the when's and how's of the Supernal
Visitation. Just know that if devotion's come and gone, it'll come
again.

What do you do when you feel interior devotion ebbing? Take
great pains to humble yourself—that's about the only thing you can
do. At the same time keep your spirits up. Why? Simple. God often
gives you in one moment what He's denied you for a long time.
That's to say, He sometimes waits for the end of your prayer before
He gives the grace of devotion; He could just as well have given it at
the beginning. Whatever, whichever, just don't get caught with a
hangdog face when the Hound of Heaven comes a-calling.

If grace were always sudden—that's to say, came when you prayed
for it—it'd catch you in your infirmity, and you wouldn't be able to
lift it off the floor. But if it came later, when hope was green and
Impatience wore *Impatiens*—that's when the grace of devotion
seems destined to come.

But what happens when devotion doesn't come? What happens when it comes but then tiptoes out the back way without your noticing it? Well, if you're looking for someone to point a finger at, blame it all on yourself and your sins.

What gets in the way of grace is often something quite small and manageable. But if it's minuscule, then it shouldn't be labeled majuscule. Except that in the matter of grace nothing's small, everything's humongous; any obstacle, whether small or large, stops the flow of good. Remove it, the flow's restored, and all of a sudden, right before your eyes, is the grace of devotion you've been seeking so strenuously.

What happens then? Immediately you've handed yourself over to God from the bottom of your heart, no longer hithering and dithering with this or that thing. Place yourself in His palm, and you'll find yourself at home with your One True Friend. Why? That's because nothing'll please or taste so well as the pleasure of the Divine Will.

Who's the sort of person grace will occasionally grace? The one who pulls his intention up to God with a simple heart as his only winch and hoists himself out of the slough of self-love.

Yes, My beloved friend, you're a vase, an empty vase, and yes, I sometimes parade around with an empty watering can. But some days the can is full, and would I bother to water you with My blessings if I thought you were full?

You must renounce more perfectly than the lowest and, using contempt of self as a tool, die more to yourself, if you ever want sudden grace to come again, to flood you till you overflow, and to save your heart from drowning.

Then you'll feel enriched, and your eyes'll wonder, and your heart'll enlarge, as Isaiah described the phenomenon (60:5), because the hand of God is with you—an expression from Acts (11:21), and you've placed yourself on that hand forever.

Behold this is the kind of person who's blessed because he seeks God with his whole heart—a thought from the Psalmist (119:2)—

and "doesn't let his soul slip into vanity," as the Psalmist described his own spiritual journey (24:4).

This person in receiving the Holy Eucharist is promised the great grace of Divine Union. That's because he doesn't dote on devotion and consolation as personal gifts to himself. All he's concerned about is the Grand Dote, that's to say, devotion and consolation only as they're applied to the glory and honor of God.

16

REJECTION

DEVOUT

O Sweetest and Loveliest of Friends, Lord Jesus, I now desire to receive You as a Devout should. You know the infirmity and necessity that I suffer; into how many evils and vices I hurl myself; how often I've sinned gravely, been tempted, disoriented, debauched.

For a remedy I come to You. For consolation and sublimation I pray to You.

I know to whom I'm speaking, the One who knows everything. All my thoughts are an open book to Him. Unfortunately for me, You're the only One who can really console and help me. You know, my Lordly Friend, the sort of things I need and the sort I don't, although whenever I do my spiritual inventory, I seem to come up short in anything labeled "Virtue."

Behold, I stand before You, poor and bare, yet demanding grace and imploring mercy. Give Your mewling mendicant something to eat, something to wear, the fire of Your love to warm my heart. Brighten my eyes with the glare of Your Presence. Sour my taste for all Terrenals; change my Gravities and Contrarieties into patience; make me condemn and forget all the creaturely things I like.

Raise up my heart to You in Heaven, and don't let me drag my bod all over the world. What do I learn from this? That You alone are the

Great Refectioner until the end of time. You alone are the Food and Drink. You alone are the Love and Joy. You alone are the Sweetness and Goodness of my life.

Would that You could ignite my wood, whip it to flame, and transmute me into Yourself. I want to be one in spirit with You, through the grace of internal union and the melting of burning love, as Paul described it in First Corinthians (6:17). Don't allow me, fasting and thirsting, to recede from You. Work with me mercifully as You have so often worked wonders with Your Saints.

Wouldn't it be a wonder if You were the Internal and indeed the Eternal Flame, as Augustine put it in his *Confessions* (10.29), and I, a mere ember of my former self! That's to say, Love purifying the heart and lighting the intellect.

17

LONGING

DEVOUT

With devotion and love, with heart and fervor, I desire to receive You, O Lord, just as many of the Saints and Devouts before this time desired to receive You in Holy Communion. Holiness of life was their chiefest concern, and they fanned the flame of devotion in the most ardent way.

O God of mine, Love Eternal, Good Entire, Felicity Interminable! I want to receive You with more desire and reverence than any of the Saints before!

I know I'm all unworthy to have these sentiments of devotion, yet I offer them to You as if I were the only one ever to have these flaming desires.

Whatever my pious if pitiful mind conceives, all these I put in front of You and offer up to You with veneration and fervor. I burningly desire to hold nothing back for myself, not even my dearest possessions.

O Lord, my God, my Creator, and my Redeemer, I desire to receive You today with affection, reverence, praise, and honor; with faith, hope, and purity.

My model is Your Most Holy Mother, the glorious Virgin Mary. When the Angel informed her of the mystery of the Incarnation, she replied in a humble and devout manner: "That's what I am, a handmaid of the Lord's. If there's more to it than that, then so be it." That's how the Evangelist Luke recorded it (1:38).

Just so, Your blessed precursor, most excellent of Saints, John the Baptist—if Luke is to be believed (1:44)—somersaulted in the joy of the Holy Spirit while still enjoying the comfort of his mother's womb. Years later as a grown man, he was able to pick Jesus out of a crowd and, according to John (3:29), speak about Him with admiration and affection. "Don't look at me! I'm only the Bridegroom's friend. He's the Bridegroom! Stop! Listen to Him! His are the words of the Joy of joys."

So too should I stop and listen. And with great and holy desire should I be spitted and broiled and presented to You en brochette.

Whence, I offer up to You all of my fellow Devouts, with their *Dulce Jubilo's*, their inflamed hearts, their ecstasies, their visions. I offer also all Virtues and Lauds, from every creature in Heaven and on Earth that has been celebrated and will be celebrated. I offer them for myself and for everyone who's been commended to me for prayer. That prayer is, may You be worthily praised by everyone and glorified in every age.

Accept my vows, Lord my God. You're Laudation and Benediction; You're Infinity and Immensity; You're Multitude and Magnitude— these are the sorts of things the Psalmist would say (150:2). You're all of these divine attributes and virtues, and more, and I offer them back to You, every single day, every single moment. And with prayers and affections, I invite and beseech all the Celestial Spirits and all Your faithful to thank You and to praise You, as You've come to expect.

Some exclamations!

May all the peoples, tribes, languages praise You!

May they magnify Your Holy and Mellifluous Name with jubilation and devotion!

May all of you celebrate the highest Sacrament with full reverence and receive it with full faith!

May they deserve to find grace and mercy in Your presence!

May they pray successfully for my sinfulness!

May they have the devotion they've desired, the union they've enjoyed, the consolation they've longed for, the refections they've tasted!

Then may they leave the Holy and Heavenly Table. Then and only then may they remember me for my poverty.

18

FAITH

JESUS

You'd do well, My dear Devout, to avoid those dreary discussions, those shaggy syllogisms, about the inner workings of this most profound Sacrament. Why? Because they come up with such funny conclusions. And, frankly, because they tend to induce doubt rather than increase faith. Which is another way of saying their conclusions may be curiouser, but are they necessarily seriouser?

A good text for this might come from Proverbs: "The person who undertakes an intellectual investigation of Majesty may well find it, only to be blinded by its glory" (3:21, 25:27).

Another way of putting it is that the Godhead has more modes of operation than Humankind has of intellection. Nonetheless, always tolerable is the pious and humble inquiry into Truth. It's prepared to learn something and strives to entertain the sane and sound opinions of the Fathers.

Blessed is the simplicity that can free itself from the intellectual entanglements of University thinking and forge ahead down Faith's plain and firm path, where every paver's a command or a commandment.

All of which is another way of saying that many Devouts in higher studies—that's to say, as Jesus son of Sirach has said, studies beyond one's competence (3:22)—lose their devotion while striving too hard to succeed intellectually.

What's needed in life, My dear friend, is faith as well as sincerity. Not depth or height, nor breadth or sweep of intellect. And certainly not mastery of the Mysteries of God.

If you don't come to grips with the world within, how do you expect to comprehend the world without?

Let God be your tutor and give your senses a good schooling in faith. Then the light of knowledge'll come. Perhaps not the full flood, but certainly flickering enough for you to complete your studies without losing your sight.

When it comes to faith and Sacrament, though, some are gravely tempted. At first blush that'd seem to be their fault, but actually, at second blush, it's the Enemy's. My suggestion? Do just the opposite of what the Devil suggests. That's to say, try to hold your water, but don't try to make sense out of commandments the Devil has turned into conundrums. Just believe in the words of God. Put your belief in His Saints and Prophets, and the Vociferous Enemy will throw up his hands in despair; the same sort of advice is found in the Letter of James (4:7).

Often, when you have to bear up under such affronts, there's some small consolation, perhaps even a compliment. That's to say, the Devil doesn't spend much of his precious time trying the virtue of Infidels and Sinners; these poor blokes he can have served up to him anytime he wants. It's always the Faithful that are the delicacies at his dinners.

Continue your intellectual journey, My friend, with simple and undoubting faith, and receive the Sacrament with the reverence of a suppliant. When your intellectual capacity reaches its natural limits, remember God's knowledge knows no bounds. When intellectual failure does happen—and it happens more frequently than Humankind likes to admit—know that God isn't the cause. You're the cause because you put your faith in yourself. Which is a roundabout way of saying the person who believes in himself has a fool for a god.

God walks in His garden still, not necessarily with soupy intellectuals from the University, but with salt-of-the-earth people from everyday life. He reveals Himself as a long-lost friend to the Humble. He teaches the Terrible Tots their *Aleph-Beth's*, as He taught the Psalmist his (119:130). He filters human knowledge for the Pure of Mind, as Luke recorded (24:25). The Curious and the Proud—well, they require special attention. He gives them grace, yes, but He just makes it harder for them to find. In conclusion—and I do have a conclusion—Human Reason is frail and fallible; True Faith, however, never fails, never falls.

Every ratiocination and investigation into the nature and work of the Sacrament ought to follow the guidelines established by Faith. That's to say, they shouldn't preempt Faith's prerogatives; nor should they infringe on any of Faith's boundaries. Why? In the realm of this Most Holy and Superexcellent Sacrament, Faith and Love rule. And it's quite clear to Me that not all of their machinations are clear to you.

DEVOUT

Nell, my reasonable, if sometimes, rambunctious friend, am I about to be smacked with another wet fish?

JESUS

No, My dearest friend. No more smelts, no more mullets, no more herrings! Just Act and Potency, Potency and Act—maybe the Schoolmen were on to something. *Eternal and Immense God turns Infinite Potency into Great and Inscrutable Acts in Heaven and on Earth.* Whatever, there just doesn't seem to be an intellectually satisfying way for you to study these Marvels; that was Job's conclusion too (5:9).

If, therefore, there were a way to taxonomize and theologize the works of God, they wouldn't be Marvels, would they? I expect the answer is no.

Nor would there be words smart enough or tart enough to describe them, now would there? Again I expect the answer no.

Again I say Amen.

Afterword

✠ ✠ ✠

THE VERSION

All versions of foreign-language classics are doomed to failure, mine included. They're intended to be, and the makers of these versions pretend that they've become, re-creations of the wonderfulness of the originals. In reality, they're pale copies, capturing only a little of the original's luster. Would it be unfair to suggest that the best version of a foreign-language original captures no more than fifty percent of the original? Or is that percentage too high?

The Translation

There are at least two kinds of versions, the translation and the para-phrase. In each the chief virtue is fidelity. The translator accomplishes this by being faithful to the Author's thought; and that's traditionally been accomplished by keeping the words and the word orders as Latinate as possible; there's always some modest festooning, that's what makes for pleasurable reading. Also it must be said that in faithful translations there's a fair amount of clotting; that's to say, where faithfulness has produced only clotted verbiage in what's supposed to be a freely flowing text.

The paraphraser, on the other hand, claims no less fidelity to the Author's thought; it's just that he or she uses contemporary idiom and vocabulary. If not as literal as a translation, the paraphrase has often be accused of being literary. Chief sign of that is a reader's laboring in vain to match each English word with each Latin word.

All of which is another way of saying that Fidelity has a lost twin, Communication. A version of a foreign-language original that doesn't consistently communicate with the average reader of the present century is, ultimately, no version at all.

Which is the better version, the translation or the paraphrase?

De gustibus non est disputandum.

The Paraphrase

Besides fidelity, as defined above, what other characteristics should a truly readable paraphrase have, and how have I responded to them?

DICTION

What happens when a Latin work with a 500-word vocabulary meets a translator with a 5,000-word—perhaps even a 50,000- or 500,000-word—vocabulary? The result may seem riotous at worst, impious at best. Whichever, it'll appear unforgivably wordy. But as British playwright Christopher Fry once said, coming to his own defense against the same charge, I use no more words than any other translator. All you have to do is count them.

As for what's appropriate in diction or vocabulary, Richard Whitford in his sixteenth-century translation provides the *locus classicus:* "Use not to speak with inkhorn terms new rhetoric, nor in dark words and hard to be understood; speak plainly that your disciples or hearers may perceive what you mean. Study not to be overmuch eloquent, nor yet in any wise barbarous. A mean style is most comely and most profitable."

In the twentieth century Ronald A. Knox expressed pretty much the same sentiment in the preface to his translation. "There are no frills about the *Imitation*. . . . It has the frill-lessness of Euclid and the Athanasian Creed."

Well, that may have been what the Great Whitford and the Great Knox said—no "inkhorn terms" and no "frills"—but that wasn't what they did in their translations. Inkhorn terms and frills galore—that's what they used if these words may be construed as "tropes" and "figures." So Kempis's original had. And so mine has, if perhaps to a higher degree.

TONE

Almost all translators have noted a certain grimness in the Latin original and shadowed their Englishings accordingly. I certainly felt it when I first read the work some forty years ago—an unbearable heaviness of being, a ghastly if ghostly pathology of the wounded soul. It was like reading, or attempting to read, Robert Burton's *Anatomy of Melancholy* (1621) or Henry Gray's *Anatomy, Descriptive and Surgical* (1856).

In rendering the work into English today, however, I've managed to find a certain lightness—perhaps it's only gallows humor—but it's there, here and there, and here's a sample: "Rely on Jesus Christ as your Lord and Master. If you don't, but rather rely on your own ability to logick your way through life, then you'll never be nominated for the *Homo Illuminatus* award!"

The translation is mine, and the passage has never been translated this way before. As such, it may be construed either as a preposterous remark, what with its being exactly the sort of honor Kempis has been shying his reader away from, or it's a humorous aside, making its serious point with some levity. I prefer the latter interpretation. And there are a fair number of similar passages throughout the work, all of which I've rendered in a rather lightened, if not enlightened, manner.

Also to this point Kempis, in his short work *De Fideli Dispensatore (On the Faithful Steward),* referred to in the foreword, prescribed a certain hilarity of expression as just right for those who gave alms or did other external works of charity. And so in paraphrasing Kempis's words about internal acts of charity in the *Imitation* I too have used what may be called a certain hilarity of expression.

GENDER

These days no book of spirituality worth its allspice is written exclusively for one gender or another. And with very good reason. Both have equal needs, both have equal access before the Lord, and both are favored by the Lord. And so I thought, as I began this paraphrase, I'd follow the general guidelines of gender-inclusive language.

My task as "paraphaser," at least as I saw it, was to "recreate" the original work. That has come to involve interpreting the time-honored text not as a continuous prose narrative, as some of the previous translations have led us to believe, but rather as a set of detailed notes for the use of a spiritual director, who himself drew from a hundred sources.

Hence, the narrative drive, if I may call it that, has turned out to be one monk addressing other monks and would-be monks on a variety of monkish topics.

Double hence, I had to create a voice for Kempis, and my text has come to sound like Kempis directly addressing his spiritual charges.

Triple hence, it's become a dramatic monologue of sorts, except in Books Three and Four, when it becomes a dialog between two males, the Lord Jesus and a Devout.

Have no fear; this isn't the record of private revelation between the Lord and Kempis. It was just a literary genre, a Platonic dialog in which two personages speak; as Socrates and Ion in *The Ion;* as Socrates, Hermogenes, and Cratylus in *The Cratylus*. The thing to remember is that all the voices in the philosophical dialogues are Plato's and all the voices in this spiritual treatise are Kempis's.

The principle here is that the greater the particularity or historicity, the greater the clarity or intelligibility. By recreating the monkish world of the fourteenth and fifteenth centuries in the Netherlands, I've made it more accessible to twenty-first-century readers, whether monk or not, living somewhere in the English-reading world. Or so I hope.

All of which is the long way of saying, alas, my paraphrase isn't gender-inclusive. Nonetheless, my hope, as is that of all the other transgressors in this regard, is that women may still read my *Imitation,* appreciate the paraphraser's tradeoff of gender inclusivity for greater clarity, and find some enjoyment and some instruction in this humble volume.

Still, I have a great sadness about this. But what wonders await us all, male and female readers alike, when a woman writer, both handy with Latin and heady with English, translates the *Imitatio* as seen through the eyes of one of the Sistern of the Common Life. After all, the *Imitatio* was their spirituality as much as the Brethren's!

SCRIPTURE

Kempis has directly cited Scripture comparatively few times, but he's alluded to Scripture hundreds of times. Hence, the truly modern paraphrase should incorporate into the text itself, in one way or another, all biblical citations and as many allusions as can be found. And so I have.

A further word about Scripture. For too many centuries the *Imitation* has appeared to be a compendium of the teaching of the liturgically oriented churches, especially Roman Catholicism. And of course the fourth book, "The Sacrament of the Altar," does little to change that impression. But I'd like to point out that some paragraphs from the eleventh chapter of that book are of paramount interest to readers from the Bible-oriented churches.

My body's a prison, and the view from my cell is grim. I survive, but barely. I have to do without things in this wretched state, but two things I just can't live without. Food and Light. And You, Dear Lord, You bring them to me in the middle of the night.

Food? Your Sacred Body, which revives my sagging mind and body.

Light? Your Divine Word. As the Psalmist has sung in similar circumstances, it's a lamp for my shackled feet (119:105).

Without the Food and without the Light, I wither. Without the Bread and without the Bible, I wander. Without the Sacrament of Life and the Book of Life, I perish.

From my cell I see—or think I see—an altar. A Holy Table from which rises Holy Church in all her splendor. On one side is the Holy Bread, that's to say, the precious Body of Christ. On the other, the Holy Bible, that's to say, the Divine Law that contains Holy Doctrine, teaches right faith, and leads even the imprisoned soul through the veil of veils to the Holy of Holies, as the Letter to the Hebrews has led us to expect (6:19).

Hence, one hopes that it's not too much for the Bible-oriented readers to suppose that Jesus is present to them as much in the Scripture as He is in the Sacrament for liturgically oriented readers. With that sort of insight, Bible-oriented readers will surely find, in that troublesome Book Four, much to edify, much to nourish.

Still another word about Scripture. All scriptural quotations have been freshly translated into English from the Latin Vulgate, the translation from Greek to Latin done by Jerome in the fourth century. This was the translation copied by Kempis in the fifteenth century and cited by him throughout the *Imitation of Christ*. All scriptural references to the Vulgate have been adjusted, where necessary, to reflect the new versification and numeration appearing now in the New Revised Standard Version.

As an authentic version of the Bible, the Vulgate certainly enjoys the umbrella protection of inerrancy, but that may be no balm to Bible-oriented readers of the *Imitation*. The Latin scriptural translations—or at least my Englishing of them—often don't seem to correspond to the Bible translations of our own day. There are at least two reasons for that.

First, Jerome translated from the Greek of the Septuagint; I'm translating from the Latin of Jerome. That means that Jerome could translate a Greek metaphor with a Latin metaphor; and I could translate that very same Latin metaphor with an English metaphor. Occasionally that has resulted in quite a distance in wording, but hopefully not in meaning, between my English and the Greek.

If I may belabor an example from Book One, Chapter 3, of the *De Imitatione;* which is as follows:

KEMPIS: *Beatae aures quae venas divini susurri suscipiunt.*

LITERAL ENGLISH: Blessed are the ears that pick up wisps of the divine whisper.

In this passage Kempis wasn't quoting Scripture directly, but he might very well've been alluding briefly to 3 Kings 19:12 in the Latin Vulgate; that would be 1 Kings 19:12 in the New Revised Standard Version, which is as follows.

VULGATE: *Et post ignem sibilus aurae tenuis.*

LITERAL ENGLISH: And after the fire a tenuous whistle of the ear.

KING JAMES VERSION: And after the fire, a still small voice.

NEW REVISED STANDARD VERSION: And after the fire a sound of sheer silence.

With Kempis's Latin and the Vulgate's Latin in mind, therefore, the passage could be Englished in at least two ways.

GRIFFIN #1: Blessed is the soul that hears the murmur of conversation with the Lord.

GRIFFIN #2: Blessed are the ears that pick up the Godly Whisperer, if I may borrow an expression from 1 Kings (19:12), and at the same time block out the Worldly Whisperer!

Hopefully, this example indicates the difficulties one may run into when tracking down biblical quotations or allusions. But it also shows the increased possibilities of rendering them in translation.

Second, Kempis used scriptural references in an easy, offhand way. Some critics have said that he was misquoting; others, that he was

misremembering; neither very flattering appraisals. I'd rather say
that he was paraphrasing, playing with the language. And so I've
done, for better or worse.

WISDOM LITERATURE

Properly, the *Imitation* seems as though it were a prayer book, and
indeed there are a fair number of prayers in it. More properly, it may
be considered a piece of wisdom literature. Most properly, it's a subgenre of wisdom literature known, perhaps unhappily, as survival
literature, in which the author has offered a number of pieces of
practical advice on how to survive Christianity as it was lived in the
monastery. Needless to say, we moderns—at least those of us who
aren't monks—read the *Imitation* just for glints on how to enrich
our lives as everyday Christians.

All of which is preface to my pointing out that wisdom literature is
part sapience, part sappiness. That's to say, it often contains the felicitous expression of homely truths. Read too many of these wisdoms
at one sitting, though, and this sort of literature begins to cloy. And
in that it's not unlike divinity fudge. The first piece is supreme; the
second, divine; but by the third, one can feel the fur beginning to
grow on the roof of one's mouth.

The cloying factor in wisdom diction seems to come from an
abundance of assonance and consonance with an occasional emission
of dissonance, parallelisms, rhyming words or syllables, and repeti-
tions of all sorts. That's to say, these word figures are like circus per-
formers; they're a bit out of the ordinary, flashy yet flashing, but their
kind intent is to please.

Kempis's *Imitatio* is no exception; neither is my *Imitation*. I hasten to point out that it wasn't always possible to be assonant or con-
sonant where Kempis was. But accumulatively, the final amount is
about the same in the translation as in the original. Any dissonance
is mine alone. But the inevitable conclusion is, whatever the lan-

guage, no one can speed-read wisdom. That's to say, readers shouldn't be surprised if they can read the *Imitation* only in small snatches.

FRIENDSHIP LITERATURE

The relationship that Kempis establishes with his charges is that of instructor to student, drill sergeant to raw recruit, novice master to novice, and my translation strives to make that clear. But the instruction has to do, in large part, with the Devout's forming a bond, a friendship, if not with the drill sergeant, then with Jesus; and so the Devout strives in Books One and Two of the *Imitation*.

In Books Three and Four the relationship deepens. That's to say, they turn into Platonic dialogs between the Lord and the Devout. The love between the two is expressed in the hottest possible terms. But in translating I've decided to use the diction not of mystical love, but of friendship love. The *Imitatio* is definitely not a torchy treatise by Mechthild of Magdeburg or Hugh of St. Victor, Meister Eckhart or Marguerite Porete.

Rather, the *Imitation* is part of another subgenre, friendship literature. Cicero (d. 43 B.C.) wrote a memorable essay on the subject; so did Aelred of Rievaulx (d. 1167) and Nicholas of Cusa (d. 1461), right on down to the present century. In his *The Four Loves* C. S. Lewis (d. 1963) devoted the third of his four to the love of friendship; male friendship, really, for he found nothing more wonderful than the sound of male laughter echoing. I daresay Kempis would paraphrase Lewis to the effect that there was nothing more wonderful than the sound of male prayer chanting.

Hence, I've tried to render the red-hot language of mystical love as it appears in the *Imitation* more in the light of, and indeed in the terms of, for better or worse, friendship between males. It mayn't be gender inclusive, but it does manage to hose down the affections in that bastion of masculinity, the monastery, where particular friendships were to be avoided at all costs.

In this regard, Kempis often excused himself early from the daily recreation in common. His reason? A prior engagement. When pressed for further clarification? He had a friend waiting. Of course, it was Jesus Himself who was waiting for His fine earthly friend. Hence, Kempis hied himself to that warm chatsworthy place he'd set up so many years before; that's to say, the room within his room, his soul.

MEDIEVAL THEOLOGY

In fourteenth-century Europe God was harsh, wielding the cruel scourges of disease and war, trying to whack his followers back into line. At least that has seemed to be the spirituality of the time. The operative image was Jesus being crowned with thorns and nailed to the cross. For those who followed Jesus the only way was the *Via Crucis,* that's to say, the Way of the Cross. That the New Testament had much the same thing to say made the message even more convincing. What was being described in pulpits was also appearing in such paintings. Andrea Mantegna's *Ecce Homo* and Antonello da Messina's *Christ at the Pillory.* Simultaneously, Dramaturgy was rearing its shaggy head. Rascally dramatizations of holy subjects were being turned out of the cathedrals into the courtyards. Clerics were no longer the actors. Various guilds did the underwriting as long as their guildsmen appeared in the plays.

What kind of plays?

The morality play flourished in the fifteenth century. Perhaps the earliest was born in Kempis's part of the world: *Elckerlyc* in Dutch, *Jedermann* in German, *Everyman* in English. Basically it's an allegory, that literary or dramatic genre in which the characters are personifications of abstractions. In this instance, Death tells Everyman he's going to die, but to soften the blow, he may take a friend along for the journey. Fellowship, Kindred, Worldly Goods, Good Deeds, and Others, all are flattered to be asked, but in the end only Good Deeds takes Everyman's hand in hers as they go to the grave and the inevitable

Judgment beyond. A sober work, yes, and an instructive one, worth more than a hundred sermons, but at the same quite entertaining.

Not long after the appearance of the morality play came the miracle and mystery plays, springing up all over the European continent as well as the British Isles. God is also the chief character. He's just, but He's often jolly. Indeed, He runs the gamut of human emotions from friendship to generosity, from sacrifice to Sacrament, even to pouting when He, the Lord and Tailor of the Universe, always seems to come in second to the World, the Flesh, and the Devil.

Speaking of the Devil, to whom we owe a fair measure of our human misery, I hasten to point out that he was seen then not as a desperate creature on a desperate errand, not as the fast-talking slip-sliding creature in the Primal Garden, but as a comic figure wearing red. A worthy successor to the Braggart Soldier of Roman comedy, he was pompous, full of bombast, striding back and forth, swearing and forswearing, tut-tutting one-on-one temptation while grandiosely proposing to tempt the whole world in one extravagant swoop!

Of course, a wide range of verbal, even vegetable, abuse was hurled at him by the other characters and, no doubt, the rowdy audience. When he was finally dispatched from the stage, it wasn't with a wooden sword or a *deus ex machina;* it was with a good, swift kick in the arse! Riotously entertaining, yes, and yet not altogether fanciful from a theological point of view. It was here that theology and dramaturgy became one, if only for a few sweet hours.

Although much of this was happening in Kempis's era, he apparently knew none of it. Yet that hasn't prevented me from dipping into these dramaturgical resources whenever it seemed necessary to lighten Kempis's sometimes ruthless pursuit of the Cross. He failed—perhaps it's more accurate to say, his notes failed—to distinguish between the proper self-esteem necessary for survival as a human being and the considerably lower, if perhaps more efficient, spiritual esteem necessary for survival as a monk. In defense of Kempis, I'd say that, complementing his notes, he probably made the necessary distinctions whenever he was addressing the young and impressionable. But I, having no such homogeneous audience, must make my emendations in the text of my translation. There's no mistaking where they appear.

By what license do I do this? By Kempis's own. As he gathered his predecessors' papers, drew from them for his own lectures, and eventually for the grand anthology that would be *De Imitatione Christi,* he edited and amended them where he felt it necessary for any one of a variety of reasons. And so have I, albeit in mercifully few places, all of them evident.

ALLEGORY

Flourishing in the text of the *Imitation* are a superabundance of virtues and vices; that's to say, nouns representing abstract qualities. According to C. S. Lewis in *The Allegory of Love,* the medieval mind was entertained by such words, especially when they were found in works that developed a moral or allegorical meaning. Most of the nouns are familiar to the modern reader in name only; few are defined, and then only descriptively. Hence, managing this horde became a huge project. But one solution did present itself; that was, for one example, to treat faith as a person and to capitalize it accordingly. The result was that a cluttered paragraph could be paraphrased into something smooth and clear to the modern reader who has no knowledge whatsoever of the works and pomps of medieval allegory.

When Virtue strides into the room, Vainglory vanishes. When Heavenly Grace and True Charity sweep into the room, Virid Envy turns up her nose, High Anxiety has a fit, Particular Friendship is beside himself. We all know why. Grace and Charity have this way of clearing the floor of crooks and cranks, thus releasing all the warmths of the soul. (Book 3, Chapter 9)

COMMUNICATION

The final characteristic of the truly modern paraphrase has to do with communication. It must be in an English idiom that can be understood by a large, literarily heterogeneous group in more than one English-reading country. And if such a paraphrase has the occasional vintage word, figure, or reference, and if it has something of Kempis's piping voice urging his spiritual charges onward and upward in their pursuit of the spiritual life, then perhaps this paraphrase could be considered appropriate for the twenty-first century. And so I hope it is.

Bibliography

✠ ✠ ✠

THOMAS À KEMPIS

Opera Omnia. Edited by J. Pohl. 7 vols. Freibourg: Herder, 1902–22.

The Chronicles of the Canons Regular of Mount St. Agnes. Translated by J. P. Arthur. London: Kegan, Paul, Trench & Trübner, 1906.

The Founders of the New Devotion, Being the Lives of Gerard Groote, Florentius Radewin and Their Followers. Translated by J. P. Arthur. London: 1905.

A Meditation on the Incarnation of Christ: Sermons on the Life and Passion of Our Lord, and Of Hearing and Speaking Good Words. Translated by Dom Vincent Scully, C.R.L. London: Kegan, Paul, Trench & Trübner, 1907.

Meditations on the Life of Christ. Translated and edited by the Venerable Archdeacon Wright and the Rev. S. Kettlewell. With a Preface by the latter. New York: Dutton, 1892.

STUDIES

Butler D. *Thomas à Kempis: A Religious Study*. London: Anderson & Ferrier, 1908.

Cruise, F. R. *Thomas à Kempis: Notes of a Visit to the Scenes in Which His Life Was Spent*. London: K. Paul, 1887.

Durant, Will. *The Reformation: A History of European Civilization from Wyclif to Calvin: 1300–1564*. New York: Simon and Schuster, 1957.

Huizinga, Johan. *The Waning of the Middle Ages: A Study of the Forms of Life, Thought, and Art in France and the Netherlands in the Dawn of the Renaissance.* New York: Doubleday, Anchor Books, 1954 (1949).

Hyma, Albert. *The Brethren of the Common Life.* Grand Rapids, MI: Eerdmans, 1950.

——. *The Christian Renaissance: A History of the "Devotio Moderna."* First ed. New York, 1925. Second ed. Hamden, CT: Archon Books, 1965.

Kettlewell, Samuel. *Thomas à Kempis and the Brothers of Common Life.* London: K. Paul, Trench, 1882.

Montmorency, J. E. G. de. *Thomas à Kempis: His Age and His Book.* London: Methuen, 1906.

Raitt, Jill, with Bernard McGinn and John Meyendorff, eds. *Christian Spirituality: High Middle Ages and Reformation.* Vol. 2, World Spirituality series. New York: Crossroad, 1987.

Scully, Vincent. *Life of the Venerable Thomas à Kempis, Canon Regular of St. Augustine.* Introduction by Francis Cruise. London: Washbourne, 1902.

Tuchman, Barbara W. *A Distant Mirror: The Calamitous 14th Century.* New York: Knopf, 1978.

Van Engen, J., ed. *Devotio Moderna: Basic Writings.* Preface by Heiko A. Oberman. New York: Paulist Press, 1988.

Wellner, Bernard, S.J. *A Dictionary of Scholastic Philosophy.* Second edition. Milwaukee: Bruce, 1966.

ARTICLES, CHAPTERS, ESSAYS,
INTRODUCTIONS, PREFACES

Alberts, Wybe Jappe. "Brethren of the Common Life." *New Catholic Encyclopedia* 2 (1967): 788–90.

Bangley, Bernard, trans. "Foreword," "Afterword," *Growing in His Image: The Imitation of Christ by Thomas à Kempis.* Wheaton, IL: Harold Shaw, 1983. Pp. 9–15, 151–55.

Burrows, Mark. "Devotio Moderna: Reforming Piety in the Later Middle Ages." Chap. 4 of *Spiritual Traditions for the Contemporary Church.*

Edited by Robin Maas and Gabriel O'Donnell, O.P. Nashville: Abingdon, 1990. Pp. 109–32.

Creasy, William C., trans. "Introduction," *The Imitation of Christ, Thomas à Kempis.* Notre Dame, IN: Ave Maria Press, 1989. Pp. 11–27.

Cunneen, Sally. "Preface," *The Imitation of Christ.* Translated by Joseph N. Tylenda, S.J. New York: Vintage Books, 1998. Pp. xv-xxvi.

García-Villoslada, Ricardo, S.J. "Devotio Moderna," *New Catholic Encyclopedia* 4 (1967): 831–32.

Gardiner, Harold C., S.J. "Introduction," *The Imitation of Christ.* New York: Doubleday, Image Books, 1955. Pp. 5–19.

Gründler, Otto. "Devotio Moderna," *Christian Spirituality: High Middle Ages and Reformation.* Edited by Jill Raitt. New York: Crossroad, 1987. Pp. 176–93.

Helms, Hal M., trans. "Introduction," "Appendix: Rule of St. Augustine," *The Imitation of Christ by Thomas à Kempis.* Orleans, MA: Paraclete Press, 1982. Pp. xi–xix, 250–51.

Klein, Edward J., ed. "Introduction," *The Imitation of Christ: From the First Edition of an English Translation Made c. 1530 by Richard Whitford.* Harper & Brothers, 1941. Pp. xi–lx.

Knox, Ronald A. "Preface," *The Imitation of Christ by Thomas à Kempis.* Translated by Ronald A. Knox, with Michael Oakley. New York: Sheed & Ward, 1959. Pp. 5–9.

Mulhern, Philip Fabian, O.P. "Thomas à Kempis." *New Catholic Encyclopedia* 14 (1967): 121–22.

Rooney, John, trans. "Translator's Preface," *The Imitation of Christ by Thomas à Kempis.* Springfield, IL: Templegate, n.d. Pp. viii–xiv.

Scully, Vincent. "Thomas à Kempis," *The Catholic Encyclopedia* 14 (1912): 661–63.

Steere, Douglas V. *"The Imitation of Christ."* Chap. 1 of *Doors into Life, Through Five Devotional Classics.* New York: Harper & Brothers, 1981 (1948). Pp. 17–51.

Tylenda, Joseph N., S.J. "Introduction," *The Imitation of Christ in Four Books*. Wilmington, DE: Michael Glazier, 1984. Pp. 13–26.

Van Engen, John, trans. "Introduction," *Devotio Moderna: Basic Writings*. Preface by Heiko A. Oberman. New York: Paulist Press, 1988. Pp. 7–35.

Latin Words & Phrases

✠ ✠ ✠

ad nauseam: to the point of nausea, that's to say, to the point of fatigue or disgust.

amphorae: large Grecian jars or vessels, sometimes with a handle on each side of the neck.

auctoritas: in general, authority; in this context, authorship.

bona fide: in good faith.

brassica: cabbage.

Caveat lector: Let the reader beware.

cena: short meal.

coffeum (caffeum): coffee.

culter: knife.

De Amicitia: On Friendship.

De Amicitia Spiritali: On Spiritual Friendship.

de gustibus non est disputandum: literally, there's no accounting for personal tastes; figuratively, there's no real reason why one person's taste is better—or indeed worse—than another's.

De Imitatione Christi: On the Imitation of Christ.

delirium tremens: delirium accompanied by trembling.

De Petro Cuniculo: On Peter the Rabbit.

desideratum, -ata: desire(s), requirement(s).

devotio antiqua: literally, the old, perhaps establishment, devotion or religious practice; in this context, the devotion or practice that flourished in the near past, that's to say, in twelfth- and thirteenth-century Europe.

devotio moderna: literally, the new, perhaps upstart, devotion or religious practice; in this context, the devotion or practice that emerged in the Netherlands and surrounding territories in the fourteenth and fifteenth centuries.

deus ex machina: literally, a piece of stage machinery used in ancient Greek drama by which a character in distress is plucked from the stage by a friendly god; figuratively, a providential turn of events, or an unbelievable resolution to a problem.

devotio perennis: perennial devotion.

distinctio rationis ratiocinatae minor: Literally, a distinction belonging to the intelligible object *(ratio)* or aspect thought about—and such a distinction may be either *major* (nominal or mental) or *minor* (real). In other words, a virtual (metaphysical or logical) distinction with a foot in reality. Technically, "a distinction found by the mind between different aspects or multiple virtualities of the same one nature, form, or perfection where the object distinguished is actually one and indivisible, but is rich enough to present to the mind various aspects that have different meanings to our way of thinking of them. Examples include the distinction between the transcendental attributes, all of which are actually identical with being; between different divine perfections all of which in God are His simple essence; and between the sensitive, vegetative, and rational souls in man though man has only one soul (Wuellner, *Dictionary of Scholastic Philosophy,* 83–84). With this definition in mind, Kempis's point in Book Three, Chapter 43, seems very well made.

Dulce Jubilo's: hymns of jubilation.

esoterica: objects, material or otherwise, known only to a privileged few.

euphoria: an English word with a Greek root, meaning a state of well-being; if there were Latin equivalent, it would be this word; not verbatim in Kempis's Latin text, but used in translation as a correlative to *opprobria.*

exaltatio: skip for joy.

exoterica: an esoteric term for objects, material or otherwise, known by the underprivileged many, the great unwashed, etc.

exsultatio: jump for joy.

florilegia: collections or descriptions of flowers; hence when applied to words, collections of literary nosegays or quotations.

furca: fork.

Gaudium Perenne: Perennial Joy.

Homo Illuminatus: Man of the Light [Award].

homo sapiens: humankind as species, with emphasis on its ability to think, form judgments, and make proverbs.

Illuminati: people who've had an intellectually stimulating experience.

impatiens: literally, "impatient, unbearable"; botanically, a group of succulent annuals and perennials with splashy, decorative flowers used as houseplants or garden bedding; one of its species is known as Touch-me-nots.

in dulci jubilo: with joyful shout.

in excelsis: in the highest.

in flagrante delicto: literally, " in the heat of a crime"; hence, caught in the act.

in pectore: literally, "in the breast or heart"; figuratively, under wraps, under the seal of secrecy, close to the vest, behind the fan, behind the arras, *sub rosa*.

Latinitas vincit omnia: Latinity conquers everything; a poor play on the common Latin expression *Amor vincit omnia*, Love conquers everything.

Liberati: people who've had a spiritually liberating experience.

locus classicus: literally, "classical place"; in this context, the best statement on the subject.

major domo, major domus: master or mistress of a house; manager as of estate or restaurant.

mea culpa, mea culpa, mea maxima culpa: "Through my fault, though my fault, through my most grievous fault"; a phrase from the general confession of sins occurring at the beginning of the Mass; the prayer is known by its first word, the *Confiteor* (I confess).

maximas culpas: most grievous faults.

modus operandi: the way a thing or person works; a generally accepted methodology.

Mysterium Tremendum: uncapitalized, a great or overwhelming mystery; capitalized, the Mystery of mysteries for philosophers and theologians, that's to say, God.

nil admirari: literally, to stare, but not to see, that's to say, to look on disinterestedly; figuratively, indifference to the distractions of the outside world; raised to a philosophical level, it's best described by the Roman poet Horace in his *Letters* (1.6.1).

Obscurati: literally, intellectuals tainted from within or without; figuratively, spiritual persons tainted from within or without.

opprobrium, -bria: shame, disgrace.

opus interruptum: work interrupted.

ordo diei: a religious house's written list of the day's activities, featuring such items required by the religious rule as times for prayers, meals, work, and recreation.

pallium: a cloth, garment, altar cloth; a vestment consisting of a narrow circular band placed around the shoulders with a short lappet hanging from front and back; worn by the pope and conferred by the pope on primates, archbishops, and sometimes on bishops; the office or dignity of an archbishop or other high office.

peccavi: "I have sinned."

phantasma: Apparition, dream, ghost, illusion, vision.

praeteritio: a figure of thought pretending to pass over, say, a fact, thereby calling attention to it; for example, "I pass over in silence all the great crimes you've committed, not to mention all the innocent people you've slaughtered."

prandium: long meal.

pro bono, pro bono publico: work done for the common weal.

quondam: Latin adverb, "once," "formerly," "at a certain time"; English adjective, "sometime"; English noun, a former holder of an office or position, a derelict or tramp.

rapa: turnip.

restauratio: restoration.

ripiaria: collections of sentences from the Scriptures, from the Fathers of the Church, and indeed from the classics, secular as well as spiritual.

saltatio: hop for joy.

Sapientia: Latin noun, "wisdom"; capitalized, the Virtue of Wisdom or the Goddess of Wisdom; uncapitalized, wisdom in general.

scrinium: desk.

scriptorium: copy room.

Sophia: transliterated Greek noun, "wisdom"; capitalized, the Virtue of Wisdom or the Goddess of Wisdom; uncapitalized, wisdom in general.

Soror Impossibilis: the Impossible Nun.

stigma: "brand," "mark"; reproduction of a bodily wound inflicted on Jesus during His crucifixion, and sometimes said to be inflicted later on one or more of His Saints.

Summum Bonum: uncapitalized as a philosophical term, "the highest good." Capitalized as a theological term, "the highest good"; commonly understood by medieval Schoolmen to be God.

Summum Malum: a neologism of the translator's, corresponding to no known medieval philosophical or theological term; literally, "the highest, or lowest, evil"; literarily correlative with *Summum Bonum;* hence, the Devil.

Te Deum laudamus: "we praise You, O God," first words of an ancient Latin hymn of praise, generally sung on occasions of thanksgiving secular or religious.

thea: tea.

translatio antiqua: literally, ancient translation, ancient or time-honored way of translating; in this context, translation from Latin to English with heavy, or excessive, reliance on Latinate words and word-order.

translatio moderna: modern translation, modern or new way of translating; in this context, translation from Latin to English with heavy reliance on non-Latinate words and on English word-order.

translator proprius: proper translator, appropriate translator; in this context, a translator whose knowledge of Latin and English allows him or her to do a truly modern translation.

triclinium: dining room.

Via Crucis: literally, the route Jesus walked with the cross to the place of execution; figuratively, the path Jesus expects his followers to tread; devotionally, the image of Jesus carrying the cross.

vade mecum: literally, "go or come with me"; figuratively, a handbook or guidebook.

Via Domini: literally, "Lord Street"; figuratively, the Way of the Lord.

Winnie Ille Pooh: title of Latin version of *Winnie the Pooh* by A. A. Milne.

Acknowledgments

✠ ✠ ✠

For having read the manuscript as it grew and having the audacity to say they liked it at every stage, I duly acknowledge the following.

Richard Foster, several years ago, informally introduced me to a small ecumenical gathering of distinguished ladies and gentlemen in the service of the Lord. (I hasten to mention that I was present, as it were, on the spouse program.) In doing the honors, Richard casually mentioned that I loved, among other things, the *Imitation of Christ.* I was astonished at first, but then I jumped to my feet and did fifteen minutes on how much I detested the work. Then I sat down in total befuddlement.

Emilie Griffin, last year, didn't take me up on my offer to translate a chapter of the *Imitation* for inclusion in *Spiritual Classics,* an anthology she was preparing with Richard Foster. Dutifully, I wrote to the publisher of a current translation requesting permission. The publisher responded, requesting a permission fee of $600. Multiply that fee by the 52 selections in the anthology, I told my beloved wife, and one comes up with a total permissions fee of $31,200. Then, and only as a cost-cutting measure, did Emilie accept my generous offer to English a chapter of the *Imitation* for free. Book One, Chapter 20, "Solitude & Silence."

To keep my sanity while continuing to act as her amanuensis for the whole project, I kept translating more chapters, and by the time she and Richard finished the manuscript of *Spiritual Classics* and the permissions were applied for, I'd finished Book One of the *Imitation.*

Eugene Peterson had been reading portions of his Englishing of the Psalms and the New Testament for some time at the annual omnium gatherums of the Chrysostom Society, a random group of Christian writers. And each time I listened admiringly, thinking I could do that, if only someone would ask me.

Acting as an editorial consultant for Macmillan Publishing in New York, I even tried to acquire the Peterson project, a worthy successor to the J. B. Phillips translations some forty years before, or so I thought. But I failed. Or rather, Macmillan failed; the vice president of editorial wanted more religion on his list, but when confronted with it, didn't want it as much as he first thought.

When I sent Eugene the first batch of my version of the *Imitation*, it didn't take him much time to reply. "I've been using Ronald Knox's translation for thirty years—and I'm ready now to trade it in for the Griffin translation." And on receiving additional batches, he's continued to send encouraging postcards, even as he himself was finishing his Englishing of the Old Testament.

Timothy Jones and I have never met in person, but I've met him in his books, *The Art of Prayer: A Simple Guide* and *Awake My Soul: Practical Spirituality for Busy People.* I know of his background as a journalist for *Christianity Today* and as editor-in-chief of Moorings, a quondam imprint of Random House. I've reviewed his books most favorably in the public prints. "A gentle writer with a sweet, pastoral style." I described him. We've talked on the telephone several times and come to communicate occasionally by e-mail. So why should I decide to send him a batch of my *Imitation* from time to time, and why should he respond so warmly each time?

William C. Russell, S.J., and I first met on July 30, 1952, when we entered the Society of Jesus as novices. Long a Jesuit priest now, he's shamelessly liked everything I've ever written, but it's the sort of praise that one brother gives another and hence has absolutely no street value whatsoever.

His response to my first batch, or so he told me over the telephone, was to laugh out loud—so loud, in fact, that other people in his office, where he raised funds for the seminarians and retirees of the Society of Jesus in New England, came to his door to tell him to shut up.

He's a holy man, I suspect, but he always manages to disguise it well with a veneer of worldliness. The *Imitation* is his favorite spiritual book, or so he tells me, one that he returns to regularly. If he ever had the vanity that Kempis spoke of, and for which the *Imitation* is the remedy, he's long ago lost it, no matter how much he protests to the contrary.

When I confessed to him that I had this penchant for going over the top in the style I'd adopted for the *Imitation*, he replied that I should succumb to the temptation every time. That's to say, go over the top as often as possible. And so, alas, I have.

Ronald Hoppe is a monsignor in and the vicar general of the Catholic Diocese of Alexandria, Louisiana, where I've lived for the past two years. He's a round, well-educated, well-spoken fellow, a septuagenarian who, because of the priest shortage, must manage his parish and school, St. Frances Cabrini, alone and beyond the ecclesiastical retirement age. His chirrupy preaching has led me to a deeper understanding of Kempis's approach with his fifteenth century charges. That's to say, the image of Hoppe's being like a border collie nipping at the heels—and at the same time nipping at the souls—of his flock led me to apply that very same metaphor to Kempis. He's jollier, though, than Kempis, for which I'm grateful. But like Kempis and Russell, he's a citizen of two worlds. And with all this, he never strays far from his confessional—that's to say, his room within a room—to which happy place he continually invites his flock.

John Loudon of Harper San Francisco understood my project from the merest description over the phone. Citing a scholar-author of his, he even extemporized for me just what a true translation a genuine recreation would have to be. I gulped and said that was what I'd just done.

One day long ago, when there was a Macmillan in New York, I hired him as a brilliant young man who'd add to the luster of my meager reputation.

I taught him all I knew about general book publishing, which I thought was considerable. Either I was a quick teacher or he was a fast learner, but it took a comparatively short time. I think it must be the latter, for he's the pupil who's far surpassed his master.

There were others who asked to see my *Imitation* and wanted to like what they read but, for one good reason or another, couldn't. I hold your names *in pectore,* but my public thanks I can't withhold!

Memorial

✠ ✠ ✠

Thomas à Kempis died on July 25, 1471, "having completed, on the feast of St. James the Greater," says the *Chronicle of Mount St. Agnes*, "the 92nd year of his age, the 63rd of his religious life, and the 58th of his priesthood." He was buried in the monastery grounds, but two centuries after the Reformation, by which time the monastery was long destroyed, his remains were transferred to Zwolle, where they rest in the Church of St. Michael. In 1897 a marble monument was erected over them, built through subscriptions collected from all over the world. The Latin inscription on that monument seems also a fitting memorial of and to this version of his classic work.

Honori, non memoriae,
THOMAE KEMPENSIS,
cujus nomen perennius
quam monumentum

To the honor, if not the memory, of
THOMAS À KEMPIS,
whose name will last longer
than this stone.